HUMANISM WITH A HUMAN FACE

Intimacy and the Enlightenment

Howard B. Radest

PRAEGER

Westport, Connecticut
London

Library of Congress Cataloging-in-Publication Data

Radest, Howard B.
Humanism with a human face : intimacy and the Enlightenment / Howard B. Radest.
p. cm.
Includes bibliographical references and index.
ISBN 0–275–94969–9 (alk. paper)
1. Humanism. 2. Intimacy (Psychology) 3. Enlightenment. 4. Transcendentalism. I. Title.
B21.R273 1996
144—dc20 95–43764

British Library Cataloguing in Publication Data is available.

Library of Congress Catalog Card Number: 95–43764
ISBN: 0–275–94969–9

First published in 1996

Praeger Publishers, 88 Post Road West, Westport, CT 06881
An imprint of Greenwood Publishing Group, Inc.

Printed in the United States of America

The paper used in this book complies with the Permanent Paper Standard issued by the National Information Standards Organization (Z39.48–1984).

10 9 8 7 6 5 4 3 2 1

For Brendan,

Emma,

and

Jes

CONTENTS

PREFACE

We are peopled by others real and imagined, living and dead. So although much of this book is written in the first-person singular, I confess that I am a company. Indeed, that is one source of the connection between intimacy and sociability that is my theme. I am never by myself even when apparently most alone. At the same time, I know that the encounter "within" is different from the encounter "without." I know, too, that even those "same" others are met differently in the "peopled forest of my mind" and in the world out there. And finally, I know that even meeting those "same" others is a different matter when they are encountered in some shared life-world or in a common and public world. I am different too for others and for myself.

There is then an extraordinary richness in my experience of self and other that, when joined to the richness of nature and imagination, fills my life with more than enough of love and joy, challenge, fascination, and surprise. I do not need some other world elsewhere and elsewhen since I am never lonely, never without something interesting before me, and, of course, never without some other who cares. To be sure, my experience—like yours—includes its share of suffering, pain, frustration, disappointment. Nature and others can harm as well as help, frighten as well as support. I am not blind to my finitude, nor am I ignorant of the thread of tragedy that runs through experience. Yet I have confidence not so much in outcomes—which are never assured—but in next moments and next persons and next ideas. Even terror and defeat will pass away. And if, in some ultimate horror, a next moment eludes me, yet I will have learned enough, enjoyed enough, and loved enough to carry me over the gulf of holocaust to the peace of nothingness. That is the final benefit of finitude. In the last moment I know that it is indeed the last moment.

With these brief paragraphs, I have tried to encapsulate the personal faith of a Humanist. This book is a sequel to *The Devil and Secular Humanism* (Praeger, 1990), which addressed the Enlightenment roots of Humanism. Although there were hints then of the personal and transcendental qualities of Humanism, now—some five years later—I am more concerned than ever to put those qualities forward as essential to Humanism, particularly in the light of the contemporary dismissal of the "life of reason."

At the same time, my concern is stirred by more than the rise of an anti-Humanist spirit in the guise of fundamentalism, "new age," and "post-modernism." Here in the United States, but also abroad, a narrow and uncharitable view of human beings and human relationships has emerged, and it gives every sign of becoming more intense. Nationalism, sectarianism, competitiveness, and aggression are costumed once again in the clothing of virtue. The victims remain as they always have been: the poor, the helpless, the young, and the different. To be sure, this calls for a renewed sense of moral mission. Humanism, in other words, cannot retreat into its own life-world nor can it merely echo the reforms of yesterday. In the rediscovery of its voice, however, the personal and the public must intertwine. Intimacy calls for social action too.

This, then, is the context in which I try to work out the double root of Humanism—its sources in the Enlightenment and in transcendentalism. But that double root appears too in the experience of the Humanist who is not simply an actor on the stage of the world but a subject who cares and translates caring into conduct. That double root appears when the Humanist acts out the drama of reform and at the same time feels connection to self and other and world. The neglect of this "two-ness" has led, I propose, to a "shadow enlightenment" and a truncated Humanism (see Chapter 1).

Obviously I am responsible for my words and my thoughts. But I have learned much from so many around me. Indeed, the loving ways in which they have taught me were in themselves verifications of intimacy. Thus, to my colleagues at the Humanist Institute, where many of the ideas that appear here were first tried out, I am truly grateful. A number of very good friends—too numerous to mention—have read all or parts of the manuscript or have listened to my random reflections. Always supportive, they have not hesitated to share their comments and criticisms with me. For his gentle ministrations, my thanks to Bill Klee who was at age eighty-four, I used to say, my "youngest" student in the philosophy classroom and who died before I had a chance to share the final product with him. Gordon Haist, my fellow teacher and philosopher at the University of South Carolina-Beaufort, read the manuscript carefully and, as usual, provided insightful comments on every chapter.

While I was working on the manuscript, Brendan was born to Michael and Karen and Emma to Robert and Nora. If ever there was a lesson in intimacy, it was the arrival of two new grandchildren. When, to them, I join the happy, energetic, and always-bright voice of Jes, I truly know the essence and essentiality of intimacy. And as I think beyond the moment to the world in which they live, I understand too the urgency of its connection to sociability. My wife, Rita, as has been true with every other project I have undertaken, was a careful editor and above all an unfailing source of support and encouragement.

Friend and family and colleague join in building life-worlds. I have been fortunate that I have never been tempted to retreat within and ignore the public world we all share. This good fortune has not been of my own making but the gift of all those with whom I have lived and from whom I have learned. Whatever their disparate loyalties and beliefs, they have been Humanists in their associations. In a sense, they wrote this book through me, although they may not recognize my less than felicitous expression or necessarily agree with my readings of their voices. Now let me share this effort with you, the reader, who, I trust, will consult his or her experience and realize from within it the connection between intimacy and sociability that I explore here.

1

PROGRESS AND TRANSCENDENCE

REFLECTIONS

As I begin, the noise of the city, Humanism's ordinary habitation, is stilled. In the silences, I reflect on what it means to me to be a Humanist. I have heard often enough that the Humanist is distant, cold, rational to a fault. But that is not so of those I have known. Like them, I too respond to the colors and shapes and smells of an environing world. I feel a connection to things and spaces. I know that I am in the presence of and I am also part of and present to. As I write, a bird, red-headed and black-white-winged, sits on a branch outside my window. A butterfly hovers near a flower; a bee buzzes close by. Above me are the sun and white clouds. In the distance, a darkening sky promises rain and thunder and lightning. I am alone, but I am not lonely.

I dwell on people, not on things, not on ideas. I recall names and stories. I laugh quietly once again as I recall what was and imagine what might have been. I remember sharing a meal or a drink, telling stories to each other. I remember moments of humor or sadness. We talked of friends we knew who did this or that. I realize that what remains with me most of all are not the issues that once seemed so urgent but the images of those who were there. And in more sober moments, I still hear the voices and see the faces of those who are dead. I remember when we met and when we parted.

Appreciation and idea together are my Humanism. I am enriched by this two-ness of Humanism.[1] With it, I confess my sources in the world around me. It is my world; I am its creature. A child of the Enlightenment, I learned the lesson of nature, of progress, of reason. I learned that I was a person by right, and not merely a tool for the use of kings and priests. I learned that I was free. I learned that I was minded and bodied all at once. This was the Enlightenment, and we are all its outcome.

Yet when I speak of my Humanism to others, I lose my way. I am tempted, so easily tempted, to flatten experience, to talk of world and self in miserly dimension. But this is not my temptation alone. As Andrei Sakharov remarked on agreeing to sign *Humanist Manifesto II*, (1973), "I do not consider it correct from the philosophical-ethical point of view to contrapose religion and humanism, religion and scientific knowledge."[2]

When I reduce Humanism to a single voice, I become only a creature of words. Two-ness vanishes, indeed becomes the occasion of a Humanist quarrel, as if I must choose which of my parents to reject.[3] I construct an argument, not a story. My language is very much at home with such abstractness. I enjoy it much as the player enjoys the game. So it is that Humanism appears only as a text or a platform or a debate. It hides beneath a skilled—or not so skilled—playing of words. Even I, self-deceived, come to believe at times in the symbol and not the reality. I quarrel over which symbol ought to be used and which not.[4] I find myself, strange indeed, more Jesuit or Talmudist than Humanist. The result is that I fail to communicate what my Humanism really is for me. In short, the two-ness of Humanism enriches my experience, but I am often dumb—despite a torrent of words—when it comes to conveying that richness.

Consequently I understand the complaint that Humanism is "too intellectual" or "lacking in warmth." I understand those who tell me that Humanism does not sing its truth, does not speak to the pains and joys, the sufferings and celebrations that create and sustain the energies committed in the struggle for truth. I am thus made aware of a kind of Humanist schizophrenia: the suppression of the personal for the sake of the universal. So it is a commonplace to find us debating about fine points of the law yet rare indeed to find self-reference and self-exposure. Symptomatically, we stay away from biography and autobiography. Characteristically, we speak in the third person—of "it" or "they"—and are uncomfortable with the first-person singular.

Paradoxically, along with the complaint of intellectualism, I also hear that we are sentimental, unrealistic, naive. After all, the human being whom we value is at the same time a liar, a cheat, a murderer. The nature to which we respond is precarious and threatening at least as often as it is warm and enfolding. Humanism thus is open to the indictment of blindness and not just of putting abstractions in place of world.

Ironically, for this forgetful Humanism, the person becomes an abstraction too. We speak of the dignity of human beings but often fail to attach dignity to actual relations. Or we speak of human potentiality without reference to its ground in human potency, which is in turn without reference to actually potent human beings.[5] Nature too becomes a mere object instead of connection and surround. Even the claim of the uniqueness of each human being becomes an abstraction. We are thus convicted of schizophrenia in yet another way: objectifying experience and alienating ourselves from it.

When I grow aware that we have abdicated the two-ness of our roots, I feel the pain of self-betrayal. I feel the need of returning my self to myself. But I am no Whitman able to celebrate myself, as a great poet does, so this attempt to return is difficult, mute. Yet it is myself whom I need to celebrate if Humanism's achievement is to be understood and enjoyed. When instead, as is our Humanist habit, I address *the* self and *the* world in some doomed Hegelian search for things as they really are, both my cosmology and my psychology become arid. I forget that hidden in the illusion of objectivity is my personal history, my scarcely confessed dreams and angers. I delude myself, thinking to be an outsider to myself where there is no outside and no inside.[6] Yet I am present to my subject matter. The act of reasoning is a token of my passion for reason.[7]

My presence is nowhere more obvious than in my inquiry into myself—my responses, my ideas, my acts—and nowhere more quickly denied. This denial has its good Enlightenment reasons. I know how easily I can mix my desires with reality, and so I think to protect myself from wishful thinking. I know how much my hidden angers frighten me, and so I defend myself against myself. And I know that what is of myself is never only what I am but what we are, we imagine, we create. I am populated by others living and dead. As the late Abraham Maslow noted, "This kind of transcendence of time is also true in another sense, namely that I can feel friendly in a very personal and affectionate way, with Spinoza, Abraham Lincoln, Jefferson, William James, Whitehead, etc., as if they still lived. Which is to say that in specific ways they *do* still live."[8] When I speak in my own voice, I am speaking in multitudes without realizing it. I am never only myself by myself, but this admission is doubled edged: I enjoy your presence, fear your invasion. So there are many reasons for me to run to some ghostly outside and away from some cherished inside.

A Humanist psychology that accepts this separation of inside and outside is doubly faulty—mistaken in its epistemology and traitorous in its philosophy. If Humanism has any claim on me, it is because, unlike the dualisms of human history, say Platonism or Christianity, it puts together my self and my world. It is this unification of experience and place that holds for me the special appeal and the special terror of Humanism. I need not search for a world that is elsewhere, and I cannot escape from a world that is always there. But this worldliness is not, in the first place, a matter of argument, a Humanist's excursion into pseudotheological discourse, but a primitive experience. Yet I have trouble speaking of it directly, for I lack a Humanist vocabulary for intimacy.

My reflections lead me to the problem of intimacy. They lead me to try to give voice to a Humanist's experience in the having and to the effort to understand why it is so difficult a task to find my own voice, why I convey Humanism's promise so poorly that all too many are misled by our compulsive attention to externality. For all that reasoning is central to a Humanist's agenda, however, there is in it an equally significant romanticism. We know Kant but forget Emerson, celebrate Newton but ignore Freud. It is this theme of remembering and forgetting—perhaps in a way an American theme[9]—that is so much a part of the genius of Humanism and so much neglected.

BUT WE ARE BETTER THAN WE SAY!

There are moments when the two-ness of Humanism is revealed in the coming together of persons. I have, as an Ethical Culture Leader, celebrated hundreds of weddings, often with families still loyal to traditional faiths. I have listened to my colleagues—other Ethical Culture Leaders, Humanist Counselors, Humanist Unitarian/Universalist Ministers, Humanist Rabbis. The wedding guests tell me over and over again that in the marriage ceremony, we succeed in speaking directly to the joyous, and fearful, experience of loving each other. In that moment of celebration, we human beings touch each other, reach each other. The message of celebration is a common one, no matter who the celebrants may be or where they come from. This seems strange indeed, for we Humanists claim that we do not have a single canon or rite. Yet we speak in one voice, both intimate and communal, present and historic. The prosaic themes of nurture and respect take on a music and poetry as personal presence is made tangible. The witnesses to the marriage are not mere observers but are present to the celebration, are indeed members of the wedding. Suspended in that moment of celebration are those endless disputations about what Humanism stands for, and in their place is an experience of what Humanism is.[10]

I can report in the same way of my experience of memorial services and funerals. Facing life and death in some ultimate moment of separation, I realize my loneliness and feel broken apart from self and person and world. My need then is not for false promises but for the present connection: the touch of a hand, the sound of a voice, the glance of an eye. I need reminding of the world. I am recalled by the dead to the living, and out of that memory made vivid I am helped to move again forward into my life. The words are no longer mere words but tokens of relationship. Striking, too, is the common note I have heard over and over again: that it is comforting to be dealt with truthfully, although, as with all truth, we feel the pain of surrendering a beloved illusion. This knowing and surrendering build my strength when strength is needed and give me comfort when comfort is needed. Despite the presumption that eternity attracts with its promises, Humanists thus succeed in reaching to the other side of evanescence—to what follows for living when I confess that this moment is all I have and all I ever shall have.

I have known the strength of Humanism when counseling with others at times of crisis: a fatal illness, the death of a child, the breakup of a marriage, or, more grandly, the assassination of a president. In such moments, whether there are only two of us or hundreds of us, I am aware of my availability and my vulnerability. I am recalled to the essential Humanism of being a person for another person, and in those moments the roles we so easily play dissolve. I am not simply celebrant or mourner or witness or counselor, and the other person is not simply client or participant or audience. I enact what my Humanism says.

I know that I cannot live Humanism from crisis to crisis. My time is not spent only in ceremonies. Yet in what we succeed in doing and being at times of crisis there is another clue to the two-ness of Humanism. I catch on to what it means to be with a world that suffers and enjoys. I realize that community is indeed a happening—following Martin Buber—and this fits with my need to choose which ties shall bind, and where, and for how long.[11] In that, I grasp the difference between Humanism and the traditions that I have left behind. I am relieved of the oppressiveness of tribal life. Of course, I pay the price of this freedom in the flickering of connection and disconnection.

In this play of connections and disconnections of person and persons, of person and world, I am restless, energetic. Intimacy is thus taken and retaken. By contrast, the Humanism that evokes accusations of intellectualism and abstractness, or of sentimentality and naiveté, is only a shadow. Ironically, both Humanism of the word and the Humanism of sentimentality are as much a quest for certainty as the antinaturalism and anti-Humanism they claim to overthrow.

THE ENLIGHTENMENT PROJECT

To find Humanism is to refind the Enlightenment project—the continuing activity begun so dramatically in the eighteenth century. I do not want to be understood to join in a chorus of denials. I am a creature of Humanist history, which is another way of saying of modern history, Enlightenment history. I know that it is the custom these days to sneer at the Enlightenment, but as a modern Humanist, I realize that I was born in a revolutionary politics and science, a revolution in the name of the "rights of man" and under the banner of "natural philosophy." Tutored by the Enlightenment, I grew accustomed to battle with the powers that over and over again tried to repress and suppress me and mine. Despite Enlightenment cosmopolitanism, however, I learned all too well the habits of moral division into tribes, sects, nations, the habit of seeing some of my fellows as the enemy and others as the ally. Because the Enlightenment project was built on claims of truth and good, and because language was for it as potent as a cannon, I also grew accustomed to treating words as weapons, even enjoying the battle.

Oppression had a long and successful history, and Enlightenment, only a late entrant in the race, did not erase its ancient impact on me. I am inescapably modern and traditional both, and my habits are at war with themselves. Generation after generation, the powers of the world had taken away the richness of experience from our fathers and mothers, and so from me. Even intimacy—as privacy, personality, soul—fell victim to an arrogation of power, which was in fact more worldly and political than theological. In defense, human beings developed yet other traditional habits, in particular the habit of hiding away, as do all repressed peoples with their private codes and languages. I inherited those habits too. Only partly released by revolution, I still retain traditional habits of overt obedience and secret defense, keeping who and what I am hidden from all but a very few lest self and freedom be taken away from me. In short, I am myself and yet do not—cannot—entirely own myself, admit my self. This leads me to play roles out there in the world and to keep for myself alone the person I really am. And if at moments of self-revelation I allow another a glimpse of my soul, I quickly become suspicious and afraid and as quickly hide myself again.

Out of this embedded habit of concealment grew a style of living, peculiarly modern. The need for self-defense was, with everything else, moved over into a secular world and was elevated to a principle of self-interest and in turn to a destructive egoism. The market became a metaphor for the hiddenness of persons as in the radical isolation of public and personal worlds. However it happened, the habit of concealment was made legitimate in a dualist psychology of in here and out there. But without the sanction of the other side of the Judeo-Christian story—and it had its other side with the constant reminder that the soul is unique and precious to the universe itself—the self deteriorated into the merely private self. Thus, the Enlightenment was only partially successful in retaking the soul from the priests and kings. As it were, with the notion of privacy, revolution turned nasty and self-defeating. The hidden self, now reduced to the merely private self of give and get, became the only self that counted, although we used the languages of dignity without understanding that their import was the erasure of such concealment. For the rest, we simply did what was necessary and gave the appearance of what was necessary to serve our even more successfully hidden needs and desires.[12]

Yet other habits emerged over these two hundred years of conflict between the modern world and the persistent tradition. Rightly suspicious of the way the soul had, in the hands of tradition, become a means of enslavement, we directed ourselves to the world and to society. From one side, the self, always sequestered, hidden, was now protected in its hiddenness by the revolutionary idea of a right to privacy. From the other side, however, we came to believe that the only important matters of living were economic and political, where results were tangible and measurable. Our energies were to be given over to controlling the world, whether as entrepreneur or reformer. My person, however, thought to remain aloof from change, occupying the privileged position of untouchability.

Privacy was by no means an unimportant achievement, but it had a negative side as well. By a strange turn of logic, if what was important and reasonable was to be found out in the world, then what was left over therefore had to be unimportant and unreasonable. Slowly, the now-protected and liberated self was resigned to triviality. Hidden away, it was left untended, and because it was passionate and sensuous, it was convicted of wildness. With that shift in attention from soul to society, all those connections of family and community, which were suspect because of their traditionalist history, were put to one side and left untended. We became effective and frustrated all at the same time.

For the Enlightenment project, reason was embodied in the sciences, now the only legitimate road to truth and power. Reason became the preferred pathway to nature.[13] But, in the midst of extended tables, charts, descriptions, Thomas Jefferson could also write,

> The Natural Bridge, the most sublime of nature's works . . . It is on the ascent of a hill, which seems to have been cloven through its length by some great

convulsion . . . Looking down from this height about a minute, gave me a violent head ache. If the view from the top be painful and intolerable, that from below is delightful in an equal extreme. It is impossible for the emotions arising from the sublime, to be felt beyond what they are here; so beautiful an arch, so elevate, so light: and springing as it were up to heaven, the rapture of the spectator is really indescribable![14]

Like the church of tradition, the sciences were reified, made esoteric and alien, became Science. They could not succeed in speaking to the soul for, like the Latin that was too good for common folk, their language was unsuited to the experiences of ordinary living. Yet the languages of the sciences were the only languages we honored as truthful. Responsiveness to and connection with the surround were displaced. We grew frantically dumb, quantifying everything and forgetting, as Plato reminded us, that mathematics is a poetics too.[15] Something, however, was awry in such a world of mechanisms and measurements, a world literally devalued and, in a sense, even depeopled. It was simply untruthful to reduce the human being, when at his or her most rational—in the Enlightenment view most human—to the role of observer, to passivity. This habit of passivity was again an echo of a theologized human situation in spite of the Enlightenment's secularism. For the sciences, the person was only an instrument, perhaps a conduit, of the universe and its truth. When he or she tried to assert self and individuality, the sin of pride and of disobedience appeared in modern dress. Thus, the Miltonic Satan of *Paradise Lost* is fallen precisely because he will not obey and precisely because he insists on his being in-spite-of. Again, the Enlightenment project was infected by history without knowing it.

So we became forgetful of the richness of the Enlightenment project. Only now are we beginning to appreciate the radicalism of the Kantian criticism, one of the earliest efforts of the Enlightenment to correct itself. Only now do we confess that we are party to the truth, which cannot be for us without being of us. As a colleague of mine wrote,

There is a heady, intoxicating, addictive excitement in discovering, unraveling, and elucidating the fundamental relationships and processes of the universe, or at least that part of the universe to which we have access. And the roots of this are there for the mathematicians, the physicists, the chemists, the biologists . . . There is an implicit sense of direct connection with the underlying fabric of reality, a special understanding that feels almost like a privileged relationship with the cosmos, and a universality in discovery that transcends the specific. I have heard it said by friends that scientific inquiry . . . destroys the mystery and beauty of the world around us. For me and others like me, the opposite is true.[16]

As the Enlightenment's revolutionary passions faded into memory, our institutions became only social instruments for meeting personal needs in nonpersonal ways. Trying to serve family and community without intrusion into freedom, they came instead to meet the needs of clients, not of persons.[17] Yet the more skilled at lawyering and engineering we became, the less able we were to serve ourselves and others, and the unhappier was the outcome. In short, we lost our voices when it came to tenderness and love and the connections that found these for us.

Our image of persons changed too, and with that our self-image as well. Of course, we still grew and grew up with brothers and sisters, friends and relatives, and in specific places and at specific times. Yet with a liberation that lacked solidarity and history, the ideal of the cosmopolitan became a burlesque, the person ultimately unconnected to place and time. That became our vision of the future; actual connections were at best a necessity and at worst a prison; the moral imperative was separation. The revolutionary ideal of the moral equivalence of all human beings evolved into a specious individualism where equality was collapsed into sameness, and the ability to fill roles and act the part was equated with freedom of choice. Over the generations the ties of community and family had been used to overpower persons, so we threw them away in a burst of cosmopolitan energy. And with that rejection, we pushed intimacy away from our reality and quite literally gave up, and gave up on ourselves.[18]

THE PROJECT CONTINUES

We are all children of the Enlightenment, yet at the same time the struggle against the Enlightenment project grows more heated and passionate. It is not surprising that this should be so. Of course, we still tell its many stories, but they do not ring true as when we celebrate the "rights of man" and acquiesce in limiting those rights in order to "control crime," or maintain the "military," or keep welfare "racketeers" in their place. We need reminding, for all its deterioration into a shadow enlightenment, that men and women once risked life itself for the sake of freedom and reason, and in some places around the globe they still do. The reminders are hard to come by these days. Revolution was, no doubt, a public act, but it was personally felt.[19] Sadly, however, our story has grown pale in the telling.

Nothing more clearly illustrates the move away from the Humanist revolution than the notion of democracy itself. We are reminded of its vigor in those all too rare moments when it again lives for us—when we are caught in the struggle for justice or resist the violation of conscience. We are reminded too when we hear the democrat's song in Russian or Polish or Swahili or Chinese. However, we have turned democracy all too often into blind ritualism and the struggle for justice into mere lobbying and financing. Now grown routine, we forget that democracy was once the way—new in all of human history—for persons to be with each other and with the world, the new way for persons to pay attention to each other and to the world. There had been brief moments, to be sure, when it had flared and vanished, but Athenian democracy was flawed by its ethnocentrism, elitism, and sexism, and Protestant reform was flawed by its otherworldliness and authoritarianism. With the Enlightenment, however, and for the first time, all persons were invited to the feast and all persons could contribute to the feast. That double message of universal participation—to partake and to give—had never been heard before.

An Enlightenment politics invited us to change the world, and we were qualified to do so. A democratic schooling would nurture our powers and not simply turn us into a mirror, an echo, of the powers of others better and brighter than we. A liberating science would expand and organize our knowledge of the world and so was as much personal and appreciative as pragmatic.[20] Indeed, the pragmatic spirit itself was a testimony to the democratic passion and not just another name for acquisitive practicalism. Discovery and truth were, by a pragmatist's light, to be available to all who wanted them and would make the effort to get at them. Truth then was no longer the monopoly of priests, clerks, and magicians. Revolutionary institutions, in other words, were not external to us but personal outcomes in the world expressive of our native resources for developing ourselves.

I return for a moment now to those celebrations and ceremonies I spoke of before in order to heighten the contrasts between the Enlightenment project and its shadow. I am recalled by them to the democracy we find in the lived experience, those moments of coming together and moving apart when we are with others in an essential equality of being at times of love and death. Our communication in the face of crisis rests on confidence in each other and in our ability to deal with matters truthfully, when we exhibit solidarity and rationality. I rediscover the fact that I can rely on another human being, and he or she can rely upon me. That is a form of felt democracy for which the declarations and manifestos are only comments after the fact. And that is what connects the aesthetic, the responsive, and the ceremonial to the public and the revolutionary. In those rare moments, the Humanist shifts intimacy from another world to this one and from sacramental tradition into natural experience.[21]

The children of the Enlightenment, like the prisoners in Plato's cave, replace realities with shadows. Still held to Humanism by its roots in a truthful story, a uniquely modern story, I nevertheless sense the loss of excitement. How easy it is these days for us to find substitutes for Enlightenment. We flirt with spirituality as in "new age," which elevates the dualism of in-here and out-there to a personal and metaphysical principle. We regress to fundamentalism as if by telling and retelling yesterday's story in yesterday's words we can retake its reality today. We retreat to isolation in a communitarianism of separated diversities that betrays the truth hidden in the dream of cosmopolitanism, the truth of our connection to each other as a species. And we are entrapped in a ritualism exhibited by nothing so much as the way our very arguments and divisions over such matters are predictable, much as the saying of the Mass or the recitation of the creed is predictable. In all of this—and more—we demonstrate our loss of that passionate democracy that did not separate flesh and spirit, world and self.

The move from Enlightenment to its shadow is made all the more evident by the glory of the promises it once made. So it is that salvation through the sciences confronts a monstered technology that, indifferent to me and mine, seems wedded to its own imperatives. So it is that the freedoms of the democrat are converted into form without substance, into the reduction of choice to triviality, whether in political campaigns or consumerist anarchism. So it is that rationality appears as the eminently sane maniac who designs an efficient gas chamber or commits to a world-destroying weaponry.[22] Conveniently forgotten—or perhaps symptomatically repressed—are the goods actually achieved, the freedoms actually won, the inclusions actually performed in the name of Enlightenment. But it is precisely as symptom that antimodernism of left and right (e.g., as postmodernism and as fundamentalism) reveals the problem of the Enlightenment project as it enters its third century.

In one of those grand simplifying gestures of human history, the Enlightenment cut the ties to yesterday with the promise of new and better ones tomorrow. Secure in its confidence in human powers, it would, with Voltaire, "erase the infamy" of the superstitious past. In its place, now or soon, progress would enshrine the new human being in the new society. Liberation would free us to achieve and not merely to escape. But the enthusiasm of the Enlightenment promise is not matched by the reality, which remains an all-too-human reality of doubts and ambiguities. So experience now turns the simplifying gesture of Enlightenment back upon itself, challenging promise with performance.

Once upon a time, we believed that the gods could be propitiated by a song, a dance, a sacrifice. Today, demythologized and globalized, human-made events seem to have a momentum all their own. The river still overflows its banks, but, more often than not, as with the Aswan Dam, it is human blindness that invites the flood. The dust bowl grows arid and dry; the rain forests disappear. The technique that makes the flood and the desert is broadcast around the world, applied around the world, so that there are no sanctuaries, no separated places. Indeed, the Enlightenment project seems to have succeeded unto death.

FORGETTING AND REMEMBERING

As the Enlightenment project is transformed into modernism, the shadow enlightenment appears. In response, other voices are heard: if reason is the villain, then unreason is the new hero; if science destroys, then magic will create; if democracy disappoints, then unfreedom will satisfy. It is not surprising that the terrors of Holocaust should chasten hope, that the world-destroying bomb and bacterium should indict the sciences, that cold war should subvert democracy. Nor is it surprising that a world newly aware of its multitudes and variousness should retreat behind walls that, once again, need to be familiar and protective and to set us apart from the alien other. Tribes and nations, never entirely erased by the cosmopolitan impulse, reawaken like germs emerging from a spore. The move against modernism is only to be expected, and with it the move against Enlightenment and Humanism.

But it is not enough to blame the present condition of the Enlightenment project on the opportunism of its enemies. It is the promise of Enlightenment itself that increases our expectations and so abets our willingness to listen to its subverters. Disappointed, we are obstinately blind to the modern achievement that finally includes women and children and people of all colors and workers as persons who count. Instead, we complain that it is too little, or that there is insufficient gratitude, or what have you. Or we are obstinately blind to a technology that increases crop yield, that cures the sick and extends the life span. Instead, we complain that life has lost its quality where before life itself was not an option for all too many. In short, when little was awaited, then every move was a victory, every step a celebration.

In our time, anti-Humanist opportunism and unreal expectation combine to issue in despair, fear, loneliness, but these cannot be understood only as counters in an existentialist poetry. A reawakened lust for authority and a resurrected magic are not just instruments of power and manipulation by corrupted individuals either. For many reasons the person finds himself or herself on the margin, alienated, victimized, and often by the very powers that are said to be humanity's allies. In the name of helping, society and government nurture helplessness. In the name of knowing, science and technology nurture social control. More deeply still, in the name of liberation, the shadow enlightenment nurtures rootlessness and abandonment. Nietzsche was not merely playing at nihilism when he addressed this shadow enlightenment:

> The only thing inquiry has accomplished has been to raze wall after wall of outer fortifications which the ascetic ideal has succeeded in building around itself . . . Or does anyone seriously believe that the defeat of, say, theological astronomy spelled the defeat of the ideal? Does anyone believe that man has grown less hungry for a transcendental solution to life's riddle simply because life has become more casual, peripheral, expendable, in the visible order of things? Has not man's determination to belittle himself developed apace precisely since Copernicus? Alas, his belief that he was unique and irreplaceable in the hierarchy of beings has been shattered for good: he has become an animal quite literally and without reservations; he who, according to his earlier belief had been almost God ("child of God," "God's own image"). Ever since Copernicus man has been rolling down an incline, faster and faster, away from the center—whither? Into the void? Into the "piercing sense of his emptiness?"[23]

So it is possible to draw a radical indictment of Humanism,[24] one that touches more seriously on the issue of modernism than is imagined by its enemies. In point is the fact that a shadow enlightenment, like a Humanism of the word, characterizes modernity. The indictment reveals that neither Enlightenment nor Humanism has been truthful to itself.

When Nietzsche proclaimed the "death of God" or when Dostoevsky concluded that now "everything is permissible," they were calling attention to, responding to what happened when Enlightenment evolved into its shadow. To understand that response, we need to avoid reducing God to a simple-minded anthropomorphic entity and to argue (endlessly) the question of is and is not. The god idea served us well and not just badly. In summary, three claims are associated with God in human experience. First, God ensures the existence of the world and provides a background reality of order, structure, and permanence for a natural reality that is as disorderly as it is orderly and that is ultimately impermanent. Second, God offers assurance to persons, not so much by warranting good outcomes but by being a source of meaning and purpose. Third, God makes the natural universe intelligible. Without God, then—and we are used to having God around whether he exists or not—the universe is but an accident, and we are but an accident. If there is no God, then how shall human beings be served in their need and before the threat of accident?

We human beings have not yet learned to live in an accidental universe. We still look backward in longing. We are secularized only along certain narrowed pathways, in business, work life, law, government, recreation. We treat secularity as a convenience of arenas rather than as a displacement of realities.[25]

Must we then choose between pointless battle against the past and demoralizing surrender of the Enlightenment project and Humanist faith?[26] The arid responses to Humanism, spirituality, fundamentalism, communitarianism, and ritualism simply echo the habits of an alienated world and alienated people. In turn, we become angry at ourselves and uninteresting to others. But these flirtations with unreason are only symptoms, and their telltale is the nasty dogmatism with which they are held.

Yet for all these recurrent rehearsals of old wine in new bottles, we cannot ignore them either. The passions they stir in us, the walls they erect between us, our compulsive return to them over and over again, suggest that they are serious indeed even for the children of the Enlightenment. They beg for a diagnosis. Briefly put, as we flirt with spirituality—and which of us has not—we announce our longing for love and care. We cry out for help in dealing with the fears, doubts, and anxieties that today seem to grow even more oppressive. When we turn backward, we confess our need for reliable truths to live by and with. In our romance with community, we seek connections that demonstrate our need for them precisely by the rarity of their occurrence. Reminded from time to time that connections do happen, we are all the more oppressed by their infrequency. We want to be recognized and to recognize others—that is the achievement of community and its narrative—but instead we are often driven away.

In short, our behaviors tell us that we are in need of the Humanist ideal that once turned revolution and reform into personal experiences and personal experience into revolution and reform. Our behaviors teach us that we have put apart what was together, self and world, self and other, in here and out there. This would seem to call then for a Humanist "cure of souls," a normal therapy for Humanists. Of course, I understand the dangers of using the image of therapy. I worry that giving a psychological turn to Humanism risks the reduction of interpersonal relationships to dependency or to uncritical sentimentality. Nor am I unmindful of the fact that the language of therapy invites the anti-Humanist to accuse me of sickness.

At the same time, I know that the anti-Humanist exploits the disconnections of modern living by urging the surrender of the world itself. I know, too, that out of our loneliness, we are tempted to accept the invitation. How else to explain the manifest popularity of those esoteric cults that encourage separation and of those fundamentalist movements that turn to another world. Sadly, it is precisely among cultist and fundamentalist that we find the greatest success in reaching to our need of connection. Slavery and exploitation wearing familiar and not-so-familiar costume rise again. We must find ways of drawing upon the passionate democracy of the Humanist for a secular and modern and even normal "cure of souls."

The seeds of such a Humanist therapy are found in the naturalism that unites us with our world. Rationality too was its celebration, announcing reliable ways of expressing the qualities of our passionate attachment to the world, an attachment deeply rooted in our desire to know and, with it, to do. Revolution and reform celebrated our ability to enter the world as participants and not simply as victims. Once upon a time our struggle led us to the joys of free inquiry and to storm the barricades in its name. A normal therapy thus is guided by the unity of self and world, passion and action, attachment and participation.

A normal therapy is really a form of mutuality—of teaching and learning. I initiate it by engaging in acts that make me ready for others, by making myself accessible to others, finally by breaking the age-old habit of hiddenness. This calls for the silence of spaces, the forgotten surround, and for listening to the voices of others and of the world.[27] Thereby I make spaces for others; I announce my welcome. I invite others into my world so that it becomes a shared world, and I seek their invitation as well. I resist the Humanism of the word and, for a time at least, am prepared simply to be present. Strangely, as I listen and grow silent—and listening and silence are always a problem for the Humanist—I invite not only others but myself.

With such a therapy, I become newly accessible to myself. Of course, the activity of silence can easily deteriorate into mere withdrawal. I need then to put myself deliberately into places and spaces that evoke my response. I not only listen but appreciate. I grasp the riches of the world's offerings. I seek moments of aloneness precisely to prepare myself to be with others again. Or I treat my associations in work and play as instances of solidarity, seeking to move away from taking others merely as their roles, or as the services they provide, or as the functions they perform. I look for persons within their roles, confident that although hidden they are there. I try to break the chains of interchangeability that a collection of roles imposes on me. I replace ritual greetings with conversation, routine acknowledgment with recognition. In short, I put myself in the position of being a person in the presence of other persons. Not least of all, I believe in the possibility of finding persons, of being a person.

Such a therapy entails its politics, and so the activities of intimacy push us toward reform in a new way. The world around us must be shaped to permit, even encourage, a pedagogy of intimacy. It is no mere frill to build an environment of beautiful objects and open spaces. Nor is it only a matter of social justice to struggle for the widest distribution of the time and wealth that are prerequisite to my ability to be with others. The barriers of geography and language that close us off from each other call for a schooling that equips us to enjoy the riches of a pluralist and diverse world. As with any other pedagogy, there are skills to be learned and powers to be shared.

Freed of community by birth, I am in position of shaping my biography. Of course, it would be arrogant and false to claim absolute powers of self-creation in some existentialist pipedream. Biology will have its way, as will accident and surprise. But a pedagogy of intimacy readies me for happenings. As a Humanist, I still retain that confidence in my self, in others, and in the world. I have turned away from the allure of another place. Now I must mean it. I grasp, finally, the coherence that a passionate democracy gives to the Enlightenment project.

NOTES

1. While phrased as a call to reconstruct religion, *Humanist Manifesto I* (1933) identified this two-ness in its introduction,

> Today man's larger understanding of the universe, his scientific achievements, and his deeper appreciation of brotherhood have created a situation which requires a new statement of the means and purposes of religion. Such a vital, fearless, and frank religion capable of furnishing adequate social goals and personal satisfactions may appear to many people as a complete break with the past.

2. From a letter to Paul Kurtz, in "Sakharov: A Humanist Galileo," *Free Inquiry* 10, no. 2 (Spring 1990): 46.

3. This quarrel takes many forms but most often is reduced to a debate between "secularists" and "religionists." Thus, in an editorial, Don Page commented on the founding of the International Humanist and Ethical Union:

> Nicholas Walter's statement is from an atheist and freethinker who has worked for many years in the British humanist movement. He makes it clear that, while advocating the right of people to be religious or non-religious, he himself finds little need for religion or the religious outlook. . . . Joseph Chuman, on the other hand, explains the position of the non-theist who describes himself as "religious" because of his ethical and aesthetic concerns. . . . It is very clear, for example, that [Julian] Huxley and [Jaap] Van Praag intended to found a movement based on a humanism which accommodates these concerns

International Humanism (October 1991): 1.

4. For a discussion of the "game of either/or" see Howard B. Radest, "Companionship (A Metaphor for Humanism)," *Humanism Today*, no. 4 (1988): 61–77. See also Howard B. Radest, *The Devil and Secular Humanism* (New York: Praeger, 1990), pp. 49–64.

5. Again, the Humanist misses the connection, in this instance between an abstracted Enlightenment and the Humanism of the Renaissance.

6. It is more than a hundred years since William James published *The Principles of Psychology* (1890; reprinted, New York: Dover, 1950) with its discussion of the stream of consciousness. It is nearly fifty years since the death of John Dewey, who waged a lifelong war against dualism. Yet the unifications of matter and spirit, self and world, still elude us and still often elude Humanists who "know" better.

7. I hope I am not misunderstood when I identify the essential subjectivity of experience. Perhaps the point becomes clearer when I suggest that it is Kantian, not Dionysian. For further notes on the role of the subject when seen through Kantian eyes, see Howard B. Radest, "The Humanist Imagination: From Ethics to Aesthetics," *Journal of Humanism and Ethical Religion* 2, no. 1 (Fall 1989): 39–58.

8. Abraham H. Maslow, "Various Meanings of Transcendence," 1968, p. 2, unpublished note, revised and published in Donald Cutler, ed., *The Religious Situation* (Boston: Beacon, 1969).

9. As I reflected on our neglect of Emerson and Whitman, of William James and Josiah Royce and George Santayana—which is only partially corrected by the attention John Dewey receives in Humanist circles—I was struck by the thought that American Humanisms differ from their European and British counterparts by picking up this romantic strain. Yet a post-Enlightenment Humanism must acknowledge its double root, and in this American Humanists are better placed than their European colleagues.

10. For illustrations of this point, see Khoren Arisian, *The New Wedding* (New York: Vintage, 1973); Algernon D. Black, *Without Burnt Offerings* (New York: Viking, 1974); Arthur Dobrin and Kenneth Briggs, *Getting Married the Way You Want* (Englewood Cliffs, N.J.: Prentice-Hall, 1974); Roger E. Greeley, ed., *The Best of Humanism* (Buffalo, N.Y.: Prometheus, 1988); Corliss Lamont, *A Humanist Wedding* (Buffalo, N.Y.: American Humanist Association, 1978); Sherwin T. Wine, *Celebration* (Buffalo, N.Y.: Prometheus, 1988). See also "The Aesthetics of Humanism," *Humanism Today* 2 (1986).

11. See Martin Buber, *I And Thou*, trans. Ronald Gregor Smith (New York: Scribner and Sons, 1958).

12. In another connection on the same point, I noted the following:

> The public bias of the ethics of Humanism sets the intimate aside, reduces it to the "private" and protects it as nearly untouchable. So, as it were, it excludes intimacy from the moral scrutiny of others, who on Humanist grounds, are strangers. Ironically, even the "private" becomes a legal category as in "a man's home is his castle," or as in the laws attending to marriage, the obligations of parenthood, the

> notion of "private" property, and the like. Humanist ethics then has trouble dealing with the personal and the intimate which are only hinted at in the notion of privacy. . . . Its legalist bias not only forces an inordinate attention to analysis and language itself but makes it difficult for Humanism to account for more intuitive and experience-based moral categories like love, concern, care, and sacrifice.

Howard B. Radest, "Doing Good: Humanism and The Liberal Temptation," *Humanism Today* 5 (1989): 28–29.

13. Nature was, of course, a significant Enlightenment symbol, but, unlike the nature that was responsive and responded to, nature was instead a political vehicle in the challenge to tradition and history and the scene of impersonal forces and powers and laws as in the sciences. Nature lacked what Emerson, among others, tried to restore to the Enlightenment project: an actual presence and a dramatic presentation. Thus, for the Enlightenment,

> supported by both reason and experience, nature became its own authority. The challenges it posed to the authority of tradition covered a wide field. It challenged the legacy of medieval science, the power of organized religion, and the feudal class-based institutions of state and society. But nature in the Enlightenment was effective against these traditions not only because it was backed by reason and experience: it had collected so many affirmative meanings in the history of European thought that it was available to be enrolled in nearly any campaign at hand. What is more, the eighteenth century was peculiarly suited for nature. It was a concept that took a position against institutions and social conventions that were deteriorating from within and attacked from without.

Charles A. Miller, *Jefferson And Nature* (Baltimore, Md.: Johns Hopkins University Press, 1993), p. 8.

14. Thomas Jefferson, *Notes on the State of Virginia: The Portable Thomas Jefferson*, ed. Merrill D. Peterson (New York: Viking Penguin, 1975), pp. 54–55.

15. For example, see Plato, "Timaeus," *The Dialogues of Plato*, trans. Benjamin Jowett (New York: Random House, 1937), 2: 3–68.

16. Jane F. Koretz, "Work As Meaning: A Passion for Science," *Humanism Today* 6 (1991): 129.

17. For a discussion of this pattern and of efforts to break out of it, see Howard B. Radest, *Community Service: Encounter of Strangers* (Westport, Conn.: Praeger, 1993).

18. In *Individualism Old and New* (1929–1930; New York: Capricorn, 1962), John Dewey undertakes a critical analysis of the causes and consequences of this specious individualism. He notes,

> The "joining" habit of the average American, and his excessive sociability, may well have an explanation like that of conformity. They, too, testify to nature's abhorrence of the vacuum which the passing of the older individualism has produced. We should not be so averse to solitude if we had, when we were alone, the companionship of communal thought built into our mental habits. In the absence of this communion, there is the need for reinforcement by external contact. Our sociability is largely an effort to find substitutes for that normal consciousness of

connection and union that proceeds from being a sustained and sustaining member of a social whole. (pp. 87–88).

19. I turn to Walt Whitman to catch this sense of public reform personally felt:

> I sit and look out upon all the sorrows of the world, and upon all
> oppression and shame;
> I hear secret convulsive sobs from young men, at anguish with themselves,
> remorseful after deeds done;
> I see, in low life, the mother misused by her children, dying,
> neglected, gaunt, desperate;
> I see the wife misused by her husband—I see the treacherous seducer
> of young women;
> I mark the ranklings of jealousy and unrequited love, attempted to be hid—
> I see these sights on the earth;
> I see the workings of battle, pestilence, tyranny—I see martyrs and prisoners;
> I observe a famine at sea—I observe sailors casting lots who shall be kill'd,
> to preserve the lives of the rest;
> I observe the slights and degradations cast by arrogant persons upon
> laborers, the poor, and upon negroes and the like;
> All these—All the meanness and agony without end, I sitting look out upon,
> See, hear, and am silent.

"I Sit and Look Out" (1860), in *Leaves of Grass* (Philadelphia: David McKay, 1990), pp. 179–180.

20. A broader and more generous view of the sciences as a human activity is evident in the actual activities of scientists. For a Humanist, John Dewey catches the spirit of the enterprise when, typically, he writes,

> Because the free working of mind is one of the greatest joys open to men, the scientific attitude, incorporated in individual mind, is something which adds enormously to one's enjoyment of existence. The delights of thinking, of inquiry, are not widely enjoyed at the present time. But the few who experience them would hardly exchange them for other pleasures. Yet, they are not as restricted in quality as they are in the number of those who share them. That is to say, as long as "scientific" thinking confines itself to technical fields, it lacks full scope and varied material. Its subject-matter is technical to the degree in which application in human life is shut out. The mind that is hampered by fear lest something old and precious be destroyed is the mind that experiences fear of science. He who has this fear cannot find reward and peace in the discovery of new truths and the projection of new ideals. He does not walk the earth freely, because he is obsessed by the need of protecting some private possession of belief and taste. For the love of private possessions is not confined to material goods.

Individualism Old and New, pp. 161–162.

21. Erich Fromm, by way of example, describes the naturalization of conscience as follows:

> Humanistic conscience is not the internalized voice of an authority whom we are eager to please and afraid of displeasing. It is our own voice, present in every human being and independent of external sanctions and rewards. . . . It is the voice of our true selves which summons us back to our selves, to live productively, to develop fully and harmoniously—that is, to become what we potentially are. . . . If love can be defined as the affirmation of the potentialities and the care for, and the respect of, the uniqueness of the loved person, humanistic conscience can be justly called *the voice of our loving care for ourselves.*

Man for Himself (New York: Rinehart, 1947), pp. 158–159.

22. Jurgen Habermas makes the point in a similar way:

> The distance between expert cultures and the broader public grows greater. . . . This problem was first seen in all its acuteness in the eighteenth century; it called into being the project of Enlightenment. . . . Enlighteners cast in the mold of a Condorcet had the extravagant expectation that the arts and sciences would promote not only the control of natural forces but also interpretations of the world and of ourself, moral progress, the justice of social institutions, even the happiness of humankind.
>
> The twentieth century has left little of this optimism intact.

Jurgen Habermas, *The Theory of Communicative Action*, vol. 2: *Lifeworld and System: A Critique of Functionalist Reason*, trans. Thomas McCarthy (Boston: Beacon Press, 1987), pp. 326–327.

23. Friedrich Nietzsche, *The Geneology of Morals* (1887), trans. Francis Golffing (New York: Doubleday Anchor Books, 1956), pp. 291–292.

24. Recently, the faculty of the Humanist Institute has been exploring the legitimacy of criticism of modernism. In preparation for that discussion, I was asked to draft an indictment of Humanism that, under the title, "An Indictment: Summa Contra Humanismus," appears along with various responses in *Humanism Today* 9, 1995.

25. Habermas, for example, makes the point when he writes,

> To the degree that the Protestant ethic of the calling ceased to place its stamp on the private conduct of life, the methodical-rational way in which bourgeois strata led their lives was displaced by the utilitarian life-style of "specialists without spirit" and the aesthetic-hedonistic life-style of "sensualists without heart," that is, by two complementary ways of life that soon became mass phenomena. The two life-styles can be strikingly represented by different personality types, but they can also take hold of the same person. With this fragmentation of the person, individuals lose their ability to give their life histories a certain degree of consistent direction.

Habermas, *Theory of Communicative Action*, 2: 323.

26. I use the word *faith* with hesitation because it stirs unwanted and unnecessary associations with traditional religious vocabularies. Yet I know of no more adequate term for describing the attitude, stance, and confidence of a person toward the world in which he or she lives, the position taken, as it were, toward the as yet—and always—invisible future. For useful and important discussions

of this term and its relationship to Humanism, see Beverley M. Earles, "The Faith Dimension of Humanism" (Ph.D. diss., Victoria University, 1989), and Wilfred Cantwell Smith, *Faith and Belief* (Princeton, N.J.: Princeton University Press, 1979).

27. Again, I know the risk of addressing themes like silence and meditation that for Humanists carry the burden of destructive and oppressive associations. Nevertheless, I am not content to permit the capture of human values or of valuable human capacities by traditionalists. I am reminded of Emerson's comments on solitude:

> To go into solitude, a man needs to retire as much from his chamber as from society. I am not solitary whilst I read and write, though nobody is with me. But if a man would be alone, let him look at the stars. The rays that come from those heavenly worlds will separate between him and what he touches. One might think the atmosphere was made transparent with this design, to give man, in the heavenly bodies, the perpetual presence of the sublime. Seen in the streets of the cities, how great they are! If the stars should appear one night in a thousand years, how would men believe and adore; and preserve for many generations rememberance of the city of God which had been shown! But every night they come out, these envoys of beauty, and light the universe with their admonishing smile.
>
> . . . But all natural objects make a kindred impression, when the mind is open to their influence. Nature never wears a mean appearance. Neither does the wisest man extort her secret, and lose his curiosity by finding out all her perfection. Nature never became a toy to a wise spirit. The flowers, the animals, the mountains reflect the wisdom of his best hour, as much as they had delighted the simplicity of his childhood. When we speak of nature in this manner, we have a distinct but most poetical sense of mind.

Ralph Waldo Emerson, "Nature" (1836), in *Selected Essays*, ed. Larzer Ziff (New York: Penguin, 1982), p. 37.

2

THE DEATH AND BIRTH OF A DREAM

PREJUDICES

Controversy still surrounds socialism, so it is only fair to alert readers to my prejudices. I am still a creature of the left, although I did not embrace a united front, romanticize "Papa Joe" (Stalin), or flirt with a variety of near-communist options like the 1948 Henry Wallace presidential candidacy and its brief incarnation of the Progressive party. I believe that American socialism lived in a world that never was and that the American Communist party had neither substance nor integrity. Of course, socialists like Norman Thomas (does anyone remember him or Eugene Debs?) and more recently Michael Harrington contributed to society in ways that we scarcely appreciated then or recall today. And I am not unmindful of the fact that many American communists—certainly before the Hitler-Stalin Pact but not only then—came to their loyalties out of a deep sense of moral idealism. In more recent memory, I was appalled by American imperialism in Southeast Asia and Latin America but at the same time did not believe that Fidel Castro was merely an "agrarian reformer" or that Ho Chi Minh was a democratic idol or that the "sayings" of Chairman Mao (Tse-tung) should replace those of Jefferson, Lincoln, Locke, or Rousseau.

I confess that I cannot conceive a Humanism that is not seized with the issues of political economy, but that does not demand the sacrifice of intimacy to power. If a Leninist realism claimed that "you can't make an omelet without breaking eggs," the Humanist voice recalls that the "eggs" are human beings. To be sure, I know Humanists who claim that politics and economics are irrelevant to Humanism, who have, as it were, surrendered all hope of the Enlightenment project. They would, in a secular reincarnation of the Gospels, "render unto Caesar the things that are Caesar's and unto God the things that are God's." I know too that there is more than one conceivable political partner for Humanism. Nevertheless, there are limits; for example, I know of no Humanist fascists or theocrats. I know still other Humanists who will not engage in the messiness of political economy. These views, which I call Humanist parochialism, Humanist pluralism, and Humanist opportunism, arise from the shadow enlightenment and opt for social passivity. I am grateful then that events have denied us permission to rely on time-worn, shop-worn notions taken from another place and another time.

SOLIDARITY

Although I want to relocate intimacy into Humanism, I have not given up on social reform. That would be to replace one impoverished Humanism with another, turning sentiment into sentimentality and romance into romanticism.[1] I am instead searching for the widest integration of rationality and intimacy. It is these together that give birth to ideas, which return me to a richer Humanism. I am not alone in my passion for ideas. Indeed, in some grand Emersonian manner,[2] our response to nature exhibits us to each other, establishes our kinship. I am, in other words, an aesthetic being long before I learn to speak about feeling evocation, taste, and beauty. Thus John Dewey commented on Keats's lines, "Beauty is truth, truth, beauty":

> In spite of the elliptical character of Keats' statements, two points emerge. One of them is his conviction that "reasonings" have an origin like that of the movements of a wild creature toward its goal, and they may become spontaneous, "instinctive," and when they become instinctive are sensuous and immediate, poetic. The other side of this conviction is his belief that no "reasoning" as reasoning, that is, as excluding imagination and sense, can reach truth. Even "the greatest philosopher" exercises an animal-like preference to guide his thinking to its conclusions. He selects and puts aside as his imaginative sentiments move. "Reason" at its height cannot attain complete grasp and a self-contained assurance. It must fall back upon imagination—upon the embodiment of ideas in emotionally charged sense.[3]

Were our aesthetic sensibility absent, ideas would not simply be abstract but empty. I would be a manipulator of mere signs, as the computer or calculator manipulates signs. But these would lack anchorage outside the manipulations. Except in the most superficial sense, I really would not *have* ideas at all; my ideas would lack reference. Indeed, John Dewey, although I think he exaggerated for effect, went so far as to remark, "In short, the history of human experience is a history of the development of the arts."[4]

I realize that this world is my home in all its loveliness and fascination. I enjoy it, am awed by it, fear it, am playful within it, am alternately serious and foolish about it. Beneath the achievements of the sciences and the arts, there is my connectedness to and appreciation of the world, a connection felt directly in moments of crisis and celebration. Because I have this sense of things, I am affronted by those who—in yet another dismissal of the Enlightenment project—tell me I am only "passing through" or that I am "in the world but not of it." If I thought to name a Humanist heresy, it would be that disdain of our place and space. My quarrel with so many of the traditions, East and West, is not about God's being or nonbeing, not about fate, not about heaven or hell, but about this disjunction between world appreciation and world rejection. Of course, a "sense of injustice" leads me to revolution and reform. A sense of fittingness, however, gives these an enriched content. That a politics should flow from this is not surprising, and that it should be the object of attack is not surprising either. So we take a look at socialism by way of example.

Given the manifest failures of Marxism-Leninism, Stalinism, and a command economy, we all too quickly dismiss socialism, one of the Enlightenment's more interesting incarnations. Other claimants for the socialist title, however, existed well before Karl Marx, who dismissed them as merely "utopian" or "bourgeois." Still other socialisms have evolved, announcing their family membership by calling themselves democratic socialism and social democracy. Still more recently, "self-governing socialism" developed in Yugoslavia,[5] although the death of Marshal Tito, the failure to establish a successor leadership, the breakup of Yugoslavia, and the horrors of Bosnia-Herzogovina have clearly aborted the effort. The story of socialism has by no means ended despite the fall of the Berlin Wall and the dissolution of the U.S.S.R., and despite the illusion that universal salvation is to be found in the "free" market.[6] Symptomatic of its Enlightenment roots, socialism tried to develop a scientific sociology and political economy. The effort did not succeed. Marxist predictions, for example, often came after the fact as vindications and interpretations, not as verifications. If not really "scientific," however, Marxism had at least the merits of objectivity and relevance. So,

> if anyone should insist on a "scientific" rationale for socialism—an orthodox Marxist, perhaps or an orthodox monetarist—then the answer must be: no such science exists for human choice and action. . . . Does this disclaimer leave socialists all at sea, in dark and fog, and without map or compass? On the contrary. All opinions are not created equal, and distinctions will still be made between truth and falsehood. Loyalty to a cause becomes dangerously sectarian, however, whenever exclusive claims are made to religious or scientific authority.[7]

Although Marxism claimed a sense of history and faulted its predecessors for having none, it was a history that *philosophes* like Condorcet would have recognized.[8] Following Hegel, it was a history that demonstrated the working out of spirit, of the idea, in actual time and place. Of course, "spirit" for the Marxist was transubstantiated, became "material," as in the "forms of production" and as in Marx's claim to "stand Hegel on his head." But the Enlightenment project's commitment to progress remained essentially unchanged, as did confidence in its inevitability. As recently as the 1960s U.S.S.R. premier Khrushchev informed the West, "We will bury you." This was not so much a threat—which was the way we read it—but a historicist conclusion. This historicism continued right up to the breakup of the U.S.S.R. In 1986, it appeared for example, when Ivan Frolov, former president of the Council of Philosophic Societies in the Soviet Union, proposed a "new" Marxist Humanism.[9]

With its claim to be "scientific," its Baconian connection of knowledge and power, and its progressive sense of history, Marxism was clearly a child of the Enlightenment. In its attentiveness to the person in nature as in its analysis of productivity and alienation, it reflected the two-ness of Humanism. Nor is an aesthetic reference all that aberrant either. For example, Cornel West remarks:

> Marx's own debts to the Romantics' preoccupation with many-sided personality and full-fledged individuality (as in Friedrich Schiller's *Letters on Aesthetic Education*) and to the early socialists' focus on universal suffrage, womens' rights, abolitionism, and workplace democracy intrigued me. I became convinced that Marx's own intellectual development should be understood in terms of this fascinating tension between the moral conviction of the flowering of individuality under wholesale democratic socio-economic and political conditions and the theoretical concern of explaining scientifically the dynamics and tendencies of profit-driven capitalist societies that foster a narrow individualism and a truncated political democracy.[10]

It was just this ethical and aesthetic sensibility that vanished as Marxism deteriorated into the arid dialectics of Marxist "criticism" and the depersonalized activities of Marxist bureaucrats. Marxism, like liberalism and reform, also exhibited the shadow enlightenment.

Socialism, as in its criticism of alienation, is a passion posing as a science. Calvin Schrag writes,

> Admittedly, Marx himself did not work out the ethical posture of his new notion of *praxis* as sensuous human activity. It would seem, however, that his notion of *praxis* lends itself neither to a teleological nor to a deontological typology. In fact, it opens up the avenue to a radical critique of traditional value theory. *Praxis* is governed neither by objective ends nor by transempirical oughts. It deploys a pre-objective field of concerns in which a functioning intentionality of aspirations and expectations responds to the concrete conditions of the times.[11]

Alienation is the subtext beneath the talk of class warfare and capitalist exploitation.[12] But today we realize that it is an industrial, corporate, and bureaucratic society that separates person from person, person from world, and person from self. These separations are real enough in all advanced social systems. I live in a world of many, many things and, am encouraged in the illusion that their acquisition is all that ultimately matters. I live in a world that tempts me more and more to respond to persons as things, to use them, own them, literally to objectify them. As the world grows more crowded and as my skill as manipulator improves, it is likely indeed that I will treat everyone but myself as object. Finally, this habit of perception and action overwhelms me, and I come to treat myself as a thing too.

At the same time, I am a sensuous and physical being. My imagination is nurtured by the tangibilities of classical and Renaissance Humanisms. I am like Archimedes, seeking a lever to move the universe and da Vinci, enjoying the tension and release of muscle and sinew and bone. I am with Franklin flying a kite and Roebling building a bridge. But as I grow more perfect in a technology that began in the cave, I can easily forget its mundane roots in human needs and human playfulness. All too soon, I can even objectify myself in the varied roles I play, understand myself through a script I do not author and that finally has no author. I lose not only others and world but myself; I become genuinely and finally an alien. By contrast, I am led by the Marxist notion of solidarity from which its critique of alienation grows, in yet another way to the two-ness of Humanism.[13] Thus the context within which I consider the so-called death of socialism as an instance of the shadow enlightenment.

IT WAS A FAMOUS VICTORY

I recall the gleefulness that was all too visible at the fall of the Berlin Wall, the drama of Solidarity in Poland, the *glasnost* and *perestroika* of Mikhail Gorbachev, the liberation of East European states, and finally the dissolution of the Soviet Union. Glee has now given way to horror at ethnic cleansing in the former Yugoslavia, near–civil war in the former Soviet republics, and the rise of orthodoxy and Islamic fundamentalism in the East. With the successful election of Vladimir Zhirinovsky and his party to a sizable plurality in the Russian parliament in 1994, radical nationalism has again seduced millions of Russians with the promise of a new adventurism reminiscent of the "glories" of the czar. Nor have we heard the last of the old communist left, now ironically known as "conservative." Yet American "triumphalism" persists. Were I Aeschylus or Sophocles, I would surely hear echoes of that *hubris* that announces the fall of princes and principalities.

It is not surprising—but it is surely troubling—that the "victory" of the forces of "freedom" reinforces a certain blindness to our own problems of poverty and exploitation, of environmental and societal decay. Our "victory" therefore becomes a way of hiding from what is going on—a circus, an amusement. What is lacking above all is a decent sense of human solidarity, a sense of shared fate and shared concern. Indeed, even as we announce that we will aid Eastern Europe and Russia in their effort to build a new society, we insist that its shape must be determined by the virtues of the "free market," our virtues. Our "democracy," then, masks an exercise of wealth and power.[14]

Surely we can criticize the naiveté of those, like Lincoln Steffens in the 1920s, who believed they had "seen the future and it works." Yes, communism is the "God that failed." But a Humanist's response to a loss of faith is a certain sadness as hope is once again betrayed. We need to remind ourselves that Marx was a moralist and that Marxists were moral idealists. Of course, they costumed their dream in the turgid polemics of dialectical materialism and dubious claims of science. But in a world filled with poverty, exploitation, and inequity, they committed to the achievement of global, political, and economic justice. A dream betrayed is a cause for sadness, not rejoicing.

The sorry condition of Eastern Europe and the Soviet Union (and of Latin American communism too) should not lead us to ignore the achievements of Marx and of Marxists. Of course, these were flawed, yet with their moral outrage at an industrialism indifferent to human beings, Marxists lived with the sense of universal social justice that shaped the Enlightenment project, an attempt to rework its ideas in the new social and industrial framework that the eighteenth century had not yet encountered.[15] Thus, with communities fragmented by an adventurous industrialism, "alienation"[16] remains a feature of a still-unreconstructed industrialism. To this day industrial organization has difficulty recognizing that human beings are present in a workplace that is too often designed and continues to be designed for robots.

Under conditions of concentrated wealth and power, distributive justice remains a puzzlement and political freedom often an empty promise. Marx, like Adam Smith, knew that the substance of social life had to be political economy. We instead divided these from each other, as if we could have participatory democracy in politics and ego-driven anarchy in economics. Marx and the Marxists understood too that rationality is not a disembodied activity, that reason is led and misled by context and interest and social location. They understood that my "reason" could be shaped to serve the ends of others without my being aware that this was being done.

The notions of class consciousness and false consciousness became mere propaganda tools of bureaucratic *apparatchiks*. At the same time, the notion of class still has its analytic power despite our American blindness to it.[17] The effort to transcend class, to locate human solidarity in the natural world—again a reprise of the universalism of the Enlightenment project—had never before been attempted in a secular political economy. The Roman Empire, after all, excluded women, slaves, and aliens. The catholicism of the Church left this world to its miseries as it proclaimed universal membership in the community of the faithful for all the "children of God." Finally, in a world that demeaned both work and worker, the effort to legitimize and not merely sentimentalize the dignity of labor remains a necessary ideal.

It is not unimportant to read the signs of what lies ahead in Eastern Europe before we celebrate our "victory." Traditional anti-Semitism reappears, replacing the institutional anti-Semitism of communist Moscow.[18] When coupled with the Church's maneuvering for power as in Poland or Rumania and an aggressive Eastern Orthodoxy and Islam, the repression that follows the fall of communism should not be underestimated. Barbara Stanosz, professor emeritus in the philosophy department at Warsaw University, describes the rising influence of the Catholic Church:

> The legislative and executive branches have provided enormous benefits to the Church: special tax privileges and property rights not accorded individuals; privileged access to television and radio frequencies; dispensation to engage in political propaganda; introducing even stronger provisions of teaching the

catechism in public schools; adopting legal provisions that open the way for religious censorship in the media . . . ; and adopting legislation that penalizes abortion (both patient and doctor) and restricts divorce.

. . . The army has been clericalised, with priests now playing the role of the former political commissars; the Church hierarchy is regularly "consulted" on the filling of state posts . . . ; religious symbols and icons have been introduced into the building of all public institutions.[19]

Another reports reads,

With Moscow disintegrating . . . Mr. Marupov [member, Russian Ministry, Internal Affairs] says its time to carve out a fundamentalist religious state like neighboring Iran. It would encompass a vast area—inhabited by 50 million Moslems—that borders on Iran, Afghanistan, and China. Mullahs would preside over restored religious courts outlawed since Lenin's day.[20]

We do not seem much better placed. Right-wing coalitions, fundamentalist religions, and neofascist adventurism are on the rise; an honorable conservatism is trapped by the right-wing populism of its putative allies[21]; historic forms of limiting freedom of expression and conscience grow more and more frequent. The market economy has yet to deal with problems of poverty, the maldistribution of social goods, and the decay of what is called the "infrastructure" of society. In short, "it was a famous victory," but good has not triumphed nor is evil vanquished.

HUMANISM AND SOCIALISM

It is helpful to recall the historic affinity of Humanism and socialism. Examples abound: the informal connections of Humanism with Fabian socialism in late nineteenth-century England; the social democratic commitments of most of the founding leadership of the Dutch Humanist movement that grew from the Resistance to Nazi occupation after World War II; the "radical" Humanism of M. N. Roy, founder of the Radical Humanist Association in India; the critical Marxism of the Humanist "philosophic section" in Yugoslavia; and, not least of all, *Humanist Manifesto I* (1933) in the United States, which said,

Fourteenth: The Humanists are firmly convinced that existing acquisitive and profit-motivated society has shown itself to be inadequate and that a radical change in methods, controls, and motives must be instituted. A socialized and cooperative economic order must be established to the end that the equitable distribution of the means of life be possible.

Humanism, however, never did have an affinity for Marxism-Leninism and certainly not for Stalinism, both of which may be seen as anti-Humanisms. Symptomatically, Humanists drew a line of development between Marx's 1844 manuscripts and *Das Kapital* and read Marx through the perspectives of liberation.[22] Nor did notions like economic determinism and dialectical materialism, terms of Marxist scholasticism, find a home in the Humanist vocabulary. Instead, Humanists recognized the insights that shaped socialism and above all responded to the sense of moral outrage that elicited the Marxist canon. We can still hear the Humanist song in these words of a contemporary British socialist:

> The ideal socialist, to say nothing of a good many real ones, has a fire in her belly and a moral hymn in her heart. Perhaps not so many can now remember the tune, and the words are long since forgotten, but the centrality of the normative cutting edge of socialism's critique of the status quo cannot be too heavily emphasised. Whatever else is distinctive of socialism it must have, centrally, a morally informed vision of a better life. It must have that cutting edge to its attack on Capital that comes from commanding the moral high ground.[23]

Humanists joined in attacking a system that concentrated wealth and power in fewer and fewer hands and exploited the weak while claiming that these arrangements were alternatively necessary or ultimately moral, and sometimes both. On the affirmative side, they were committed to the dignity of labor, to the support of labor organizations—in their pioneering moments at least—and to broad-based programs of social welfare. Socialism addressed these with an intellectuality and moral sensitivity that Humanists could identify with. Indeed, for some Humanists—and for many of its critics too—socialism was only "Humanism" with another name. For others, with socialism in the field, Humanism had no need to do any basic political economic homework of its own.

Most Humanists in the United States, however, found the ideological language of socialism incongenial and opted for the reformist's agenda.[24] From time to time this even seemed to work out, particularly during the age of reform, Teddy Roosevelt's Bull Moose, and above all during Franklin Roosevelt's New Deal. But the reformers learned that reforms more often than not took an ironic twist.[25] Reform, in other words, was often frustrated and too often frustrating, not least of all because it left the reformer without sensible connections from event to event, issue to issue, and so with laudable sentiment but little reason. To be sure, today the Clinton administration is more humanely minded than its recent predecessors, but the problem of "this reform or that" is already quite visible. With its apparent retreat after the 1994 elections and a Republican-conservative victory, reform has become even more problematic. Indeed, practicalism—what can pass the Congress and appease the public at any given moment—leads to the unintelligible and the ineffective, as in the efforts at punitive welfare reform and rigid criminal justice policies. All of this is then given the name of a centrist "new" democracy or a conservative "Contract with America," as if a common label could hide the confusions.

By contrast, socialism provided a political economic rationale that Humanism had not enjoyed since the exciting initiating days of the Enlightenment project. To be sure, Humanists were "democrats," but they had failed to develop the commitment to democracy into an effective and distinctive Humanist politics. Instead, based in the moods and styles of American religious radicalism and liberal academicism, American Humanism tended to adopt the reformist habits of the former and the philosophic habits of the latter. A piecemeal Humanism was the outcome. Its European and Asian counterparts were, on the other hand, quite content to let their Humanism be one thing and their socialism another, as long as the two were understood to be in partnership. Above all, a distinctive and independent Humanist social ethics did not emerge, let alone its connection to the passions of the personal life. The subversion of socialism today unmasks a critical weakness in modern Humanism: its failure to address political economy in its own name. Thus, its legitimacy as a child of the Enlightenment project is itself in question.

HUMANISM IN THE SHADOWS?

Intellectual elitism, ideological antireligion, and communalism have tempted Humanists away from the Enlightenment project. Many Humanists follow Voltaire's satiric advice to Candide: "Tend to your own garden." Thus, ideological Humanism feeds on a diet of anticlericalism, antitheism, and antireligion and scarcely attends to the celebration of human powers and commitment to participatory democracy that witnessed the birth of Enlightenment. This Humanism is almost exclusively committed to freedom of inquiry and conscience and to a notion of reason said to be uniquely exhibited in the sciences. Actions derived from these premises, like preserving the separation of church and state, are legitimized; other social agendas are simply uninteresting. Indeed Humanism on these grounds can make common cause with all but fascism and totalitarianism. It is, however, quite likely to take on a libertarian coloration. In a reversal of Humanist habits, this ideological Humanism has suddenly discovered the virtues of capitalism and the ideal possibilities of the "free market."[26]

Humanism thus conceived surrenders nearly all commitment to human connectedness. The great Enlightenment trinity—liberty, equality, community—is reduced to a single ideal. From within this singularity, equality is viewed with suspicion, and community is reduced to a contract for the delivery of services. To be fair, Humanists so inclined urge individualism as the most likely way, "in the long run," to achieve a genuine solidarity and a genuine good life. The two-ness of Humanism thus hides in the shadows but does not vanish. That actual needs and actual sufferings exist is not denied either. Ideological Humanism echoes Adam Smith's faith in the benign outcomes of an invisible hand and surrenders the attempt to apply reason to the "problems of men." Deserting the larger society, Humanism is best located in the academy or its near relatives. For it, modern Humanism's engagement with the world is over, and a new Humanism must take its place that makes no pretense to popular appeal or social concern and that represses the passion that gave birth to Humanism's affinity for socialism in the first place.

If ideological Humanism moves in the direction of "rugged" individualism, other Humanists, and particularly in the United States, opt for the continuation of left liberalism. This is the Humanism of alliances and coalitions, the Humanism that simply participates as one of many interest groups. Apart from a generalized sentiment of humanity, however, little that is identifiably Humanist as such characterizes it. In fact, for the sake of alliances, Humanist ideas are often muted lest allies be offended. For Humanist liberalism, the personal presence of the reformer is surrendered too. In its place we find the typical paraphernalia of the interest group: resolution passing, meeting going, letter sending, and money raising. As with interest groups generally, action is delegated to agents and surrogates. Such a Humanism of alliances appears as a ghost of its origins in a vigorous and personally felt reformist impulse. Because its concerns are problem oriented, we may also call it a technocratic Humanism. The vision of a good life is reserved to the private attentions of Humanists by themselves. Just as ideological Humanism narrows the range to intellectuals, technocratic Humanism narrows the range to the "like-minded" and this "like-mindedness" is defined in the shallowest possible terms.

As Humanists lose confidence in a widely shared moral vision, a localized communal Humanism joins the individual with others in gathered communities of belief. Often miscalled "religious," this Humanism builds on psychologies of personal development and an unspecified notion of spirituality. It is, however, just another instance of the shadow enlightenment, a retreat from universal Humanist ideals: cosmopolitanism, anger at social injustice, and passion for social redress. The center of this communal Humanism is affect, not cognition. To the annoyance of ideological Humanists, communal Humanism borrows the language of faith and the forms of congregational religion. To the annoyance of technocratic Humanists, communal Humanism seems blind to the urgencies of social conscience. But whatever their differences, these three Humanisms do not confess the departure they have made from the Enlightenment project: the restriction of Humanism to a select population and the surrender of the Enlightenment claim to address the needs and hopes of all persons in all places and for all time.

With these moves, the significance of the "death of socialism" becomes even more apparent. Humanism's kinship with socialism kept political economy in play in the Humanist arena and lent Humanism a compatible and credible political economy. With socialism's "death," however, Humanism descends into the shadow enlightenment, which warrants the sneering postmodern reference to it as a merely "local" narrative. Bereft of a political economy, Humanism loses its hold on a broadly conceived social reality. It becomes only another "saved community."

WHY NOT THE FREE MARKET?

Many Humanists see in the "free market" and in modern capitalism a likely partner for Humanism. As Richard Schmitt summed it up,

> According to the Secular Humanist Declaration: "a free society should also encourage some measure of economic freedom. . . . This means that individuals and groups should be able to compete in the marketplace. . . . The right to private property is a human right without which other human beings are nugatory. . . . "
>
> . . . If that appears to be a strong claim, it is by no means unusual. In fact there is a solid consensus among political philosophers that agrees with the Secular Humanist Declaration. Thus, Ronald Dworkin believes that in the eyes of the liberal, the best society, one that is genuinely free, allows each member to follow his or her conception of the good life as long as all others are allowed the same freedom. . . . Milton Friedman echoes this claim: "Capitalism is a necessary condition for political freedom." Rawls agrees with that as does Nozick. A free society, everyone seems to believe requires a free market—that is a capitalist economic system.[27]

But it is well to recall "free market" history. Capitalism entered the lists proudly proclaiming that morality was only a personal matter; it explicitly and deliberately broke apart the two-ness of Humanism. In public life, as Bernard de Mandeville put it in *The Fable of the Bees*, "private vices, public virtue." Self-interest was the best guide to social policy and the engine of social development. Of course, we might see the "free market" with Lord Keynes as the celebration of greed and in the background—at least for Adam Smith and others—was a conviction that there was a moral sense at work in persons that would limit market adventurism. Then too, an abiding faith in the mechanics of the invisible hand taught that in the end it would all come out right. But again, Keynes reminded us, "In the long run, you're dead."

Led by an ode to ego, the story of capitalism is ambiguously one of great achievement and great misery. In the end, the worker was indeed freed of the chains of tribe and church, but he was also free to starve, and many did.[28] The release of new economic powers by capitalism was coupled with the rise of great fortunes based in corruption and thievery and the accumulation of wealth and power in fewer and fewer private hands. If the tyranny of kings and priests was undermined by the new political economy, another tyranny took its place. Indeed, its very impersonality made oppression all the more painful, for now people were told that their misery was simply the outcome of a mechanistic determinism against which there could be no appeal and with which there could be no interference. As much ask the sun to stand still or gravitation to suspend as to expect the inexorable rule of the market to give way.

It may be claimed that modern capitalism—whatever the horrors of the past—is a differently evolved creature. We correct the extremes of the free market with the countervailing powers of law and labor organization, so the wild days of capitalist buccaneering are over. Capitalism has been tamed—insofar as necessary—by prudential considerations. The "free market," then, can be permitted to proceed on its own, can be "deregulated." Moreover, it is claimed, much of the failure of the free market is due precisely to the interference of nonmarket values imposed by misguided liberals and sentimental social workers. Let things alone and all will turn out well, a claim that even Adam Smith did not make when it came to disadvantaged labor, the schools, the military, and other noneconomic but necessary services. Of course, this turn to the private sector reduces social values to economic rationality and self-interest. For example, it is doubtful that health services can be decently provided as more and more hospitals and other caregiving facilities are turned over to profit-oriented organizations.

In fact, despite the ministrations of welfare capitalism, the present condition of millions of human beings has, if anything, deteriorated. A recent photographic essay in the *New York Times* was introduced with the description, "A hundred years ago, the social reformer Jacob A. Riis documented the bleak underside of life in the city. Today, only the faces are different."[29] And the *Wall Street Journal* reported,

> The number of Americans below the poverty line increased in 1990 by two million, or nearly 6% according to the Census Bureau. In addition, inflation-adjusted median household income declined for the first time since 1982.
>
> The official poverty line, which varies according to such factors as family size and age, averages $13,359 for a family of four and $6,652 for an individual. Furthermore, a study released this week by the congressional Joint Economic Committee suggests that the poor no longer benefit from economic recovery to the degree that they once did.[30]

In the United States more than 33 million people are poor even by the miserly standards of the official definition. More recently, President Clinton's Council of Economic Advisers described a widening gap between rich and poor. In its report, it blamed technology, the decline of unions, a lagging minimum wage, and immigration.[31] A review of a book on the Democratic party[32] noted,

> When Mr. Reagan declared in 1983 that he wanted the United States to remain "above all . . . a country where someone can always get rich," that someone was invariably a Donald Trump or a T. Boone Pickens, not an assembly line worker from Akron or Detroit. As it turned out, the President's "just folks" *persona* masked a huge bias in favor of those at the very top. Indeed, the Edsalls point out that the policies of the Reagan Administration regarding taxes, wages, unions, banking and antitrust produced one of the most dramatic redistributions of wealth in our nation's history.
>
> "In terms of income alone," they write, "those at the high end of the distribution experienced huge gains during the decade of the 1980s, as the top one percent saw average family income grow by 75 percent, from $313,206 in 1980 to $548,970 in 1990 (both figures in 1990 dollars); while all those families falling in the bottom 90 percent saw average income grow by just 7 percent, from $27,451 to $29,334." Not surprisingly, the lower one went on the income scale, the worse things became. Families at the bottom 10 percent saw their average incomes *decline* during the 1980's, from $4,791 to $4,295.[33]

The situation gets worse.[34] The number of homeless people on the streets increases; the costs of medical care are prohibitive; earning an income above the poverty level requires even the "prosperous" middle class to have more than a single wage earner—a relatively new phenomenon in contemporary industrial America although long familiar to rural families and to the poor. The effects on latchkey children—a growing group whose existence began to be remarked during World War II—cannot be estimated in economic terms alone. Despite complaints of the loss of family values, little is done to deal with this situation, although the rhetoric of punishment—of unwed mothers, of irresponsible fathers, and so forth—grows louder and louder. It is commonplace that young people today envision a less-than-prosperous future and dream less than glorious dreams. The fact is that the "free market" fails where it is supposed to succeed while welfare capitalism is inattentive to welfare except under crisis conditions.[35]

I suspect that some—particularly those in power—indulge in "free market" rhetoric as a device for manipulating public opinion to their own ends. After all, who cannot have anything but warm feelings toward a market where buyers and sellers who know each other exchange the goods and services they need. But this cozy language ignores the size and impersonality of things today. The megacorporation gives every evidence of behaving in a distinctly Hobbesian manner, a "war of each against all." Efforts at national and multinational control are more likely than not self-interested agreements, like the North American Free Trade Agreement (NAFTA), the Common Market, and the General Agreement on Tariffs and Trade (GATT), all agreements that can be enforced only by the collective power of megacorporations themselves. It is the latter, after all, that sit at the table, although they wear the costume of the state.

Not the least of the dilemmas of a modern "free market" is the emergence of megagovernments, which behave in many ways just like megacorporations. The distinction between private and public institutions is less than evident as modern societies evolve.[36] Indeed, it is worth asking whether government in the interests of and with the consent of the governed is really possible as corporate oligopolies and monopolies develop.

Not the least of the illusions about the "free market" is the utopianism of its advocates. But as Louis Uchitelle reminds us, "there is no such thing as a free lunch—Capitalist Lesson No. 1—and many countries are learning that the 'free market' is in large measure shorthand for transitions involving cultural dislocation, unemployment, production problems and economic and political confusion."[37] Finally, a "free market" takes a dismal view of persons. Illustratively, Robert Schaeffer writes,

> Thus it should not surprise us that, in any society, when the most productive people are systematically arrested and murdered (or, under diluted forms of socialism, driven elsewhere by high taxes and expropriation), productivity *must* fall dramatically. When the value system of disciplined achievers is declared to

be "exploitative" and criminal, no one dares to follow their example: people learn instead to emulate the irresponsibility that characterizes the proletariat, whose value system has been declared politically "correct." (After all, under capitalism the proletariat had to *earn* its place at the bottom!) And when in any society absolute power is seized by the angriest failures, it should surprise no one that what follows is plunder, instead of productivity, and revengefulness instead of magnanimity. . . . The resentful seek not merely to confiscate the wealth of those they envy, but to punish them for having enjoyed it.[38]

This division of the species into the successful, who may or may not choose to be charitable, and the envious, who live lives of resentment, might well give any Humanist pause. We hear again about the "deserving" and "undeserving" poor, repeat the Calvinist view of wealth as a token of God's grace, and verify the Nietzschean critique of Christianity as a philosophy of resentment. Only now, although with a more secular vocabulary, the Humanist joins in blaming the victim and applauding the ultimate reasonableness of institutionalized self-seeking.

THE ETHICS OF THE MATTER

This is not the place for a comprehensive discussion of Humanist ethics.[39] However, reference to ethical values is appropriate. What happens when, under "free market" inspiration, the two-ness of Humanism is broken apart. Ethics surely has to do with relationships of trust. Indeed, many business practices exhibit just such relationships. But from a moral point of view, such relationships deserve moral status only when the conduct between parties in such relationships is freely chosen. By contrast, the "free market" tends to coerce human behavior while accruing the power to do so to a smaller and smaller number of market players. That is, after all, the moral import of the successful corporate attack on labor organization in the name of the "right to work," of the development of monopoly and oligopoly, and of formulating information and using language so that only experts (e.g., lawyers and technical consultants) can understand it.

In the traditional marketplace, trust was a matter of personal knowledge and was enforced by an evolving law of contracts. The former has almost vanished, and the latter now require specialized (and expensive) interpreters as the parties to such relationships grow larger and more abstract (e.g., in collective bargaining, in buying and selling between corporate producers and individual consumers, in dealing with worker health and safety in a more and more complex technical environment). It is no accident that in the United States, where these developments have reached their height, we tend to blur the distinction between legality and morality, that is, between forced and autonomous conduct. At the same time, legal services become prohibitively costly and so cease to be available to all but the very entities that create the need for such services in the first place. An appeal from coercion thereby becomes inaccessible to most of us. The equality of the contracting parties, which shaped the notion of contract, itself becomes problematic.

Resisting coercion comes to depend on interest groups and ultimately on the continuous expansion of megagovernment as an alleged countervailing power. To be sure, as we have seen in regulatory agencies and defense procurement, for example, this power is often compromised by the fact that the same persons who populate the corporation populate the government and that the expertise needed to respond to corporate misconduct is usually available only to those already embedded in corporate reality. Apart from the resulting cynicism that subverts our trust in each other, the "free market" thus contains its own contradiction; it must generate an unfree environment in which to operate. The freedom of the "free market" turns out to be a self-interested claim on behalf of corporate entities and not a broadly conceived social and moral value. Freedom for persons is quickly lost in this give and get of great powers.

Of course, the people who work in corporate environments are as moral as those who do not. Indeed, it is striking that many of them maintain their integrity against the odds. But they are trapped by often irresistible market tendencies. Only a very few whistleblowers, at great cost to themselves and with dubious effectiveness, fight these tendencies.[40] For most of us, a certain moral blindness develops while inner disquiet persists. The "free market" claim to be the voice of freedom does not, on the record, have prima facie believability or legitimacy.

Ethics calls for fairness: the notion that human beings should be treated equitably, that as such they have rights that cannot be compromised and needs that cannot be ignored. It is a commonplace of such ideas that justice delayed is justice denied. Of course, we cannot expect all human needs to be met immediately and adequately. That is the import of human fallibility and a finite universe. However, the deliberate delay of fair treatment is another matter. The inordinate time lapse between the bringing of a lawsuit and its resolution may serve as a metaphor of such delay. Often it is a legal strategy based on the obvious fact that the corporation can afford the time and costs but individuals cannot. In some instances of medical malfeasance, for example, time even permits mortality to turn off the search for justice. The reliance of the "free market" on the mechanisms of efficiency—expertise and deep pockets—thus entails the deliberate choice of unjust behavior.

A policy of induced scarcity is also no stranger to the free market. We talk of effective demand. Typically, language is used here as elsewhere to mask reality. Only those who can afford it—effective demand, in other words—are entitled to goods and services, and only those goods and services are to be made available that someone can pay for. Needless poverty in the midst of plenty and conspicuous consumption[41] remain as challenges even to the long-run claims of "free market" proponents. The emergence of a permanent underclass in industrial nations and in the third world is an outcome of the "free market" under global conditions. Further, the megacorporation is highly mobile and is guided by judgments of self-interest and uncontrolled by judgments of harm. In a global environment it entails shifts to locations where needy workers are plentiful, wages are low, and worker protections are minimal. Once again, on moral grounds, the "free market" does not seem to be a prima facie candidate for a Humanist partnership.

Characteristic of Humanist ethics is a concern for the "other." Under capitalist tutelage this is transformed into "enlightened self-interest." However, the notion of human solidarity—a morality of care[42]—finds no place in a "free market" as such and is reserved instead for personal relationships in family and family-like settings. The latter, however, tend to vanish as relationships are transformed, after the public model of quid pro quo. Virtue is replaced by prudence. Values like loyalty, idealism, obligation, kindness, and mutuality are reduced to mere preferences. Claims of greater loyalties (e.g., to the public good) become unintelligible. Where loyalty to the firm is invoked—typically in industrial public relations and the like—prudence dictates public acquiescence. At the same time a not-so-hidden cynicism evolves. Manipulative technique is perfected in order to induce certain kinds of conduct, such as in wartime or in the competitive struggle for market share. Social life develops an inhering dishonesty while personal life is impoverished.

Moral reflection reminds us too of the distinction between the desired and the desirable. For my present purpose, I note the blurring of the market distinction between wants and needs. A market economy relies on exploiting people's wants and talks about "need creation." Entire industries—advertising, marketing, poll taking—are committed to this process. Of course, there is wisdom still in Jefferson's "the pursuit of happiness," which deliberately avoided a substantive definition of happiness. But an anarchy of things is not moral freedom either. Neither Jefferson nor his nineteenth-century liberal successors like John Stuart Mill could have imagined the materialist orgy that characterizes modern industrial society. In fact, each had in mind an implicit standard—Jefferson's honest farmer, Mill's educated British gentleman—that set the shape of the pursuit of happiness. Without such shaping—other than that imposed by market values themselves like affordability—the pursuit becomes a lesson in the triviality of everything but the values of consumption as such. The free market, in other words, undermines the meaning of choice itself by its inventive consumerism. To be sure, there is plenty of everything, and this should not in itself be sneered at as visitors from less-well-endowed societies invariably remark. But our kind of plenty also teaches tastelessness, is reinforced by impulse buying, and ultimately cheats us in its superficiality. Even more radically, freedom of choice loses most of its content and becomes a mere incantation of a political economy turned magical.

A glance—and that is all I have permitted myself—at the fate of moral values in a "free market" context suggests, therefore, the moral dubiousness of the proposed partnership with Humanism. The viciousness of Stalinism was indefensible on any ground. The vices of capitalism, however, although more subtle and certainly less brutal, are no less a matter of moral concern. The privileges of the speculator are no more and no less worthy than the privileges of the commissar. And all of this must be seen against the "free market" invitation to racketeering, which in recent memory has nearly destroyed the banks, corrupted the government, and filthied the environment. To be sure, adventurism is by no means a unique event in "free market" history. If, in mitigation, it is claimed that capitalism is not yet perfected in experience, this is as believable as the counterclaim that socialism was not really tried either.

Given the dubiousness, as I see it, of the "free market" as a morally defensible political economy and given the "death of socialism," what then can we make of the Enlightenment project? We might, in fashioning a reply, suggest with Cornel West:

> So, it is necessary to discredit the fashionable trashing of Marxist thought in the liberal academy. Besides predictable caricatures of Marxist thought by conservatives, this trashing principally proceeds from ironic skeptics and aesthetic historicists. The former shun any theory that promotes political action with purpose; for them, any social project of transformation reeks of authoritarian aims. The latter highlight wholesale contingency and indeterminacy, with little concern with how and why change and conflict take place. So we have disciples of Jacques Derrida and Michel Foucault who talk about the subtle relations of rhetoric, knowledge, and power, yet remain silent about concrete ways in which

people are empowered to resist and what can be gained by such resistance. In addition, we have the so-called "new historicists," preoccupied with "thick descriptions" of the relativity of cultural products, including those formerly neglected by traditional bourgeois male critics—while thoroughly distrustful of social *explanatory* accounts of cultural practices.[43]

Before a reply, however, we need to attend to another attack on the Enlightenment project. It appears with the surrender of universality and rationality. In other words, we need to explore what is called postmodernism and its fellow travelers.

NOTES

1. Walt Whitman illustrated a problematic romanticism:

> When I heard the learn'd astronomer;
> When the proofs, the figures, were ranged in columns before me;
> When I was shown the charts and the diagrams, to add, divide, and measure them;
> When I, sitting, heard the astronomer, where he lectured with much applause in the lecture-room,
> How soon, unaccountable, I became tired and sick;
> Till rising and gliding out, I wander'd off by myself.
> In the mystical moist night-air, and from time to time,
> Look'd up in perfect silence at the stars.

"When I Heard the Learn'd Astronomer," first published in *Drum Taps*, 1865; *Leaves of Grass* (Philadelphia: David McKay, 1900), p. 341.

2.

> The production of a work of art throws a light upon the mystery of humanity. A work of art is an abstract or epitome of the world. It is the result or expression of nature in miniature. . . . A leaf, a sunbeam, a landscape, the ocean, make an analogous impression on the mind. What is common to them all,—that perfectness and harmony, is beauty. . . . Nothing is quite beautiful alone; nothing but is beautiful in the whole. A single object is only so far beautiful as it suggests this universal grace. The poet, the painter, the sculptor, the musician, the architect, seek each to concentrate this radiance of the world on one point. . . . Thus is Art a nature passed through the alembic of man. Thus in art does Nature work through the will of a man filled with the beauty of her first works.

Ralph Waldo Emerson, *Nature*, in *Selected Essays of Emerson*, ed. Larzer Ziff (New York: Penguin, 1982), p. 47.

3. John Dewey, "The Live Creature and 'Etherial Things,' " in *The Philosophy of John Dewey*, ed. John J. McDermott (Chicago: University of Chicago Press, 1981), p. 553.

4. John Dewey, *Experience and Nature* (New York: Putnam, 1929), in *Philosophy of John Dewey*, p. 322.

5. See, for example, *Self-Governing Socialism, A Reader*, ed. Branko Horvat, Mihailo Markovic, and Rudi Supek (White Plains, N.Y.: International Arts and Sciences Press, 1975).

6. An interesting and useful brief article illustrates this point. See Amanda Bennett, "U.S. Marxists Thrive Despite Communism's Demise," *Wall Street Journal*, September 6, 1994.

7. Scott Tucker, "The Good Fight," *Humanist* 54, no. 2 (March–April 1994): 12.

8. The Marquis de Condorcet was a mathematician and philosopher who played an active role in the French Revolution and was one of the first victims of the Terror. His master work was *Esquisse d'un Tableau Historique des Progress de L'esprit Humain* (Historical sketch of the progress of the human spirit). I was introduced to Condorcet's work when completing my master's essay at the New School for Social Research (New York, 1951).

9. Ivan Frolov, *Man-Science-Humanism: A New Synthesis* (Moscow: Progress Publishers, 1986).

10. Cornel West, *The Ethical Dimensions of Marxist Thought* (New York: Monthly Review Press, 1991), p. xxii.

11. Calvin O. Schrag, *Radical Reflections and the Origin of the Human Sciences* (West Lafayette, Ind.: Purdue University Press, 1980), p. 39.

12. For example, consider the following passage from Karl Marx, *Economic and Philosophic Manuscripts* (1844),

> That which exists for me through the medium of *money*, that which I can pay for . . . that *I am*. . . . My own power is as great as the power of money. The properties of money are my own . . . properties and faculties. What *I am* and *can do* is therefore, not at all determined by my individuality. *I am* ugly, but I can buy the *most beautiful* woman for myself. Consequently, I am not *ugly* for the effect of *ugliness* . . . is annulled by money. As an individual, I am *lame*, but money provides me with twenty-four legs. Therefore I am not lame. I am a detestable, dishonorable, unscrupulous and stupid man but money is honored and so also is its possessor. Money is the highest good, and so its possessor is good. Besides, money saves me the trouble of being dishonest; therefore I am presumed honest. I am *stupid* but since money is the *real mind* of things, how should its possessor be stupid? Moreover, he can buy talented people for himself, and is not he who has power over the talented more talented than they? I who can have, through the power of money, *everything* for which the human heart longs, do I not possess all human abilities? Does not money, therefore, transform all my incapacities into their opposites?

Trans. and ed. T. B. Bottomore, in Erich Fromm, *Marx's Concept of Man* (New York: Ungar, 1961), pp. 165–166.

13. Erich Fromm in his introduction to the above makes a similar point from the insights he derives by integrating Marx and Freud.

14. In a revealing series of articles in the *Wall Street Journal*, February 23–24, 1994, the point is made that much of the aid the West and the United States claim to be providing is more often than not beneficial to us:

> By early 1993, the 24 richest nations of the West had made paper pledges of $70 billion to East European countries from Estonia to Albania. . . .
>
> What happened to it? . . .
>
> The answer is discouraging. Aid has been fired like scattershot at a flitting bird. Replacing communism with capitalism has been far trickier than the bricks-and-mortar salvaging of postwar Europe. Many aid dollars benefit donors more than donees. And many, laden with conditions, sit unused.

Barry Newman, "West Pledges Billions of Aid to Poland—Where Did It All Go?" *Wall Street Journal*, February 23, 1994, p. 1.

15. Jean Amery rightly, I think, identified Marx with a clear line of Enlightenment development. He wrote,

> Here we stand, critically minded intellectuals, and whatever intellectual freedom we possess, we owe to the Enlighteners: from Montesquieu to Freud, from Locke, Condorcet, and Diderot to Marx, Feuerbach and Russell. . . . We need only to go back for a moment to the condition of the world and the mind before the onset of the Enlightenment and with horror we will perceive fear: fear of the unleashed powers of nature, fear of bodily pain, for which there was no relief, fear of the evil eye, of gods, idols, and demons, fear of the rulers whose sadistic exercise of power was not curbed by law, fear of one's own fear, which arose from the unconscious and made man the slave to his "id."

Radical Humanism: Selected Essays by Jean Amery, ed. and trans. Sidney and Stella P. Rosenfeld (Purdue, Ind.: Indiana University Press, 1984), p. 137.

16. The idea is not confined to philosophic texts. See, for example, Bob Davis and Dana Milbank, "If the U.S. Work Ethic Is Fading, Alienation May Be the Main Reason," *Wall Street Journal*, February 7, 1992, p. 1.

17. "Class" is not simply an intellectualist category. For example, the article "Working Class Culture Erodes Britain's Rank in a Unified Europe," *Wall Street Journal*, February 11, 1992, p. 1, describes the social reality and the consequences of what might appear as merely an abstraction.

18. Mary Rossabi, a teacher at the Ethical Culture Fieldston Schools, (founded in 1878 by the NY Society for Ethical Culture) reported on her experience as a visiting instructor in Leningrad:

> As Gorbachev opened Pandora's box, freedom of expression emerged in various guises. People could worship more freely in the churches and synagogues, and a convent had just opened in Leningrad. But the negative side of *glasnost* also surfaced in the anti-Semitic, pro-Russian group Pamiat or Memory. This small but vociferous group held its meetings in front of Kazan Cathedral on the Nevsky Prospekt. It attributed to the Jews many of its country's social ills, and though few

regarded its diatribes as particularly threatening, others saw them as a portent or symptom of future difficulties—pogroms, civil wars, or revolution.

"The Six Paradoxes of Socialism," *Independent School* (Winter 1991): 32.

19. Barbara Stanosz, "Poland: Emerging Democracy or Religious State?" *International Humanist News* 1, no. 4 (December 1993): 6.

20. Craig Forman, "Moslems Seek Theocracy in the USSR," *Wall Street Journal*, October 9, 1991, p. A12.

21. For example, Albert R. Hunt, "The Religious Right Is a GOP Albatross," *Wall Street Journal*, June 9, 1994.

22. For example, see Gajo Petrovic, *Marx in the Mid-Twentieth Century* (Garden City, N.Y.: Doubleday Anchor Books, 1967), particularly "The Continuity of Marx's Thought," pp. 35–51.

23. Michael Luntley, *The Meaning of Socialism* (Chicago: Open Court, 1991), p. 3.

24. Felix Adler, the founder of the Ethical Culture Societies, warned of the dangers of unintelligible reform, of "this reform or that" without theory and a comprehensive view of social reality. But he was an exception, and his idealist theory of vocationalism did not capture the interest or loyalty of even those in his own ethical culture movement.

25. For fuller discussion of this theme, see Howard Radest, *The Devil and Secular Humanism* (New York: Praeger, 1990), chap. 6.

26. A helpful and revealing discussion of this theme can be found in *Free Inquiry* 9, no. 4 (Fall 1989). Paul Kurtz, "Libertarianism or Socialism: Where Do Secular Humanists Stand?"

27. Richard Schmitt, "Humanism and Socialism," *Free Inquiry* 9, no. 4 (Fall 1989): 16.

28. For example, we would do well to look again at Frederick Engels, *The Condition of the Working Class in England* (1892) (London: Panther Books, 1969). Lest this source be considered too partisan, reports of the various British Royal Commissions of the period can be consulted. Within the Humanist tradition, it would repay us to look again at the motivations of those who founded the settlement house movement in the United States, such as the Ethical Culture movement's Stanton Coit and John Lovejoy Elliott.

29. "New York in the Nineties," contemporary photographs by Fred R. Conrad, text by Sam Roberts, *New York Times Magazine*, September 29, 1991.

30. Timothy Noah, "Number of Poor Americans Is Up 6%, Real Income Is Off 1.7%, Agency Says," *Wall Street Journal*, September 27, 1991.

31. Paulette Thomas, "Widening Rich-Poor Gap Is a Threat to the 'Social Fabric,' White House Says," *Wall Street Journal*, February 15, 1994, p. 2.

32. Thomas Edsall Byrne with Mary D. Edsall, *Chain Reaction: The Impact of Race, Rights, and Taxes on American Politics* (New York: Norton, 1991).

33. David Oshinsky, "What Became of the Democrats?" *New York Times Book Review*, October 20, 1991, p. 26.

34. Despite the election of a new administration in 1992, structural features of our social system do not show signs of changing. Thus, we boast of a "recovery," but our "new" jobs are poorly paid; of increases in "productivity," but wages lag behind the inflation rate. The poor now include many once thought securely in the middle class. See Gwen Ifill, "Whose Welfare? The Poor, They Are Different and in '92, Ever More Invisible," *New York Times Week in Review*, January 19, 1992, p. 1. With the 1994 election, the rhetoric of change increased, but the changes proposed only confirm a move backward to the private world of nineteenth-century America: orphanages, private charity, less government, punitive welfare policies, and so forth.

35. See, for example, Christopher Jencks, *Rethinking Social Policy* (Cambridge, Mass.: Harvard University Press, 1992).

36. Rhetorical and ideological distinctions only mask these structures. So, for example, an article in the *Wall Street Journal*, by Michael R. Sesit and Robert Steiner, with barely a nod to the capitalist-communist distinction, points out: "Money Managers Pick China over India for Investment," January 12, 1993, p. B1.

37. "But Just Who Is That Fairy Godmother?" *New York Times*, September 29, 1991.

38. Robert Scheaffer, "Socialism Is Incompatible with Humanism," *Free Inquiry* 9, no. 4 (Fall 1989): 20.

39. A helpful anthology on this subject is Morris B. Storer, ed. *Humanist Ethics* (Buffalo: Prometheus Press, 1980).

40. As Marcy Mason writes,

> And historically, whistle-blowers have paid a very high price for their good deeds. Of the 1,700 whistle-blowers interviewed by Edna Ottney, a quality assurance engineer who has investigated employee concerns in the nuclear power industry since 1985, 90% experienced negative fallout. Other studies concur—including the most recent, a survey of 35 Australian whistle-blowers published in the *British Medical Journal* last September. The study found eight of the whistle-blowers had lost their jobs as a result of their actions, 10 had been demoted, 10 had resigned or retired early because of ill health related to victimization, 15 were taking prescribed medication to deal with the stress, and 17 had considered suicide.

"The Curse of Whistle-Blowing," *Wall Street Journal*, March 15, 1994, p. 18A.

41. The phrase is Thorstein Veblen's. A modern parable may be found in Connie Bruck, *The Predators' Ball* (*The Inside Story of Drexel Burnham and the Rise of the Junk Bond Raiders*) (New York: Penguin Books, 1988 (trade), 1989 (paperback).

42. Labor unions in their formation spoke of worker solidarity. Marx described the human being as a "species being." For a significant modern rendering of the theme, for which we can be grateful to feminist thought, see Nel Noddings, *Caring, A Feminine Approach to Ethics and Moral Education* (Berkeley: University of California Press, 1984).

43. West, *Ethical Dimensions*, p. xxii.

3

STRANGE ENEMIES

TARGET: THE ENLIGHTENMENT PROJECT

With the "death of socialism," the Enlightenment project is pronounced dead too. But the obituary is premature. Moreover, the passion of the announcement points to another kind of fact, not so much of history or ideology but of faith. To be sure, postmodernism is clothed in academic and philosophic dress. With "new age," the claims of *esoterica* recall similar metaphysical adventures. Even where, as in fundamentalism, the battleground seems to be God and cosmos, the reality is still psychological. In other words, with the alleged death of the Enlightenment project and, more particularly, with the passions that attach to its demise, we are in the presence of a profound dismay of culture. The shadow enlightenment feeds these very rejections and is itself another rejection. This reveals that the Enlightenment becomes its own enemy as it deteriorates into scientism, rationalism, or secularism.

Holding on to the promises of the modern age is very difficult in a time of fragmentation. Yet while each of us lives in his or her own village, we live in a global village too. Of course, epistemological puzzles persist, at least for the philosophizing mind: our inability to demonstrate that we can "know" another human being or that he or she can truly "know" us; our inability to demonstrate that we can "know" the world. But we give evidence in practice that we share common features of consciousness, hope, and fear despite the fact that we inhabit different life-worlds. It is a mark of the vitality of modernism despite its undertakers that the struggle for human rights is global, that the sciences are everywhere, that democracy attracts our energies and loyalties. Perhaps, too, it is our very commonality that is frightening, just as looking in a mirror can be frightening.

The attack on the Enlightenment project is real enough. To be sure, the attack comes from religious fundamentalism in the name of the truth, while the postmoderns deliver it from the other side in the name of the "subject." So-called new age joins them in an unlikely consensus. It is found joyfully dismembering hard-won victories for rationality. But the circle that embraces these three closes. When postmodern and new age and fundamentalist meet, they recognize each other as kindred spirits joined in their disdain of reason, democracy, and science. Of course, fundamentalists, new agers, and postmodernists do not speak with a single voice, but they share in the attack on Humanism and on modernism. Deafened by the noisiness of these disparate enemies, Humanism grows defensive, fails to capture the originality of its own voice, and finally succumbs by imitating its enemies.

When we are defensive, the vices of enemies and the virtues of friends are exaggerated. So the Humanist boasts naively of rationality's transformative powers. True, with rationality, the authority of kings and priests and scribes was subverted. I am, because rational, at last genuinely free. I can, as we say, "make up my own mind." Ignored, however, is the fact that rationality can itself become tyranny. It can wear the costume of authoritarianism when, as with the "free market," it is reduced to the calculations of self-interest, or when, as with bureaucracy, it is converted into standard operations. Doing things by the numbers becomes not merely our habit but our god, and we worship it, whether our attention is on measuring intelligence or balancing the books. At such points, authority reveals itself everywhere in new costume, as in the power to confine freedom to choices put by experts who, in setting the problem, also set its solutions. Coming to us in the guise of rationality, this new authoritarianism is very seductive. Just like its predecessors, it claims to speak with the irresistible voice of the universe and its laws; it deteriorates into a theology of reason. Even more deadly is the fact that the theologians of reason do not acknowledge their status as keepers of the faith but pretend that they are merely messengers of the way things are. Indeed, it all sounds very familiar.

This unconfessed theology of reason has its roots in the philosophic imagination. Cartesianism, the early signal of modernism, retreated within the human mind in order to find the world. Strip away all incidentals in order to arrive at one single indubitable and universal truth: "I doubt, therefore I am"; "I think therefore I am." In an adventurous move, the modernist thus claims that it is possible to deduce from the outcome of radical doubt the entire being of being, the ultimate mathematization of all that is, was, and ever shall be.[1] This rationalism incarnates in another way a recurring human dream. The search for the one truth of it all has led us to explore the fascinations of idealism and materialism and all the other isms that have tempted us to seek out ever more monistic intelligibilities. At the same time, this dream has, more often than not, blinded us to the riches of the particular. It is by encouraging a disdain for the singular that the greater fault of the theology of reason is revealed.

For the Enlightenment project, we were one species not only as a biological but as a moral fact. The separations of race and class, of tribe and nation, were to be dissolved by that fact, and with it those angers and destructions that had made us alien to each other. Erected as the promise of inclusive community, universality served as a critical solvent for old habits of division. Conquest and rule by superiors over inferiors could no longer be legitimized as the natural way of things human. Delegitimizing this moral hierarchy could not of itself change human conduct all at once, but it opened the door to the rightfulness of participation; it liberated the struggle to be free from the curse of sin. For all its glory, however, the dream of reason was revealed too as blind to the variousness of the species itself. Moreover, it was blinded by inherited prejudice. Children and slaves were denied participation, although the former would eventually qualify and the latter did not deserve to, or at least not yet.[2] Nothing revealed this blindness more clearly, however, than the language of the "rights of *man*." The Enlightenment spoke of "fraternity" or "brotherhood" and thus ignored—without realizing it—the larger part of the species itself.

To be sure, the Enlightenment project had a more hopeful philosophic anthropology too, and this would ultimately serve to widen the circle of inclusiveness to women and children and would destroy all justification for slavery. No longer would it be possible to doom the human being through the generations to this or that servile occupation, to condemn him or her for eternity to live out the drama of sin and salvation. Each human being was an original empowered to choose and capable of doing so. Nor could choice be rightfully taken away in the name of virtue or even of good sense. Individuality, in short, meant the right to make your own mistakes and to resist those who tried to override your choices, even if for your own good. Individuality thus had its own harshness, and it was welcomed and feared as freedom is welcomed and feared.

At the same time, however, individuality deteriorated into individualism, the conversion of ideal into idolatry. Forgotten, even denied, was the embeddedness of persons in connections. Individualism moved individuality from the arena of sociability into the cave of privacy. This radical separateness invited tyranny back to the table, for in separateness there was also vulnerability. Ironically, the separated individual came to desire nothing so much as to be like the other in order, no doubt, to be liked by the other and at the same time to enjoy the benefit of anonymity. Individualism, in other words, bereft of legitimate social connections, replaced them with uncritical connections—like similarity and conformity—and made these attractive. Little wonder that "mass man" became a popular description, and little wonder that romantic critiques of Enlightenment in the name of an even more radical individualism appeared. Of course, Enlightenment figures from Jefferson to Mill warned of the tyranny of majorities. But this, the evolving shadow enlightenment ignored, flattening the picture of Enlightenment even more.

The sociable individuality of the Enlightenment project was ultimately surrendered to nihilism. Paradigmatically, Nietzsche thus became the first hero of antimodernism:

> He stands not only "beyond good and evil" but beyond all tradition. . . . We must accept him for what he was: the prophet of a new day that never dawned, of a joyful wisdom that was not achieved, of a dance that was never danced.[3]

With nihilism, authority was invited in again through the back door. For, echoing Dostoyevsky, if nothing and everything were permitted, then so too with power, which had neither definition nor limits. Indeed, nothingness encouraged the seizure of power, for anything was emotionally preferable to the emptiness between. Humanism, now given a new enemy to oppose in the totalitarian impulses of the age, could ignore the urgency of its own reconstruction. In yet another way, then, the shadow enlightenment replaced the Enlightenment project.

It was one of the achievements of the Enlightenment project to mark the shift of human attentiveness from another world to this one. Secularity, in other words, while confining us to a single universe, liberated us to act and live in that universe in ways not possible when a super universe could intervene arbitrarily in this one. No longer caught between two worlds, an uneasy traveler without resting place in either, the human being now had his or her own place. Another world might exist, and eternity might await us, but here and now was sufficient, and acting here and now was satisfying. Mysterious powers need not be seduced by sacrifice and prayer into helping us. Above all, control need not be ceded to the priest and kings, the worldly agents of those superworldly powers.

As with the other values of the Enlightenment project, however, secularity turned into secularism. Dogmatism appeared in new form. At the same time, the secular arena under industrial conditions became a scene of mere muchness without selectivity and without taste. Control deteriorated too, becoming mere action without ends and without ideals. A radical separation of public and personal worlds located action in the former and direction in the latter, and no one could show how the two might reasonably flow into each other. Hence the puzzles of the "is" and the "ought," the strange notion that values existed anywhere but here. Once again, the shadow enlightenment replaced the Enlightenment project, which had, after all, lived by a moral, political, and aesthetic ideal even as it boasted its allegiance to mechanics and to the "new" science.

Rationality, universality, and secularity revealed the soul of the Enlightenment project, for each of these was a passion as well as an idea. Each revealed, too, in its deterioration, the shadow enlightenment, the consequence of shifting from dynamic to static form, from personal to objective style. For all the claim of the Enlightenment project to break with the past, it could not escape its moment in history. Yet the denial that it had a history—the Newtonian commitment to universal and unchangeable natural law everywhere—intended a blindness to circumstance. As a result, the limitations of the Enlightenment project were over the horizon, invisible to all but hostile critics who converted this limitation into accusation. The Enlightenment project at its birth exhibited gender bias, race bias, culture bias. It was a creature of the seventeenth and eighteenth centuries, which explains but does not excuse. Compounded by the colonialism of European nations and given the absence of all but near-mythic information about people and practices in sub-Saharan Africa, distant Asia, and South and Central America, it is understandable that cultural and racial arrogance should find support in this illiteracy. Given the centuries-long tradition of fixed role and occupation, it is understandable too that gender blindness should find support in social practice.

At the same time, illiteracy was a target of the Enlightenment project—hence its idealization of education and free inquiry as self-correcting activities. Failure to carry the attack on ignorance deeply enough, however, tells us that the victory of Enlightenment was prematurely declared. In other words, the failure to defend it against its circumstance gave birth to those regressions that are found in the quarrel between the attackers of modernism and the defenders of a shadow enlightenment.

Finally, the Enlightenment project may be convicted of a deadly sobriety. Skepticism, which demands a sense of humor and a sense of place, did not extend far enough to shape its temperament and mood; the

Enlightenment, lacking a sense of humor, was not serious enough, not radical enough. Forgetting how to laugh at itself, it invited a dogmatism that fed Humanism's enemies and blocked humility, which tutored the Enlightenment's children in arrogance. The "terror" in other words was, sadly, a child of the Enlightenment project too. Thus, the shadow enlightenment replaced philosophy with ideology just as it shifted from dialectics to didactics.

FUNDAMENTALISM REVISITED

Among the rejections of the Enlightenment project is fundamentalism.[4] Certainly those who have lived through the vicissitudes of America's political religions in the past two decades are aware of its spreading influence. To be sure, the Moral Majority has been dissolved and many of fundamentalism's spokesmen discredited by their personal peccadilloes. Yet the call for a moral crusade against the unbeliever is still heard, as in Patrick Buchanan's address to the 1992 Republican National Convention. Admittedly he was met with dismay in conservative quarters, but his voice, and others like it, is by no means stilled. Whether it be the struggle over abortion or evolution or "family values," religious dogmatics have shaped the current public debate. Indeed with the elections of 1994 and the preliminaries of the 1996 presidential campaign, the alliance of religiosity, moralism, and politics continues to enjoy a national audience.[5] Of course, this is not unique in American history. Nativism, know-nothingism, and anticommunism, among others, has each had its turn as a vehicle for this alliance.

Fundamentalism, of course, is neither peculiarly American nor only contemporary.[6] Religiopolitical impulses—many of them fundamentalist—stir violent nationalisms in India, Ireland, Israel, Iran, the former Soviet Union, and the former Yugoslavia, to name but a few. We may expect, too, that tomorrow will bring news of reawakened or newly founded religious fundamentalisms elsewhere around the globe. The joining of sect and politics is, after all, a historic source of political power and emotional safety. Every generation has its crusades, and ours is no exception. The variety and sources of these battles to the death—for that is how fundamentalists see it—are embedded in patterns of culture, and in particular are aroused today by the features of modernity. Fundamentalism today gives little sign of weakening as long as modernity retains its cultural presence. It is nourished by the fact that we live in a diverse and secular society that has yet to confront the problem of the person. In other words, none of us wants to live in a technologized world that seems dedicated to replace persons with objects. Fundamentalism builds upon that aversion.

It is not surprising that fundamentalism remains a contender for the power, wealth, and loyalty of institutions and persons. By contrast, the Enlightenment is no longer capable of speaking out of the élan of revolution. The passion for reason is quieted, and so the old battle for the soul continues, while the Enlightenment, reduced to its shadow, hardly knows how to enter the lists. Reduced to relying on the standard public defenses of freedom of conscience and free inquiry, it does not meet the need of the present, which is miscast as a problem of reason, that is, a problem of liberty or law. The issue, however, is neither law nor fact but personal meaning. Of course, First Amendment protections against the alliance of church and state are indispensable, but ultimately, they are frail defenses against the passions stirred by the god of the fundamentalist. Passion, in other words, does not yield to the calm of rationality.

Meaning, passion, and resistance to the modern do not exhaust the complicated story of fundamentalism, as Martin E. Marty and R. Scott Appleby reveal so effectively in their comprehensive study of it.[7] Yet in its antimodernism, it can be understood as a single "hypothetical family":

> All these movements arise as a response to modern, secular, pluralistic societies that have disrupted both the cultural certainties and the familial support networks of preindustrial or small town societies. Thus fundamentalisms seem to be a way of coping with the experience of chaos, the loss of identity, meaning and secure social structures created by the rapid introduction of modern social and political patterns, secularism, scientific culture and economic development.[8]

The unity of religion and politics is a mark of fundamentalism, although tactical judgments may mute the connection. Politics like religion, takes different forms in different countries and in different times, so fundamentalism may be communalist in some places, organize political parties in others, and be quietistic in still others. It may, given the occasion, make common cause with the democrat or the dictator. Its dogmatism continues to be reflected, however, in a leader principle and in the literal use of simplified texts, which serve more as "mantras" than as expositions. These texts need not be traditional despite the biblical literalism we are used to in Protestant America. We are quite likely to find current writings, particularly by charismatic leaders or "wise men," claiming sacred inspiration. In any event, the texts are more dramatic than critical and are invitations to action, not reflection.

Seen globally, it is misleading to think that fundamentalism is rooted only in religions of the word. Even among us, however, the text only seems to take center stage. Direct personal experience is in fact the mark of fundamentalist faith. In this derogation of the text as a meaningful document in its own right, we have one of those interesting cross-over points to the postmodern whose deconstruction is but another way of saying the same thing. Above all, it is the subjective experience and not the objective reading that really counts. Fundamentalism, like new age, is a practice, a way of living, and not just of believing. The missing two-ness that marks the shadow enlightenment is radically evident in fundamentalism, only now it is the intimate that casts out the sociable.

Of course, fundamentalism has its own complexities. But beneath these, the naked duality of good and evil is always present. The arguments of theology are surrendered to the truth of the way. Ideas as such play little part, although fundamentalism, even if anti-intellectual, is psychologically sophisticated. Of course, cultural diversity provides some surprising turns as would not be unexpected in a "movement" that ranges from TV evangelism to Buddhist, Hindu, and Islamic fundamentalisms. God plays his role. But he is a presence and not a matter of dispute or demonstration. Fundamentalism is thus essentially antisecular even when it seeks control of the secular situation. At times, to be sure, political, social, or economic priorities may deemphasize cosmic matters. Militancy and aggression inhere in fundamentalist lifestyles, and this leads out to the public arena. Everywhere there is the "enemy" who is simultaneously existential and cosmic. Above all, people find fulfillment and purpose in the loyalty and activism demanded by fundamentalist movements. Not surprisingly, then, fundamentalism is a global and growing phenomenon, as antimodernism is a global and growing phenomenon.

News of fundamentalism seems only the latest intelligence about an old anti-Humanism that refuses to surrender to the force of modern ideas. But as a mirror of modernism, fundamentalism reveals painful truths about the rest of us. We fail to realize this because, typically, all of us—and not just "sectarians"—talk to the convinced. We use our own symbols, perform our own rites, enact our own practices; we claim universality and practice parochialism. Since we fail to realize this fact, we are surprised when we encounter communities where our word is not the common sense of the matter. In that encounter, we are surprised at the virulence of the attack on us. At the same time, we are unsurprised at the aggressiveness of our own defenses, which we simply see as doing the right thing. So it is that fundamentalism holds a mirror up to the modernist's behavior because of the contrasts it sharpens and the similarities it announces. We need a less parochial literacy, and not merely in order to provide ourselves with ammunition for debate.

Consider, by way of example, the urgency of developing global policies of population planning. This requires technological sophistication and economic resources. But for fundamentalism, science is the work of Satan, and control is a matter of God's will. Our problems are the compounded outcomes of false ideas made politically potent. The curricula of our schools are shaped by local school boards and by textbook publishers. A fundamentalist agenda joined with organizational skill and passionate commitment already affects what we teach and do not teach, the books we buy and do not buy, the teachers we hire and do not hire. For school board members, teachers, and administrators, this agenda forces one of two outcomes: we either compromise our integrity by playing down certain issues—the study of evolutionary biology in high schools or the study of the positive and negative role of religion in history and society—or we refrain from criticism in the name of toleration. Meanwhile, the fundamentalist conscience is untroubled. Preaching the "truth" unhindered is its moral commandment. It is, after all, God's truth, and so merely human devices like First Amendment protections must give way.

Fundamentalism is not only a reverse image of modernity but an attack on it. Unlike traditionalism, orthodoxy, and conservatism, fundamentalism is present centered and sees itself as "fighting the good fight." It is in its own view the church militant of the modern age. Indeed, this is a source of its appeal. Since modernism understands the inevitability of the mixture of good and evil, fundamentalism offers moral relief in the midst of confusion. The themes of the Enlightenment project—individuality, diversity, secularity, and toleration—are read as signs of Satan. They befuddle the mind and the conscience with questions and alternatives and doubts. Since scientific inquiry, liberalism, developmental schooling, and rationality are the rallying points of modernism, these are also taken as the work of the enemy. In short, the Humanist is demonized or pitied and condemned as a victim of the devil. This reading of the drama of modernity, while played out on the stage of social and political practice, is felt personally as a loss of meaning.

Fundamentalism avoids the complexities of history for the simplicities of cosmos. Unafflicted by situational relativism and moral dilemmas, the fundamentalist "knows" good and evil. Indeed, the guarantor of knowledge is the creator of the universe itself. The frail, stumbling, and always inadequate efforts of the merely human cannot compete. That such a picture is appealing should not surprise us. Indeed, just as the modern world develops around its strongest resources—science, technology, democracy—it multiplies our insecurities and blurs our certainties. The process of modernity is thus a puzzlement. How else can we interpret the confusion of liberty with "lifestyles" that is diversity gone mad, the paradoxes of creative destruction nurtured in the technologies of war, or the tyrannies of mass movements strengthened by mass media. We may see in these moments a transition to a newer and better world, particularly in the millennial mood of the year 2000. But the transition seems to prolong itself indefinitely, and its confusions seem to grow, not diminish.

Fundamentalism announces itself as an appealing alternative. Delivered by a leadership secured by the universe itself, it describes our destiny without equivocation. In short, its appeal is to overcoming our marginality and in particular the alienation that accompanies the very successes of a corporate and technical world. Here, finally, fundamentalism reveals itself as meaningful. As Rosemary Reuther sums it up:

> What are the common characteristics of the "fundamentalist type"? . . . All these movements arise as a response to modern, secular, pluralistic societies that have disrupted both the cultural certainties and the familial support networks of preindustrial or small town societies. Thus fundamentalisms seem to be a way of coping with the experience of chaos, the loss of identity, meaning and secure social structures created by the rapid introduction of modern social and political patterns, secularism, scientific culture and economic development.[9]

Alienation gives no sign of lessening, so it is not surprising that fundamentalism should grow as a response. Nor is it possible to argue it away as if fundamentalism were only an alternative philosophy. It is not so much that fundamentalism is unreasonable but that it is eminently practical, and so fine points of disputation are simply irrelevant. Amid the terrors of being lost in a world that has no maps for its territories—and new territories spring up everywhere—fundamentalism provides a way of living that makes sense in a world that does not.

Fundamentalism is not only popular but populist. It may appeal to the young in some countries where an establishment politics carries on exclusionist strategies. It may appeal to the countryside where the city seems needlessly to complicate life and destroy historic virtues. It may appeal to traditionalists where radicalism has uprooted historic securities. Even traditionalists feel lost when our sense of the past changes so rapidly. But whatever the substance of the appeal—which varies with each country, each culture, and each age—the pattern emerges. Fundamentalism reduces experience to satisfying and personalized practices and warrants them with eternity itself. To see fundamentalism as an intellectual mistake or the dying gasp of the past is to ignore its contemporaneousness. Even as fundamentalism is a persistent strain in human history, it is always of the moment.

Finally, then, the question is not how we shall dispute with fundamentalism's antimodernist ideas, as Humanists mistakenly believe, but how we shall address marginality and alienation without surrendering to absolutism and fanaticism. Sadly, the modern discourse teaches scientism, not science; worships technologism, and fails to appreciate technology; confuses democratic forms—votes and political parties—with democratic substance. Thus, in its attack on the modern, fundamentalism, unwittingly to be sure, points the way toward the reconstruction of the Enlightenment project.

THE "NEW" AGE

As I move from the cosmic dualism of fundamentalism into the new age, I enter a crazy-quilt universe. Indeed, even to say *universe* presumes what new age denies, and in this denial it bridges to the radical nihilism of postmodernism. This new age move into happy chaos offers both comic and cosmic relief. How else to respond to a *mélange* that includes crystals that heal, optimism that ignores, personal powers that have no limits, intuitions that know everything, channeling, reincarnation, witchcraft, and on and on. The sobriety of the Enlightenment project and the deadliness of fundamentalism give way to a new age that is good-natured, welcoming, nonjudgmental. In this, it reveals its source in the temperament of the sixties. By contrast, however, the Age of Aquarius, from which so much of today's new age arises, seems almost monomaniacal. Indeed, remembering the likelihood of pain and death in Southeast Asia, the sixties had a seriousness that its experimentalism and musicality could not hide. It was, nevertheless, that Aquarian adventure in a culture that seemed madly homicidal and suicidal—how else, looking backward, to interpret the Vietnam War and its children—that opened the doorway to today's affection for esoterica as lifestyle.

But laughter and comic relief, important as they are for our sanity, do not catch on to the fact that the new age enterprise is serious in its import. Desperate for meaning, new age is, like fundamentalism, a rejection of the modern world.

To be sure, *new age* is a convenient term for a disparate collection of views and prescriptions. Given its motley character, it is not a single movement. Found under its banner are charlatans and scholars, people out for a buck, and searchers for a better way. Indeed, any attempt to speak of new age as a single thing or in the compass of a few pages is bound to mislead. Any summary of its positions must run the risk of simplifying its psychological and cultural complexity. Nevertheless, new age, if only in its rejections, is rightly seen as antimodern, antirational, antiscience, antitechnology. While not intentionally antidemocratic—indeed in its assignment of near-limitless powers to any and all persons, it seems almost a parody of democracy—its antipolitical characteristics invite the manipulator and the authoritarian. Democracy, after all, needs critical participation and reasoned judgment. But by denying criticism and reasoning, new age encourages victimization and racketeering, all the while keeping everyone busy in an unintended reincarnation of the "bread and circuses" that have traditionally been the strategy of tyrants.

For new agers, there are common villains but disparate heroes. Not the least of the villainy is to be found in rationality and its variations. Nourished by recent research into left and right brain activity, new age may—when it suits—even draw here and there on the sciences in an interesting but contradictory performance. Thus, creativity is not only celebrated but scientifically verified, and analysis is decried as evidence of a truncated use of human abilities. Of course, neurobiology is quickly converted into self-serving commentary:

> This left brain/right brain concern has been an important part of the New Age movement, and we see it in basic New Age terminology. For example, New Agers commonly define the word "analytic" as "narrow minded," "empirical" as "superficial," "objective" as "petty" and "rational" as "arrogant." On the other hand, they define "esoteric" as "truthful," "inarticulate" as "profound" and "irrational" as "sensitive."[10]

To be sure, it is possible to be unreasonable about reason, to convert rationality into dogmatism, and, as feminists have rightly pointed out, to mask a power play as rationality. But the warfare between "creativity" and "rationality" does not make sense after a glance at the record of creative achievement in the arts and in the sciences. Were we to follow the new age, however, we would opt for a permanent and species-wide schizophrenia as left and right brain mobilized against each other.

Ironically, given its predilection for splitting the person, holism, another new age catchword, is presented as a cure for analytic one-sidedness. Typically, as in "holistic" medicine, new age stresses the ability of the person to heal himself or herself, but at the same time it blames the individual when healing efforts fail. Disease, in other words, is evidence of an inadequate use of one's own powers, a failure of will. Apart from the obvious practical dangers of rejecting scientific medicine, the holism of new age turns out to be conceptually as one-sided as the views it seeks to replace.[11] To be sure, it is the better part of therapeutic wisdom to work for the health of the patient and not just the cure of the disease, a wisdom all too easily ignored in today's technologized medicine. So as with all other antimodernisms, there is a seed of truth in new age criticism.

New age also acquires a certain legitimacy for those of us who see the validity of feminism and its attack on modern political and religious institutions as instances of patriarchy and rationalism. Accusations of racial arrogance, of gender bias, and of ethnocentrism ring true. Not a little guilt attaches to those of us who are Western white males, which leads us in turn to mute our doubts in fear that we merely corroborate the misguidedness of our culture. Perhaps then—the thought is never far from the mind—my skepticism about the claims of ecofeminism, neopaganism, and witchcraft are only further instances of a masculine desire to remain in power. I am trapped thus between legitimate and illegitimate critiques of science, democracy, and rationality. I hesitate for fear that what I announce as the difference between them is only self-serving. Indeed, it is just that disarming of critical ability that is one of the greater dangers of new age.

In a similar way, I am trapped by the new age attentiveness to spirituality. Critical of the shadow enlightenment's one-sidedness, I respond to the allure of transcendence. I hear the call of loving and hoping and dreaming, and I grasp the power of ideals and beauties. I am aware of how flat the world becomes when these are exiled to the merely subjective.

Yet I stand convicted too of perpetuating the shadow enlightenment, of isolating intimacy from sociality. Spirituality thus speaks to my need, leading me to forget its roots in dualism, its affinity for otherworldliness, and its usefulness to tyranny. To be sure, there is a certain gentleness of spirit in new age, which surely has little sympathy for tyranny. But then the invitation to authority is seldom given openly and freely and is most often hidden by fear and confusion. There is an insidious kindliness in new age spirituality, which destroys the unity of imagination and intelligence. Typically, "A New Age Manifesto" reads:

> Every human being has a spiritual essence. . . . Consciousness is not some by-product of biological processes. . . . The body doesn't "have a soul;" rather, the soul temporarily has a body. . . .
>
> . . . The evidence points to the spiritual realms being more basic and less illusory than the physical plane. Many believe the physical plane will exist long

after we are gone, when, in truth, we will exist long after the physical universe is gone.[12]

As with earlier efforts to naturalize the spirit, new age pretends to have its own scientific rationale, nor is the appeal to science without precedent. Nineteenth-century spiritualism, for example, interpreted efforts to validate the existence of a spirit world as the introduction of science into the study of religion. As James Turner reminds us, "Spiritualism's distinctive doctrine was communication with the spirits of the dead, its animus doggedly scientific, peculiar as this combination may now sound. . . . For Spiritualists wanted to carry the enterprise of natural theology to its ultimate conclusion; to provide empirical verification, rigorously scientific, of spiritual reality."[13]

Among new age sources are the speculative insights of Carl Jung, whose psychology builds from Freud's unconscious to the symbolic traces of racial consciousness said to be found in the interpretation of dreams.[14] In a different way, third force or humanistic psychologies provide yet another basis for the wilder flights of new age imagination. Drawing on the work of Abraham Maslow and Carl Rogers, new agers reject behaviorist mechanism and Freudian pessimism. In the language of "peak experience" and "client-centered" therapy, they find an anthropology that seems congenial, although neither Maslow nor Rogers would, I think, take much comfort in their latter-day descendants.[15] Long before the new age, Maslow wrote,

> Just as dangerous are some of the critics of orthodox science who find it too skeptical, too cool and non-human, and then reject it altogether as a danger to human values. They become "anti-scientific" and even anti-intellectual. This is a real danger among some psychotherapists and clinical psychologists, among artists, among some seriously religious people, among some of the people who are interested in Zen, in Taoism, in existentialism, "experientialism," and the like. Their alternative to science is often sheer freakishness and cultishness, uncritical and selfish exaltation of the mere personal experiencing, over-reliance on impulsivity . . . , arbitrary whimsicality, and emotionality, unskeptical enthusiasm, and finally navel-watching and solipsism.[16]

Finally, new age finds in the Gaia hypothesis[17] a justification of some of its more interesting flights of fancy. Forgotten in all of these efforts to connect to the sciences is respect for the hypothetical and awareness of the precarious nature of the speculative. The new age is unrecognizable as classical science to be sure, but it is unrecognizable as radical science too.

The intellectual roots of new age are really to be found in literature and comparative anthropology—again, I notice a bridge to the postmoderns—and, in particular, in a renewed interest in symbol, myth, and narrative. Preeminently, the work of Joseph Campbell provides new age with critical and academic respectability, although I think he would have hesitated to identify himself with his more enthusiastic readers.[18] As Beverley Earles notes,

> And while some academics readily dismiss him [Campbell] as a lightweight, Campbell nevertheless has the distinction of having educated an enormous number of people in the myths of the planet. Furthermore, he has done it in such a way that many readers become personally engaged in those myths and thereby experience something universally human yet at the same time intensely personal. Indeed, Campbell believes that the discovery of human universals is the discovery of the deeply personal and the means of discovery is the understanding and experience of myth. He argues, for example, that one of the most important universals that one can experience in myth is the person of the hero. No matter who the hero is (Jesus, Buddha, the Humanist's Prometheus, or whoever), the basic experience is the same says Campbell: an engaged reader identifies with the hero's experiences so that while the hero is coming to the realization of her own identity, so too is the reader. "Not only are all [the] stories one story, but the one story is one's own."[19]

I admit that there is a certain appeal in all of this new age adventurism. It provides a joyous extremism without apparent risk. It allows us to take an intellectual holiday since the canons of evidence, of noncontradiction, of social and political responsibility, are all put to one side. At the same time, it encourages an unambiguous address to the personal as such, and by justifying so great a variety of life choices, it provides for the idiosyncratic, which is taken as the mark of being a personality. Above all, it offers a ready source of helping practices and avoids the doubts and hesitations that a critique of practices inevitably brings. In all of this, new age appeals to the desire for liberation without politics and the dream of potency without effort. Insofar as it attends to intuition, to the "nonverbal" encounter, it offers a welcome vacation from the noisiness and busyness of a culture of objects and objectifications.

Even its racketeering has a good-natured quality to it—a kind of laughter that permits new age to be both serious and comic all at once. A visit to one of the many new age emporiums reveals this interesting combination of earnestness and humor, of taking one's self seriously mixed in with laissez-faire competitiveness. However, by pretending to be apolitical, by exaggerating the powers of mind and spirit, by offering personal salvation, new age isolates and desocializes. In that it is programatically antimodern. Personalist and anti-intellectual as both fundamentalism and postmodernism are too, new age meets the individual in a time of a dismay of culture. But in its rejections, it leaves the puzzles of the world untouched while pretending to solve the puzzles of the person apart from the world. As its participants dream the dream, however, others seize the powers of the world to do with as they wish. Nothing reveals this more than the fact that new age is primarily a youthful—or of those anxious to insist on their youthfulness—and middle-class activity, an activity of the comfortable who can neither abide nor dispense with the superficiality of their comforts. Ultimately, then, new age invites destruction without knowing it. In this, it fails to meet the crisis of modernity, which is found in the apartness of sociality and intimacy. Of course, as the feminist movements have it, "the personal is the political," but for "new age" the personal is the personal—only that and nothing more.

THE POSTMODERN

Like fundamentalism and new age, postmodernism rejects the Enlightenment project all the while contending, without realizing it, with the shadow enlightenment. Postmodernism attacks science, reason, and democracy, and in its more radical formulations it denies that there is the possibility of truth or even the actuality of fact.

Unlike my criticism of fundamentalism and my amusement at new age, when I face the postmodern, I find myself growing more aggressive. I announce almost angrily that I am a "white, middle class, Western male" but do not apologize for what I am. I am a Humanist, and I do not apologize for that either. Of course, I do not deny that racism, male chauvinism, and ethnocentrism are intellectual and moral disasters but I do not see these as sins of modernity as such. Indeed, inspired by Enlightenment ideals, many of us have been engaged with just these issues over the years personally, politically, and intellectually.[20] That success has not always attended these efforts is undeniable, but that they have only been exercises in bad faith is nonsense.

Even where, as among some of the postmoderns, an alternative politics is toyed with, its roots in negation forecast its triviality. Thus:

"Derrida's influence has been disastrous," Roger Kimball, a conservative critic and author of "Tenured Radicals," proclaims. "He has helped foster a sort of anemic nihilism, which has given imprimature to squads of imitators who no longer feel that what they are engaged in is a search for truth, who would find that notion risible."

Though Derrida considers himself a member of the democratic left, critics on the left haven't necessarily been any kinder. Some have charged that all this emphasis on the "impossible," on what we can't know, threatens to leave us paralyzed, "standing"—like poor Bartleby—"mute and solitary" before the world's injustices. Derrida's response—needless to say one more time—is that if the world were as simple, untangled and uncontradictory as his critics on both the left and the right want it to be, political and ethical decisions would be so straightforward as to have no interest or meaning. Tangled, in other words, are the health of politics—and the health of art, too, deconstructionists would argue.[21]

Of course, I do not deny the possibility of self-delusion, a delusion that turns *my* position into *the* position, *my* world into *the* world. I understood Karl Marx very well when he spoke of "false consciousness" or Max Weber when he spoke of "ideology."[22] But obviously I did not need the postmoderns for that either. I still know, from the evidence around the globe, that rationality, freedom, and equality are generalizable human values and that science and democracy are institutions for their realization. Yes, these are *my* values, but they are confirmable beyond *my* subjectivity, *my* culture, *my* history.[23] I still value a sense of objectivity, particularly since I have seen what a reasonless passion for "Race" and "Blood" and "Kultur" (always revealed by the use of uppercase letters) has done to us: Holocaust, ethnic cleansing, and religious wars.[24] Having declared myself against the postmodern, therefore, let me take this declaration apart—"deconstruct" it, if you will—particularly in the light of what is generally called the postmodern rejection of modernism and Humanism.

I begin with a prejudice against the postmodern, but I have my reasons. For example, postmodern language—for all its pretentiousness about words, and archaeology and deconstruction—seems deliberately designed to confuse and mislead. To be fair—fairness is another Enlightenment legacy and no doubt a modernist illusion—a more sympathetic critic might see it differently:

> an important point Michel Foucault makes in "The Discourse on Language" when he speaks of a "will to truth" which wills what is sayable instead of what the sayable does. Foucault contends that the will to truth arose "between Hesiod and Plato" in the form of a discourse on the true, and that it arose by excluding the ritualised discourse of earlier Greek poets which ". . . held sway over all and was pronounced by men who spoke as of right, according to ritual, . . . carrying men along with it and thus weaving itself into the fabric of fate." The point is that

exclusive concern for what is said rules out the use of discourse for the exercise of power.[25]

On either interpretation—elitism or inoculation against power—postmodern discourse rules out communication; language becomes an exercise in alternating subjective structures without intersubjective content. Despite a claimed concern for persons, this deliberately obscurantist style reveals that only certain persons really count; perhaps only one person really counts. Further, the disdain of reason demonstrated in the abuse of language is not simply an abstractionist's argument. More significant, the abuse of language reveals itself in conduct and above all in whether and how we can speak to each other. Conversation becomes nearly impossible—at best an exchange of elaborated grunts. The postmodern message is thus masked by verbal pyrotechnics that serve to hide us from each other and to hide ideas from inquiries. Thus, my less than charitable reading of the fact that postmoderns deny the possibility, the meaning, and even the notion of truth itself. As Pauline Rosenau remarks, "There is a general 'privatization of individual concerns.' In a post-modern age, everybody has his/her own truth based on each individual's personal experience. All that remains is individual opinion."[26]

Paradoxically, however, the postmodernists ask me to listen to them, although on their own premises, I cannot understand why I should. I can hear them only if I have agreed, in advance, that truth is a nullity, in which case it is impossible to say what it is that I am hearing. Perhaps there is a discovery or two to be found in postmodern views, but these remain hidden too—deliberately hidden, I think. Further, like the university sophomore who has come upon a new "discipline"—the first-year psychology student comes to mind—postmodern language works hard to convey an impression of profundity, as if to speak "clearly and distinctly" could be only to speak superficially.[27] Thus, a rejection by way of genre, of Descartes, the arch villain of reason. The so-called play on words of postmodern style self-consciously expects the reader to pay serious attention, for a lapse of attention ensures a missed point. At the same time, paying attention is only an egoist's exercise without an intersubjective performance. The "author" vanishes, says the more radical postmodernist. He or she becomes a nonperson, so I have no way of consulting anyone but myself as reader-turned-author. The play of the postmodern then is not playful in its destruction of connection, including the connection sought by the postmodern itself in new forms of communication. As if in confirmation of this rather uncharitable reading, Derrida writes,

> The movements of deconstruction do not destroy structures from the outside. They are not possible and effective, nor can they take accurate aim, except by inhabiting those structures. Inhabiting them *in a certain way*, because one always inhabits, and all the more when one does not suspect it. Operating necessarily from the inside, borrowing all the strategic and economic resources of subversion from the old structure, borrowing them structurally, that is to say without being able to isolate their elements and atoms, the enterprise of deconstruction always in a certain way falls prey to its own work.[28]

This move of language to the edge of unintelligibility is all the more ironic since the root of the postmodern claim in the work of Heidegger is to strip away 2,500 years of "metaphysics" in order to return to "being" as such and to escape the "language games" that have plagued us since Plato. Having thus dismissed rationality, the postmodern turns to myth, poetry, and metaphor as entries to being. But an examination of the texts reveals that the postmodern is more often than not unpoetic and confuses myth with obscurity. Calvin Schrag thus is able to write,

> Foucault's archaeology of the human sciences culminates in a transformation of the representational prose of science and its world of things into a poeticized "being of language" and its anaclastic world of words. Allegedly, having shown that the representative model of language has been dismantled by the discontinuous movement of *episteme* through the history of the human sciences, Foucault then proclaims in a somewhat oracular fashion that we have not achieved that epistemological space that discloses the poetic *arche* of the sciences of man. The ultimate conclusion of Foucault's reflections on the origin of the human sciences is an inversion of positivism; the language of science itself is reduced to poetry.[29]

That the France of Descartes, Voltaire, and Rousseau and the Germany of Goethe and Schiller should produce such linguistic escapades is sadly funny. And even if, as I am told by my European colleagues, postmodernism is "on its way out," it remains for us to see what its successor will be like following the influence of this latest excursion into obscurity for its own sake. Most puzzling of all, however, is the announced postmodern allegiance to that great pre-post-modern hero, Friedrich Nietzsche, who was a genuine master of language and metaphor.[30]

If postmodern language—like structuralism before it—displays a disrespect for persons and ideas, the notions that are implicitly conveyed are even more doubtful. Yet these notions remain very popular at least among academics, although, when pressed, the academic resorts to hints and suggestions rather than to definitions and descriptions. All too many of us with an intellectualist bent, having despaired of the world and its problems, are thus beguiled by postmodernism. In this, we are kin to the less academicized who find their homes in fundamentalism and new age. In common with these neighbors, postmodernism fascinates us by its disdain for the inherited world, indeed its disdain for any inheritance. Again, citing Foucault,

> To be brief, then, let us say that history in its traditional form undertook to "memorize" the *monuments* of the past, transform them into *documents* and lend speech to those traces which, in themselves, are often not verbal, or which say in silence something other than what they actually say; in our time, history is that which transforms *documents* into *monuments*. In that area where, in the past, history deciphered the traces left by men, it now deploys a mass of elements that have to be grouped, made relevant, placed in relation to one another to form totalities. There was a time when archeology, as a discipline devoted to silent monuments, inert traces, objects without context, and things left by the past, aspired to the condition of history, and attained meaning only through the restitution of a historical discourse; it might be said, to play on words a little, that in our time history aspires to the condition of archeology, to the intrinsic description of the monument.[31]

So as Heidegger reached back past 2,500 years of history to an original moment, postmoderns try to make a similar leap—except that, in their own terms, they really have nowhere to begin and nowhere to land. As Gordon Haist remarks,

> But in the end, the image . . . is misleading because, unlike modern science, postmodernism does not lay claim to a predecessor culture whose own truths it stands against, and against which it is maliciously partial. "A work can become modern only if it is first postmodern," Lyotard writes; "Post modernism thus understood is not modernism at its end but in the nascent state, and this state is constant." So, rather than cynicism, we would keep better counsel to look toward . . . a return of the sophist. . . . Postmodernism does not have a truth about which to be cynical, but if anything, a cynicism . . . about which to be true.[32]

In justification of their radical nihilism, postmoderns appeal to our distrust of the competence—or what is interpreted as the claim of competence—of our inheritance, classic and modern. They repeat the familiar litany of failures of science, of technology, of democracy.[33] Many of us, of course, share in that distrust. It is this that drives us to look for anything that promises a response to the terrors of our experience.

What is it that we hear when we try to search out the "truths" of postmodernism? Universal claims of any sort—including this one—are at fault simply because they are universal. So the Enlightenment with its dream of "all" persons is, at best a "local" event mistakenly universalized. This, I am told by the postmodernist, feeds on the great error of "foundationalism," the Cartesian arrogance of searching for a unifying idea that can characterize literally everything. A counsel of humility, no doubt—as if events do not teach humility every day—but the postmodernist takes the matter beyond sensibility to ontology. Thus dismissed is the great revolutionary trinity—liberty, equality, fraternity—and the great physical imagery of space and time and movement. Indeed, Foucault goes so far as to trace an inherent connection between an "age of reason" and existential (i.e., normal) insanity:

> In the landscape of unreason where the sixteenth century had located it, madness concealed a meaning and an origin that were obscurely moral. Its secrecy related it to sin. . . . In the second half of the eighteenth century, madness was no longer recognized in what brings man closer to an immemorial fall or an indefinitely present animality; it was, on the contrary, situated in those distances man takes in regard to himself, to his world, to all that is offered by the immediacy of nature; madness became possible in that milieu where man's relations with his feelings, with time, with others are altered; madness was possible because of everything which, in man's life and development, is a break with the immediate. Madness was no longer of the order of nature or of the Fall, but of a new order.[34]

To be sure, hesitation about universal claims is always advisable, as is a respect for differentiation and otherness.[35] But I did not need the postmoderns to tell me that I am "human, all too human."

Scientific truth claims, I learn from the postmodernist, are at best commonly held opinion—even social opinion—found in disparate lifeworlds. But this postmodernist appeal to "social opinion" is distant indeed from Charles Peirce's ideal "scientific community" or Josiah Royce's "holy community." For the postmodern, science is only another cultural narrative, another metaphor.[36] This is, of course, to confuse theory creation with literature and insight with verification. But that is all right too, since we are also told that history, like science, is only another metaphor. Of course, theory is always under challenge among scientists, but that challenge is not merely aesthetic, political, or idiosyncratic. It is ontological and arises from an abiding respect for what is. So despite his or her pretensions, even a postmodern walks on the ground, breathes air, drinks water, understands perspective and distance, distinguishes hard and soft, solid and liquid—that is, encounters what is just like us more ordinary souls—and it is the "what is" in elaborated form that initiates, grounds, and tests theory.[37] Even a postmodern can hear a child in pain, see a man starving, a woman abused.[38] Even a postmodern uses a printing press and a technical distribution system and relies on these to get the word out.

The world—not *my* world—turns false theory out, as "special creation" and "spontaneous generation" and "geocentrism" were turned out. It is not true that one science story simply follows another as tastes change. A paradigm shift is not a move from one fairy tale to its successor. In other words, if the sciences have arrogated to themselves a monopoly of truth—or better, if scientists have been encouraged in their arrogance for political and mythic reasons—I did not need the postmoderns to tell me that truth is where you find it and where it finds you—and not always in a laboratory or a formula.

Continuing its attack on the Enlightenment, freedom turns out to be merely a Western moral idea. If a culture wishes to keep its priests and shamans and head men (note that it is mostly men who are referred to, despite a postmodern nod to the feminine), why, then, freedom is as good as slavery, only different. The magic word for some postmoderns is *community*, but little is said about the differences between oppressive and liberating community; little is said about the community that nurtures persons and the community that defeats them. Such distinctions can be made only when rationality and evidence are admitted, but now these have been excluded as merely Western. Community is, however, not self-defining or an end in itself, and it must come to judgment. But how shall we judge? Indeed, without criteria, any community is equivalent—morally, politically—to any other. Thus, something serious is at stake in this approach to things. It is much more than a troublesome rhetoric.

The attack on science and freedom coagulates around a disdain for reason, which is known only as "arid" reason. That this attack confuses reason with rationalism is hardly noticed. Postmoderns here accord with those theologians of reason who are merely dogmatists disguised as rationalists. Both buy into the reduction of reason to mere formalism. Of course, the reason of mathematics and logic is not to be sneered at, but this does not exhaust the ranges of rationality. It is as if Hegel had not already attacked and subverted a univocal reason. It is as if Bertrand Russell and Charles Peirce had not already opened the doorway to an enrichment of reasoning. It is as if John Stuart Mill had not offered an experimental logic and John Dewey a generous notion of inquiry. To be sure, these are all "Western white males," but that is to use a deserved social criticism to invalidate an idea, to turn all ideas, as it were, into biographical idiosyncrasies.

That the poet too is a devotee of reason is ignored. Yet how would a poem be if it were a mere unconnected and unintended grab bag of syllables and letters?[39] Unless that is, in his or her experiment (*ratio* again), the poet *wants* to try the grab bag. But now it is intended, and that is another matter entirely. How could we respond to a poem (or a play or a song or a symphony or a painting) if it failed its shaping intelligence? Reason in its various inventive guises appears in minimalism, in free verse, in op art, in impressionism and cubism and nonobjective art, and, yes, even in postmodernism in architecture and painting. The ancient warfare between reason and passion is declared once again in the attack on modernism. So rationality is merely the ultimate Western male value and as such merely the figure of a local narrative—and a poor one at that, given the pretensions of reason and its failures.[40]

Finally, neither "success" nor "failure" is a usable idea since these require a standard of judgment and a sense of development, both of which vanish under postmodern ministrations. But then, contradiction does not bother postmoderns all that much. At best, then, we are left with discomfort, a kind of philosophic indigestion. At the same time, we are left with a mock-heroic individual living in his or her personal world, adventuring now this way or that but never into a world "out there," which, after all, is simply denied.[41] Like the fundamentalist and the new ager, the postmodern drives the person away from other persons. If the shadow enlightenment forsakes two-ness for the world, the deniers of the Enlightenment project forsake two-ness for the magic of innerness.

NOTES

1. It is unfortunate that Descartes's *Meditations* are explored only by philosophers. Its cultural magnificence is thus buried in endless technical arguments about the legitimacy of the logic of the project or about the fine points of the transition from doubting to being. The daring notion of finding in one's mind the absolute basis of everything is hardly explored except in adversarial confrontation of rationalists and empiricists or in the hostilities of the postmoderns.

2. Symptomatically, Thomas Jefferson struggled to deal with the slavery question and the race question. At times an advocate of emancipation, at other times a compromiser, he nevertheless held to the notion of the ultimate inferiority of blacks—so much so that his solution was, finally, to expatriate the freed slaves to a land of their own where they would not contaminate their betters. See *Notes on the State of Virginia*, in *The Portable Thomas Jefferson*, ed. Merrill D. Peterson (New York: Viking Penguin, 1977), pp. 186–187 passim.

3. Jean Amery, *Radical Humanism*, ed. and trans. Sidney Rosenfeld and Stella P. Rosenfeld (Bloomington: Indiana University Press, 1984), pp. 97–98.

4. In an earlier essay, *The Devil and Secular Humanism* (New York: Praeger, 1990), I explored in more direct and extended fashion the relationships between Humanism and fundamentalism. Here I want to add some other ideas, particularly in the context of the recapture of the two-ness of Humanism, the connectedness of the intimate and the public, the intuitive and the rational.

5. For example, I received just prior to the 1994 elections a mailing addressed to "Christian voters" signed by Pat Robertson as founder and president of the Christian Coalition. His letter began, "Do you think your Congressman and two Senators are doing a good job of representing *your values* in Washington?" The expected appeal for funds was aimed at the strategic goal of mobilizing "40,000,000 Christian voters" for 1996. See also Leslie Kaufman, "Antipolitics '94, Life Beyond God," *New York Times Magazine*, October 16, 1994.

6. In addition to the well-reported instances of Islamic fundamentalism in Iran and Lebanon, examples are plentiful elsewhere. Thus, the *kokugaku* (National Studies) movement that began in nineteenth-century Japan developed out of Shinto and was antirationalist and ethnocentric. In Israel, we find the *'edah haredit* (ultraorthodox) and *Gush Emmunim* (Bloc of the Faithful). Sikh fundamentalism is violently active in India. Indeed, no modern society seems able to avoid religious fundamentalism.

7. Martin E. Marty and R. Scott Appleby, *Fundamentalisms Observed* (Chicago: University of Chicago Press, 1991).

8. Rosemary Radford Reuther, "A World on Fire with Faith" (review of *Fundamentalisms Observed*), *New York Times Book Review*, January 26, 1992, p. 10.

9. Ibid.

10. Beverley Earles, "Humanism and the New Age: Lessons for Humanists to Learn," *Humanism Today* 7 (1992): 15. Citations are from Hans Sebald, "New Age Romanticism: The Quest for an Alternative Lifestyle as a Force of Social Change," *Humboldt Journal of Social Relations* 11, no. 2 (Spring–Summer 1984).

11. See Dana Ullman, "Holistic Health: Friend and Foe of Progressive Health Care," *International Journal of Holistic Health and Medicine* 2 (Winter 1984): 20–23.

12. J. L. Simmons, *The Emerging New Age* (Santa Fe, N.M.: Bear and Co., 1990), pp. 15–18 passim.

13. James Turner, *Without God, without Creed* (Baltimore: Johns Hopkins University Press, 1985), p. 164.

14. For example, see Carl G. Jung, *Synchronicity* (Princeton, N.J.: Princeton University Press, 1960). For a popular treatment, see John Freeman, ed., *Man and His Symbols* (Garden City, N.Y.: Doubleday, 1964).

15. For example, see Abraham Maslow, *Toward a Psychology of Being* (New York: Van Nostrand, 1968), and Carl Rogers, *On Becoming a Person* (Boston: Houghton Mifflin, 1961).

16. Abraham Maslow, *The Psychology of Science* (New York: Harper & Row, 1966), pp. xv–xvi.

17. For a sympathetic but critical discussion of the Gaia hypothesis, see Laurence Levine, "Gaia: Goddess and Idea," *Humanism Today* 6 (1991): 166–179.

18. Among other texts in a fruitful career, see Joseph Campbell, *The Hero with a Thousand Faces* (New York: Meridian Books, 1956).

19. Beverley Earles, "Humanism and the New Age," *Humanism Today* 7 (1992): 10.

20. For a discussion of reform in the liberal tradition, see Radest, *The Devil and Secular Humanism*, chap. 6, and *Community Service, Encounter with Strangers* (Westport, Conn.: 1993), chap. 4.

21. Mitchell Stephens, "Jacques Derrida," *New York Times Magazine*, January 23, 1994, p. 25.

22. The classic study of this issue and of the "sociology of knowledge" is still Karl Mannheim's *Ideology and Utopia*, trans. Edward Shils and Louis Wirth (London: Routledge & Kegan Paul, 1936).

23. Perhaps the most sympathetic treatment of what I still think is a disastrous conclusion for arbitrariness (miscalled contingency) based in the evident plurality of life-worlds is to be found in Richard Rorty's *Contingency, Irony, and Solidarity* (Cambridge: Cambridge University Press, 1989), particularly chap. 4. Most other postmodernists conclude, essentially, for nihilism miscalled freedom.

24. I know the argument can go both ways, although a look at the record (if that is still possible) would suggest that "reason" is not the villain of the twentieth century and that "unreason" is. See, for example, Pauline Marie Rosenau, *Post-Modernism and the Social Sciences* (Princeton, N.J.: Princeton University Press, 1992).

25. Gordon Haist, "The Reason of Disenchantment: A Response to the Humanist in the Post-Modern World" (paper presented at the South Carolina Philosophic Association, February 1994), p. 4.

26. Rosenau, *Post-Modernism and the Social Sciences*, p. 104.

27. Foucault goes so far as to identify clarity with blindness and, in a sense, with a madness beyond madness:

> In this sense, the Cartesian formula of doubt is certainly the great exorcism of madness. Descartes closes his eyes and plugs up his ears the better to see the true brightness of essential daylight; thus he is secured against the dazzlement of the madman who, opening his eyes, sees only night, and not seeing at all, believes he sees when he imagines. In the uniform lucidity of his closed senses, Descartes has broken with all possible fascination, and if he sees, he is certain of seeing that which he sees. While before the eyes of the madman, drunk on a light which is darkness, rise and multiply images incapable of criticizing themselves (since the madman *sees* them), but irreparably separated from being (since the madman sees *nothing*).

Michel Foucault, *Madness and Civilization*, trans. Richard Howard (New York: Vintage Books, 1973), pp. 108–109.

28. Jacques Derrida, *Of Grammatology*, trans. Gayatri Chakravorty Spivak (Baltimore: Johns Hopkins University Press, 1976), p. 24.

29. Calvin O. Schrag, *Radical Reflection and the Origin of the Human Sciences* (West Lafayette, Ind.: Purdue University Press, 1980), p. 130.

30. Recourse to Nietzsche is understandable—except that we are not permitted to "understand," that is, to reason and criticize in terms of continuities, categories, and criteria. For example, the postmodern song does indeed echo in the following:

> The forces of imagination and of Appolonian dream are saved only by the myth from indiscriminate rambling. . . . Over against this, let us consider abstract man stripped of myth, abstract education, abstract mores, abstract law, abstract government; the random vagaries of the artistic imagination unchanneled by any native myth; a culture without any fixed and consecrated play of origin, condemned to exhaust all possibilities and feed miserable and parasitically on every culture under the sun. Here we have our present age, the result of a Socratism bent on the extermination of myth. Man today, stripped of myth, stands famished among all his pasts and must dig frantically for roots, be it among the most remote antiquities.

Friedrich Nietzsche, *The Birth of Tragedy*, trans. Francis Golffing (Garden City, N.Y.: Doubleday, Anchor Books, 1966), pp. 52–53. Of course, similar things were being said elsewhere, not least of all in the United States. For example, a rereading of Emerson would be worthwhile on these same points. See "The Divinity School Address," "The American Scholar," and "Self-Reliance." Nietzsche, by the way, noted his appreciation of Emerson in *The Gay Science*. See George J. Stack, *Nietzsche and Emerson: An Elective Affinity* (Athens, Ohio: Ohio University Press, 1992).

31. Michel Foucault, *The Archeology of Knowledge*, trans. A. M. Sheridan Smith (London: Tavistock Publications, 1972), pp. 6–7.

32. Haist, "Reason," p. 5.

33. Consider in this regard, the comments of Jean Amery:

> But what I am citing are paradigmatic statements. Every one of them contains . . . irrational rage against the technical-industrial world, the wholly false conception that the historical Enlightenment was nothing but the instrument of a brutal bourgeoisie that was securing its dominion. They are blind to the obvious historical fact . . . that in the . . . bourgeois revolution there was *also* universality, that while industry and machines did harm the individual, they also freed him from the oppressiveness and dullness of the biblically accursed soil. I know the mountain peasants . . . in my native Austria and I know the American farmer. No ever so refined dialectical philosophizing can rob me of the conviction that, thanks to his machines, the latter leads a life more worthy of a human being than did the former in bygone times.

Radical Humanism, ed. and trans. Sidney Rosenfeld and Stella P. Rosenfeld (Bloomington, Ind.: Indiana University Press, 1984), p. 139.

34. Foucault, *Madness and Civilization*, pp. 219–220.

35. Again, I betray my prejudice when I suggest that William James analyzed variousness in *A Pluralistic Universe* more adequately and responsibly than the postmoderns do.

36. This "literary" interpretation of the sciences seems—but only seems—to have a legitimate parent in the work of Thomas Kuhn; see *The Structure of Scientific Revolutions* (Chicago: University of Chicago Press, 1970). Kuhn, however, retains reasonableness, method, and a return to experience (to evidence) in describing paradigm shifts and their justifications. That is all but forgotten by postmodernists. It is also helpful to realize that, without minimizing his originality, Kuhn's way of interpreting the sciences began some time ago and is not uniquely a recent event. See, for example, E. A. Burtt, *The Metaphysical Foundations of Modern Physical Science* (London: Routledge, Kegan Paul, 1924).

37. Obviously, discussions of the ways that we "do" the sciences continue. Yet this "return" to experience remains a central point despite differences of emphasis and conflicts of meaning. Still pertinent here is the pragmatic tradition beginning with Charles Peirce, "How to Make Our Ideas Clear," and continuing with John Dewey's *Logic: The Theory of Inquiry* (New York: Henry Holt and Company, 1938). Thomas Kuhn as I read him finds in experience precisely the reasons for the various historic shifts that have taken place in the sciences, shifts from doing "ordinary" science to some "new" way of doing science. He reminds me, in this regard, of Dewey's point that thinking is initiated by a "problematic" situation, that is, a discomfort, an imbalance.

38. Richard Rorty, despite his postmodernism, does urge that we refrain from "doing harm," although given the radical cultural relativism of his position, it is hard to see the reasons that anyone should listen to him unless they happen to agree (or to be born within the same life-world).

39. Archibald MacLeish wrote, "A poem should not seem but be", *Ars Poetica* (1926).

40. Noting the "linguistic turn" in modern thought, Richard Tarnas comments,

> Here in a sense the Cartesian critical intellect has reached its furthest point of development, doubting all, applying a systematic skepticism to every possible meaning. With no divine foundation to certify the Word, language possesses no privileged connection to truth. The fate of human consciousness is ineluctably nomadic, a self-aware wandering through error. The history of human thought is a history of idiosyncratic metaphorical schemes, ambiguous interpretive vocabularies having no ground beyond what is already saturated by their own metaphorical and interpretive categories. Postmodern philosophers can compare and contrast, analyze and discuss the many sets of perspectives human beings have expressed . . . but they cannot pretend to possess an extrahistorical Archimedean point from which to judge whether a given perspective validly represents the "Truth." Since there are no indubitable foundations for human knowledge, the highest value for any perspective is its capacity to be temporarily useful or edifying, emancipatory or creative—though it is recognized that in the end these valuations are themselves not justifiable by anything beyond personal and cultural taste. For justification is itself only another social practice with no foundation beyond social practice.

Richard Tarnas, *The Passion of the Western Mind* (New York: Ballantine Books, 1991), pp. 399–400.

41. For a discussion of this theme, although interpreted far more affirmatively than I do, see Robert Jay Lifton, *Human Resilience in an Age of Fragmentation* (New York: Basic Books, 1994).

4

THE EXISTENTIAL MOOD

"HELL IS OTHER PEOPLE"

The Enlightenment's enemies pretend to restore intimacy to the modern age. But they lose themselves in their own isms. They only toy with innerness, as in the new ager's consciousness game, treat it in cookie-cutter fashion, as in the fundamentalist's soul game, or resign it to relativism run wild, as in the postmodernist's subjectivity game. We need to restore intimacy, but it cannot be left to the mercies of the shadow enlightenment or to the negations of its attackers.

Let me turn then to the existential mood. This other criticism of modernism attends to soul and subject just as new age, fundamentalism, and postmodernism do. But with existentialism, I am in the presence of a less flighty effort. No doubt, this follows from the need to answer to a world where depression, war, and holocaust had subverted our sense of ourselves and where liberation had become a new tyranny. Their's is not the world of the yuppie, the religious racketeer, or the literary *poseur*.

Existentialism moved the Enlightenment project from the eighteenth century to the twentieth century. Thus, Sartre shifted Cartesianism from deductive logic to philosophical anthropology, and Kierkegaard converted the god of "nature and nature's law" into a radical "god of faith." Existential insights appeared in the guise of atheist and theist, anarchist and communist, poet and metaphysician. More elusive still, these insights were various even within the lifetime of any of existentialism's representative figures. Existentialism is thus better approached as mood than movement.

It comes to us in tonalities and temperaments rather than as an exposition of clear and distinct ideas.

Mood is reflected best in existential drama, novel, and story. As a way of standing toward the world, it is grounded in possibilities of shared experience. There is an author and an audience, an actor and a critic. For all its focus on subjectivity, the existential mood is not merely subjective. It has outcomes that can be compared, judged, complained of, praised, and altered. Its mood is finally constructive for all the language of *angst* that is typical of the existential. By contrast, constructivity is scarcely to be found in the exaggerations of postmodern literary pretensions, its precious concern for narrative, and its proclamation of the epistemic superiority of metaphor. The existential mood may be against or in spite of, but it does not desert human intelligence and action.

The existential mood moves through self-reflection to a meeting with others and with the world. From this meeting, I learn that I am who I am and yet that I am not opaque to you. The human relation is still possible, although for the religiously minded, it must be mediated by faith, and for the secular minded by act and will. Of course, I seek to hide from you, to mask myself by playing roles, to remain mute before your questions, to mislead you by lying or even by telling the truth. Yet I am, paradoxically, knowable as a fellow human being because of these strategies. I recognize you as well as myself in them, so I can penetrate your hiddenness by finding you in myself, as it were. Of course, I may choose not to do so, but then I recognize another familiar strategy: indifference. Thus, I am a social being in spite of myself. Even my masks reveal the social fact. But in the modern world, these masks press us toward a seductive exteriority—role taking and role playing—and thus take on a burden of domination that the Enlightenment project with its confidence in individuality, rationality, and revolutionary passion did not have to bear.

Of course, it is false to pretend that I must be entirely mysterious to myself or to you. At the same time, I am indeed a mystery—not only to you but to myself as well. Only I can know that I am such and such by having, feeling, and being. But I can never finally know who I am, if for no other reason than that what I know always lags behind the act of knowing itself. This is as characteristic of who I am as all those deliberate self-hidings that block me from myself and that mislead me about myself. "Self-deception," in other words, is a recurring possibility.[1]

In this partially known and partially hidden "I am," there lurks the temptation of a radical psychological atomism. In the "I am," I find my induplicability and above all my consciousness of it, my self-consciousness. I thus announce the ineradicability of intimacy. I may treat myself as an object, but it is still I that am doing the treating. I thus translate the logic of the Cartesian experiment into psychological form.[2]

When I act, I introduce myself into situations. I model the connectability of innerness and outerness. Action provides an alternative to rationalism's objectification of persons (e.g., all "men" and language like that) while denying the radical subjectivism of our so-called postmodern era. The species-wide characteristics that are embedded in our shared strategies, however, cannot tell the whole story. I am unique too in my presence at a historic and social moment. Try as I may to strip away the Aristotelian "accidents," the Cartesian "incidentals," or the empiricist's "secondary and tertiary qualities" in order to find the essential me of all me's, I cannot succeed. Much as I enter the world, it enters me in an unavoidable partnership. Sometimes, to be sure, the partnership can be angry and hostile; at other times it can be challenging and supportive. I do not exist "in general." In my particularity, I am in this moment, and I cannot be pinned down to it by general categories. In other words, the existential hunt for innerness runs to society and culture and history but ends as it begins, in autobiography.

By contrast, the shadow enlightenment variously neglects and subverts this partnership. This is demonstrated not only by the objectifications of social existence (e.g., the omnipresence of the legalist, the bureaucrat, and the behaviorist) but also by the trivialization of personality itself. In the popular media, but increasingly in more elite circles as well, being a personality means conforming to an externalized and collectivized image. Politicians are, in a Kafkaesque move, deliberately made up by others—the omnipresent, anonymous others—as are movie stars and "successful" academics. A convenient misreading of the sciences corroborates this move by a claimed neutralization of everything that is knowable, by the isolation of values from existence. Technique is all, and ends are reserved to subjectivity. This perfected technique moves us away from the ability to share widely in the things we care most about. Instead, as Sartre helps us see, it elevates alienation to high art:

I do not mind *knowing* but I do not want to *see*. . . . I do not mind knowing that Peter is dead, but I do not want to *see* him dead. . . . Proust and the inconstancies of the heart: his knowledge of his grandmother's death is a closed truth, a truth for others. . . . One day he *realizes* it, that is the definite absence of his grandmother, her no-longer-being in the world, is absence unveiled in things. How many truths useful for our action and constantly employed by us are thus closed truths, sealed letters. We foolishly call this "not having imagination." We say that the judge who condemns a criminal to ten years in jail does not *imagine* the ten years of suffering. It is not that he does not *imagine* them, he refused to verify them (visits to prisons, etc.). Thus, an "*idealist*" type of truth is created, i.e. truths that are statements about Being without contact with Being.[3]

The reduction of innerness to mere subjectivity is not without its reasons, particularly reason of self-defense. As John Dewey reminded us, experience is "precarious" and "stable." The Greeks, long ago, knew the dark and wild sides of experience, knew *thanatos* and *eros* as well as *logos*. But the conversion of fear into anxiety, and of anxiety into a cultural phenomenon—an age of anxiety, as the poet W. H. Auden put it—is a peculiarly modern event. To protect ourselves, anxiety is masked by the pseudosecurity of systemic organization or sublimated as violence and addictions. As we act out our anxieties, the outcome is trivialization and terror.

When I recall what has happened in the modern world, I frighten myself because I become aware of what I can do and of how easily I can justify what I do. Thus, the issue is not just the "rise of fascism" or the "holocaust" or the "atom bomb" but that I know myself to be capable of these acts. I know this—I "know" this—because the "I's" that performed them are not alien to me, are not "inhuman" monsters in human disguise.[4] I am caught in my own company.

Behind the masks of the living theater that replaces our actual doings and sufferings, I recognize myself, and I do not want to. The lived experience of a less bloody-minded era now becomes the experience of self-deceiving anxiety. So in defense, I alienate—in the sense of putting away from myself—my acts and the acts of others, which are seen as historic "events," as social "practices," as the work of economic "laws," or what have you. At the same time, I prepare a place for myself apart, make denial into lifestyle. And this I reveal when I escape into ever-narrowing circles of privacy. My politics becomes nonpolitical. It is neither the architectonic discipline of classical thought nor the social invention of the Enlightenment project. So too with my ethics, which is the other face of politics as both the Greeks and the Enlightenment knew and as we have forgotten. Ethics is no longer conceived as the grand drama of good and evil or as the tragic need for choosing among goods or among evils. It becomes petty moralism.

Of course, we moderns did not discover the ability to hide. Hiding is a human characteristic, a historic characteristic. Oedipus was "blind" before he blinded himself and Jesus could say, "Forgive them, Father, for they know not what they do." Nor did we moderns invent moralism and power politics. The Puritan and the Machiavellian were there long before us. If not original with us, however, we have given these traditions a frightening content. Even the highest achievements of the modern era—the marriage of science and technology, and the spread of democracy—issue in ambivalence. Feeding the hungry and curing the sick generate uncontrollable populations; housing the homeless and clothing the naked destroy the environment. The list grows. Little wonder, then, that I assign even my good deeds to agencies and institutions that act in my name and use my money. In the ironically democratic achievement of modern communication, we enjoy a wider and wider awareness of ourselves as destroyers, which cannot entirely be suppressed by our deceptions. "Our species," the sociobiologist E. O. Wilson says, "retains hereditary traits that add greatly to our destructive impact. We are tribal and aggressively territorial, intent on private space beyond minimal requirements and oriented by selfish sexual and reproductive drives. . . . The human species is, in a word, an environmental abnormality."[5]

Even that most intimate of moments, the moment of dying, becomes abstract. "All men are mortal," begins the first form of the Aristotelian syllogism. But mortality is not a logical exercise. Ritual and story have interpreted death's separations for us. Now we are stripped of ritual practice and believable story—"demythologized," as we say—left only with euphemisms that do not interpret but deny, unsuccessfully, or that attempt indefinite postponement to another world, again unsuccessfully. Despite the religiosity of our society, we live as the unbelievers that we really are.

To know how to live is, as an early wisdom had it, to know how to die. Symptomatically, however, the language of death becomes for us an exercise in blindness—the "dear departed," "passed away," and all the rest—or else death becomes a statistic. Mortuary and cosmetics industries help put death away from us in yet another way. With the modern hospital and nursing home, we die apart, socially and not just existentially. Death and dying also become intellectual and psychological toys of the new age, as in "near-death" experiences or flirtations with reincarnation.

But these attempts to banish death do not work very well. Always behind them is the reality: all men are mortal, and I am a man, and I am mortal. Knowing that I will die, the anxiety revealed in denial tells me that death is an incomprehensible and, above all, unnatural thing—else why so anxious for blindness on all sides. Now the genocide of Nazism and the body counts of Vietnam come back to haunt me. Knowing thereby that we have made death a strategem of technologized warfare or a feature of political policy, I find the denial even more terrifying, for society itself seems in on the conspiracy.

Little wonder, then, that I can easily find reasons for the move away from innerness. I find it intolerable to be told that

> all man's alibis are unacceptable; no gods are responsible for his condition; no original sin; no heredity and no environment; no race, no caste, no father, and no mother; no wrong-headed education, no governess, no teacher; not even an impulse or a disposition, a complex or a childhood trauma. Man is free, but his freedom does not look like the glorious liberty of the Enlightenment; it is no longer the gift of God. Once again, man stands alone in the universe, responsible for his condition, likely to remain in a lowly state, but free to reach above the stars.[6]

I try to run away but I do not succeed.[7] Trapped, my anxiety grows.

"GOD IS DEAD"

To be sure, the theist-atheist debate still goes on, but more as a reprise of ancient history or as an exercise in shopworn dialectics. There was a time, however, and not so long ago, when there was a lot at stake in the debate, although the ante was not so much theological as political. For too long, god ideas had been the ally of repression—the sanction for authority and power over the lives and hopes of people. Although the Christian might speak of a merciful and loving God and although the Jew might speak of a just God, the fact of the matter was that God was on the side of the battalions and the battalions belonged to the powers that be. Often the debate was really an extension of politics by other means.

There was more to it than politics, however. The Enlightenment passion against God was not merely political, anticlerical, and intellectual. The indictment of God—his alleged violation of the human being's freedom and dignity—was already evident in the angry broadsides of Tom Paine[8] and Voltaire. As with Jefferson and Joseph Priestley, the Enlightenment project tried to save Christianity by focusing on the moral figure of Jesus and on natural religion and by erasing the Christ of the cross and the God of vengeance. But it did not succeed. It was left for Nietzsche, nearly a century later, to announce publicly the failure to save Christianity:

> The thought of being in God's debt became [man's] new instrument of torture. He focused in God the last of the opposites he could find to his true and inveterate animal instincts. . . . He projected all his denials of self, nature, naturalness out of himself. . . . In such psychological cruelty we see an insanity of the will that is without parallel: Man's will to find himself guilty and unredeemably so; . . . his will to erect an ideal (God's holiness) in order to assure himself of his own

absolute unworthiness. What a mad, unhappy animal is man! . . . And if one is still able to hear . . . in this night of torment and absurdity the cry of love ring out, the cry of rapt longing, of redemption in love, he must turn away with a shudder of invincible horror. . . . Man harbors too much horrors; the earth has been a lunatic asylum for too long.[9]

While traditional language persisted, the debate over God was finally won not by reason alone but by the institutionalization of reason as science, technology, and commerce. God finally deserted his ancient allies—God was not yet dead—who, left to themselves, surrendered to the secular state or more often co-opted it. But the seeds of a new and different surrender were already contained in the fact of secularity itself. It is, by now, a very familiar story. Suffice to say, organization became its own god, strengthened now by the very technology and commerce that had ousted its predecessor. This development continues to dominate the world despite the rediscovery of sin, the successive reemergence of neo-orthodoxy, confessional religions, and fundamentalism.

But on the way to the modern idolatry of system, other and equally serious things were happening to the central themes of the Enlightenment project. This was much more troubling than a romantic revolt against the so-called rational man of the eighteenth-century *philosophe* and the classical philosopher alike. Democracy and science needed the reasonable "man" who had come down to earth from the "heaven beyond the heavens." Instead, the human being became a creature of calculations and prudence, naturally given to consult his or her perceived interests and to act upon them. Reason, in other words, was reduced to utility. The human being was, moreover, endlessly inventive in finding, making, and announcing these interests. The new-born sciences of psychology, political economy, and sociology perfected this description.

Because talk about interests came to wear the honorific "scientific," the vanishing dependability of God and of his agents on earth did not need to be all that troubling. The security offered by science and technology was available. Indeed, freedom to pursue interests became the principle of organization itself. It would be exercised predictably since interests were knowable by the new sciences. Self-interest, in other words, was not a counsel of ego run wild but of organized rationality and would provide for a sane and sensible society as well. If, on occasion, an imbalance of powers resulted, then like a thermostat, society already contained a self-adjusting mechanism, which was to be found in the interests of those on the wrong side of the balance.[10] It was important only to ensure that the free play of interests was not impeded, and all would be well. Hence the moral basis of laissez-faire, the notion of civil rights, of procedural laws, of public literacy, and all the rest of the Enlightenment's agenda.

Unfortunately, only a few short years into the modern revolution, it did not seem to be working out that way. The Marxist called attention to the fact that market mechanisms did not really correct the imbalance. Indeed, the gulf between wealth and poverty increased; the gap between power and powerlessness grew wider. Even more disconcerting was the fact that the so-called rational man did not know he or she was supposed to be rational. Interests, in other words, had a way of escaping the boundaries of reason. They could be perverse and wild and were the result of hidden motives that, when brought to the light, were shown not to be rational at all. Innerness would not be denied, but its isolation from a public world led to a kind of normal madness paralleling the madness of an idolatry of systems. Indeed, the new psychologies would trace the sources of interest to the irrational, the accidental, and the contradictory. It remained for our day, however, to elevate these to an ideal, to praise unreason as in "do your own thing" and "it's all a matter of taste" and to exalt feeling as the only sure guide to truth.

Already, Dostoyevsky had described the transformation of reason into prudence in his prophetic *Notes from Underground*:

> There's no doubt in your mind that he will learn as soon as he's rid of certain bad old habits and when common sense and science have completely re-educated human nature and directed it along the proper channels. You seem certain that man himself will give up erring *of his own free will* and will stop opposing his will to this interest. You say, moreover, that science itself will teach man . . . that he has neither will nor whim—never had, as a matter of fact—that he is something like a piano key or an organ stop; that on the other hand there are natural laws in the universe, and whatever happens to him happens outside his will, as it were, by itself, in accordance with the laws of nature. Therefore, all there is left to do is to discover these laws and man will no longer be responsible for his act. Life will be really easy for him then. . . . Then the utopian palace of crystal will be erected; then . . . well, then those will be the days of bliss.[11]

The new biology would not save rational man either. With Darwinism, hidden drives and impulses to survive shaped body, behavior, and mind. The rational animal of classical thought was replaced by forces that controlled but were not controllable. Indeed, just as the rational man of interests became describable but unintelligible, so the sciences only increased our uncertainties and thereby subverted the dream of progress that had stirred the Enlightenment project.

Reason itself was not immune to transformation. As Walter Kaufmann sums it up in writing of Nietzsche,

> Reason and the sex drive are both forms of the will to power. The sex drive, however, is an impulse, and in yielding to it in its unsublimated form, man is still the slave of his passions and has no power over them. Rationality, on the other hand, gives man mastery over himself; and as the will to power is essentially the "instinct of freedom," it can find fulfillment only through rationality. Reason is the "highest" manifestation of the will to power, in the distinct sense that through rationality it can realize its objective most fully.[12]

The enemy was not only outside the gates, as the Enlightenment had believed, but in the heart of the citadel.

In our own time—although there was warning enough in post-Newtonian mechanics (the incommensurable notions of light as particle and as wave)—physics itself, the most basic of the sciences, joined in the development of epistemological and ontological ambiguity with the arrival of indeterminacy and quantum mechanics. Nuclear destruction corroborated the evolving moral ambiguity of the sciences. And as Paul Tillich remarked, "One of the results of the flight into space and the possibility of looking down at the earth is a kind of estrangement between man and earth, an 'objectification' of the earth for man, the depriving 'her' of her 'motherly' character, her power of giving birth, of nourishing, of embracing, of keeping for herself, of calling back to herself. She becomes a large, material body to be looked at and considered as totally calculable."[13]

The offer of science as a reliable substitute for godly securities thus ran up against its own evolving theory and practice. The other themes of the Enlightenment project now became dubious too—the shadow enlightenment was well along.[14] Enlightenment itself became problematic as we began our adventures with the subconscious. With that, nihilism appears—not as in the literary and intellectualized bourgeois sport of the new age and the postmoderns but as a deeply felt psychological and historic phenomenon. Nietzsche had described it thus in "The Will to Power":

> Why has the advent of nihilism become necessary? Because the values we have had hitherto thus draw their final consequence: because nihilism represents the ultimate logical conclusion of our great values and ideals—because we must experience nihilism before we can find out what value these "values" really had.[15]

Now, in reaction to nihilism, the compulsion to develop system increased, providing a pseudosecurity and a pseudointelligibility to replace the God and the Enlightenment that were both in the shadows.

But neither the evolution of system nor the evidence of its failure tells the whole story. We have been more actively homicidal and suicidal than that. "Whither is god," Nietzsche cried. "I shall tell you. We have killed him—you and I. All of us are murderers."[16] So we announce with Zarathustra, that "God is dead," not so much as an atheist's conclusion but as a historical, psychological, and moral statement.[17] With the death of God, the possibility of a secured place for the human being vanishes, and resentful guilt takes its place. The terrifying vocabulary of the modern era moves into place: anxiety, lostness, despair, homelessness, absurdity.

To be sure, the human being still moves on his or her daily round, taking what comfort he or she can in the artifacts of a society that seems so assured in its functions. But a hidden disquiet is also evident. What we have come to call senseless violence (as if there were sensible violence) increases; power becomes an end in itself; a desperate search for meanings attracts us to the silliest and saddest offerings of cosmic and personal salvation; the grand dramas of history and destiny give way to petty experiments. A double response, then, becomes the thread of the contemporary. We are overly organized and we are bereft. "Homelessness," writes Heidegger, "is coming to be the destiny of the world."[18]

THE HIDDEN CHRISTIAN

It would seem inappropriate for a Humanist to address the puzzlements of being a Christian under modern conditions. My credentials are, to say the least, tainted by my prejudices. Of course, it is all too easy for me to attack the otherworldliness, the hypocrisy, and the institutional aggression that goes by the name of Christian. I am used to losing myself joyfully in the battle for freedom of conscience, free inquiry, and a respectful toleration. But that having been said, I would be missing the point if I left the matter of religion to institutional disputations over rights and freedoms.

I grasp the deep and despairing personal issue of faith that confronts any serious believer and the consequent criticism of both Sunday church-going and monomaniacal fundamentalism that it makes necessary. Thus, as Kierkegaard had it, traditional religion is organized and thereby becomes faithless. But I do not enjoy the discomfort of my opponents, nor am I blind to the void of meanings that they experience. I experience it too. I need not be Kierkegaard's "man of faith" in order to respond to his comment that we are what is called a "Christian" nation—but in such a sense that not a single one of us is in the character of the Christianity of the New Testament, any more than I am. . . . The illusion of a Christian nation is due doubtless to the power which number exercises over the imagination. I have not the least doubt that every single individual in the nation will be honest enough with God and with himself to say in solitary conversation, "If I must be candid, I do not deny that I am not a Christian in the New Testament sense; if I must be honest, I do not deny that my life cannot be called an effort in the direction of what the New Testament calls Christianity, in the direction of denying myself, renouncing the world, dying from it, etc.; rather the earthly and the temporal become more and more important to me with every year I live."[19]

Many of us confess the point of this criticism in our conduct—some by simply staying away from religion out of religious conviction, others by seeking the genuine belief they find missing in its conventional expressions. It is no accident that the sect is the growing edge of contemporary religion—an effort to secure the world by turning our backs to it. Traditionalism too retains its attractiveness but only as it moves toward fundamentalism. In the religious situation then, there appears a theme that transcends the lines ordinarily drawn between Humanist and religionist. A search for believable meanings, it reveals the dilemma of the human being in the presence of both the shadow enlightenment and its attackers.

"If God is dead, then all things are permitted." That, as Dostoyevsky put it, opens up the world in a radically unformed and unformable way. More radically, we are, as Paul Tillich put it, living in a time of the "shaking of the foundations":

But if we accept the message of the new reality in the Christ, we must understand that this message does not contain an easy answer, and that it does not guarantee any spiritual security. We must know that it is a real answer only if we understand it permanently in the light of our human situation, in which tragedy and hope fight each other without victory. The victory is above them. The victory came when the prayer of the psalmist was answered, "Relent, O thou Eternal"—this prayer is the prayer of mankind through all eons, and is the hidden prayer in the depth of every human soul.[20]

The foundations are shaking for the Humanist too. Reason is attacked as "patriarchy," truth as "localism," and freedom as "tyranny." I too am set back to the first days of "creation" when the "earth was a formless void and there was darkness over the deep." Of course, scientific laws, technological devices, and cultural habits anchor me in reality. Yet for all the shape and structure these bring to my life—and I do not minimize them—they miss out on the why and whither of my living; they miss out on the grand themes of purpose and destiny, and they miss out on the possibility of a shared sociability.

I lack, in other words, convincing reasons for doing this rather than that, being this rather than that. Reason becomes elusive just as ideals become elusive. As a skeptic, I know that the laws of nature and the traditions of culture might quite easily be otherwise, just as I, given a different accident of place and time, could quite easily have been otherwise. And this is so even as I reject efforts to convert science into mere narrative and to read technical ideas like indeterminacy and quantum in near-mythic terms as invitations to think that anything goes as long as enough of the society (of scientists) agrees. This move is described by William Dean:

> Conventionalism within quantum physics is best represented by John Wheeler. His approach can be understood by reference to the uncertainty principle. For Wheeler, that principle does not refer to mere technical difficulties of knowing. . . . Rather, . . . he argues that there simply is no reality apart from observers and observations and that all entities, not just humans, are observers. Wheeler puts it this way: "no elementary phenomenon is a phenomenon until it is a registered phenomenon." While here the qualifier "elementary" confines that particular dictum to microphysical worlds, in other writing Wheeler extends it to the macrophysical world. The universe, Wheeler argues, is a "self-excited circuit." He asks, "Is the architecture of existence such that only through 'observership' does the universe have a way to coming into being?" And he answers affirmatively.[21]

Facing this ontological nihilism, the notion of absurdity echoes in my mind, but it lacks the feeling of good humor.

The existential mood reaches me in yet another way as I realize that I am—an "is" without a "why." I need not go to the extremes of thinking of myself as being thrown into the world as some existentialists have put it, nor need I weep and wail in anguish because I am a given and not a reason. And yet I am not contented to be just a given, and I must have my reasons. That, it would seem, is the nature of human nature—if I can even speak that way any longer—and for that, the "religious situation" of the Christian becomes a metaphor even for a Humanist.

The traditional religious response, however, begs the question.[22] I notice that even for the man of faith, the leap into the abyss has a secured quality. If faith be false, nothing is lost that was not already lost, and if it be true, then the world is gained. Thus, in a psychological reconstruction of

"Pascal's wager," the man of faith really bets on a sure thing even if he makes the bet in "fear and trembling" and not as a calculator of the odds.[23]

Of course, the man of faith does not feel the decision as a calculation nor does he or she feel the confidence of a sure thing—hence, "fear and trembling." Kierkegaard remarks that "truth is subjectivity." Subjectivity, however, is understood as truthfulness to self, as authenticity, as the existentialist would have it. In this way, we avoid the confusions that follow the blurring of the line between truth and honesty, the erasure of the distinction between ontology and anthropology.[24] Today, however, we have indeed blurred the distinction, and subjectivity has become a parody of itself.

Kierkegaard, all the while denying that he was an insider, still reads the situation from the inside. I think of his interpretation of the story of God's demand that Abraham sacrifice his firstborn son, Isaac, and of Abraham's obedience to that demand. Kierkegaard draws the distinction between having and describing, a distinction that the shadow enlightenment minimizes and its critics exaggerate. Thus, Abraham could not know that an angel of the Lord would "stay his hand," and Isaac could not know that his father would be his murderer. But the man of faith is not a pragmatist. Both Abraham and Isaac "knew" that God's word is simply and powerfully God's word. "I am," God answered Moses from the burning bush. And with this givenness, any command is ultimately permissible although, as Job learned, not explicable. Ironically, then, it is also God's might and not just the "death of God" that opens the world to nihilism. So, contrasting the "ethical"—or what Kierkegaard calls "the universal" in a sneer at German philosophy—with the personal, Kierkegaard writes:

> Now, the story of Abraham contains such a teleological suspension of the ethical. . . . Abraham's relation to Isaac, ethically speaking, is quite simply expressed by saying that a father shall love his son more dearly than himself. . . . The difference between the tragic hero and Abraham is clearly evident. The tragic hero remains within the ethical. . . . With Abraham, the situation was different. By his act, he over-stepped the ethical entirely and possessed a higher telos outside of it. . . . He who denies himself and sacrifices himself for duty gives up the finite in order to grasp the infinite. . . . A man can become a tragic hero by his own powers—but not a knight of faith. . . . To him who follows the narrow way of faith, no one can give counsel, him no one can understand. Faith is a miracle.[25]

But what if there is no miracle? Then the leap into the abyss is only suicide, unless, that is, life without the miracle is simply not worth having. Again, Pascal's wager returns, but with a deeply pessimistic accent. So whether the man of faith is secured in his belief or not, he or she has passed judgment on the world as it is and life as it is. They are simply not worth having. Finally, it is the question of life and world that is at stake in the religious situation, and it is this question—not its answers—that today blurs the line between religionist and Humanist.

CONDEMNED TO BE FREE

For the Enlightenment project, freedom is the value around which its other values, equality and fraternity, orbit. With it, the goods of this world are made accessible to the human being; without it, neither dignity nor community is possible. The modern theme of freedom thus develops along with the coordinate notions of personal responsibility and personal participation. Freedom, therefore, is unambiguously presented as a good. For example, in a contemporary reconstruction of the Enlightenment project, John Rawls makes liberty the first principle of a theory of justice.[26] What is missing, however, is the moral fact that sometimes we have to struggle to be free even against the good society, the democratic society. The capacity to choose and to act on my own initiative is to be self-creating, distinctive. "I am a person" acquires concrete meaning when I do not make my freedom depend on the recognition of others. I can be a revolutionary, a hermit, a nonconformist, a naysayer. Of course, I am a social being, but I cannot be forced to be a social being. If I take this seriously, then freedom as a public good becomes an ambivalent idea. That in a cruel and ironic sense is the modern hesitation that subverts the "self-evidence" of liberty.

It was not supposed to be this way. Of course, freedom was always a problem—of politics, of economics, of education, of self-development. But freedom was not supposed to be problematic. Spinoza had pointed to the fact that freedom without determinate conditions was quite literally senseless. If there is no reliable connection between cause and consequent, then my choices are, at best, acts of self-assertion. In just this way, the postmodern reduces freedom to nihilism and intelligibility to narrative. Freedom, in other words, is utterly subjectivized. But without an ontology, freedom is no longer freedom. It presumes a dependable world, no matter how minimally.[27]

In the Newtonian dawn of a few centuries ago, dependability was not an act of faith but a matter of science. With that in mind, the Enlightenment could generalize the lawfulness of the natural world to society, culture, and person. Yet I am a person and not simply "matter in motion," and I enter the scene as an agent, even a wild card. When I imagine and construct,

I am a cause—as I say, "I make things happen." But I also say that experience makes me what I am. Cause and consequent flow into each other.[28] It is not possible then to tie me down to a simple before and after. Although given, I am not fated to be one single thing or another.

Freedom thus grounded the Enlightenment distinction between person and thing. It makes sense, then, to notice that things do not have civil rights, do not participate as citizens, do not own property, do not pursue happiness, cannot be morally violated. Without that distinction, we would not bother to notice the person as such, as for thousands of years we did not notice women, children, slaves. These were, after all, only living property, living things. Ironically, however, the Newtonian metaphor forced us as well to a radical separation of person and the rest of the world in order to save freedom, now reduced to an inner freedom. The struggle to naturalize the human being could not be completed by the Enlightenment even if the distinction between person and thing was established and the otherworldliness of an earlier time was defeated.[29]

Of course, freedom may be only another self-deception. I may think I discover myself choosing and imagining but find out in some unknown way that I am not acting at all but only behaving. Were that the case, self-consciousness itself becomes a deception, and I become an object among objects again. But to borrow from Descartes, self-consciousness still does not vanish. The thought "it's an illusion" is itself thought of. I have to account for the fact that I perceive myself perceiving. Little wonder, then, that I am tempted to see myself as a member of two worlds: the world of causal chains and the world of free choosings.

Freedom, then, is problematic and not simply a problem. It is not just difficult to achieve because others seek to enslave me. Naturalist or not, I am forced to the choice that can be neither verified nor denied. Concerned to save freedom, I encounter determinacy; concerned to find reliability, I encounter contradiction. Of course, as William James suggested, I can act on the assumption that most coheres with my well-being, that is, that feels right.[30]

These few paragraphs illustrate the fact that the problematic character of freedom generates what I would call the normal puzzles of determinateness. By contrast, the romanticism of the willful individual had a certain normality to it. It fitted with coherent notions of rebellion, self-expression, creativity, innovation. Romanticism was an aesthetic confrontation with the political and the moral. But both rationality and romanticism lived in the same world and responded to each other as point and counterpoint. The scene, in other words, was ultimately unambiguous. But in the modern age, that encounter is transformed. Now the traditions of rationality, of the intelligibility of causal sequences, of the moral notion of agency, and even of the revolt against these are found in a different setting.

The modern world, as the existentialist mood would have it, loses its shape and its boundaries. Nothing is dependable, and even the notion that all things are permitted hides a cruel irony, for the permission—and with it the judgment of good and evil—relies on acting toward a purpose, and this is no longer possible either. As Sartre remarks, "Everything is indeed permitted if god does not exist, and man is in consequence forlorn, for he cannot find anything to depend upon either within or outside himself. He discovers forthwith that he is without excuse."[31] It is little wonder then that the man of faith leaps into the abyss, that the man of will acts without acting on anything. Absent determinateness and freedom as imagining and choosing also vanishes. And determinateness is now said to be absent! In its place, nihilism expresses but does not produce, evokes but cannot respond. Even the language in which I try to say this betrays me, for language needs a structure, and this itself is up for grabs. The existential mood, then, even leads to speechlessness, which is why, if caught at all, it is better caught in poetry than in prose. In short, the normal puzzles of freedom give way to the contemporary problematic of the meaning of freedom and, too, of the meaningfulness of freedom.

Obviously, the existential mood is given to exaggeration, although the postmodern turns that exaggeration into philosophy. At the same time, it reads experience as the encounter with ultimate unreasonableness, not just in the world but in myself. My intentions do not square with my actions, my actions with their outcomes, my outcomes with my plans. Even when I think to bring these together in some rare moment of coherence, the world out there not only disappoints and defeats me—that is nothing new—but actually contradicts me. In other words, I may do the reasonable thing, but now the outcome is, by nature, a surprise. As Albert Camus writes in *The Fall*,

> Do you know that in my little village, during a punitive operation, a German officer courteously asked an old woman to please choose which of her two sons would be shot as a hostage? Choose!—can you imagine that? That one? No, this one. And see him go. Let's not dwell on it, but believe me, monsieur, any surprise is possible. I knew a pure heart who rejected distrust. He was a pacifist and libertarian and loved all humanity and the animals with an equal love. An exceptional soul, that's certain. Well, during the last wars of religion in Europe he had retired to the country. He had written on his threshold: "Wherever you come from, come in and be welcome." Who do you think answered that noble invitation? The militia, who made themselves at home and disemboweled him.[32]

Disconnection is everywhere and so the compulsive and even pathetic drive to connect, to hide, to trivialize. I cannot escape. This world is incontrovertibly present, whether I like it or not, want it or not. It goes right on. This is the penultimate insult. The world goes right on, precisely by ignoring me, by treating me as an object. And then, the final insult: I too go right on, ignoring myself, treating myself as an object. I arrive then at the tragicomic result: I am free, but free to do what? All that is left is a defiant heroism, but it is a heroism without conquest or defeat, indifferent to the lost categories of good and evil, sense and nonsense. As Sartre put it,

> That is the idea I shall try to convey when I say that man is condemned to be free. Condemned, because he did not create himself . . . because, once thrown into the world, he is responsible for everything he does . . . man, with no support and no aid, is condemned every moment to invent man.[33]

Freedom becomes its opposite, becomes the inability to achieve an end in the world. Even if I believe that I can invent myself, I have no sensible excuse for doing so even once let alone over and over again. But I cannot help myself. I still do it. In that, I am indeed condemned to be free.

AUTHENTICITY

I can try to surrender my freedom, but even that calls for a choice. But since I am who I am, I am unwilling to remain a captive. My expectations of the pleasures of captivity are not met since my opposite, my master, is also my oppressor. So I resist. Catching myself resisting, however, I choose again to surrender. It is easier than remaining free. But I must then surrender, over and over again. The existential comedy continues. Or I can try to find peace in inactivity, in going along. However, this does not work either. The day dream world of acquiescence is interrupted, uninvited, by a thought, a feeling, a suggestion. Unwittingly, I respond. I criticize, react. I catch myself and try to become passive again, to empty myself even of thought. But the emptiness does not remain unfilled for very long. My mind, as we say, wanders and in its wandering stumbles upon things. So I learn that contemplation is really a discipline—a deliberate, difficult, and complicated pursuit. It is not passive at all. But that is just what I have been trying to avoid. So the cycle continues. Or finally, I can choose suicide, one final act and then nothingness. But in the attempt, Hamlet-like, I hesitate. I am beset by "what ifs." Even if I overcome my hesitation, I have still to choose. My last act is still my freedom. Even in my denials, I am caught being free.

The ironic reading of experience that is embedded in the existential mood leads finally to the notion of authenticity. Wherever I turn, I am still free. Perhaps nothing else can be said about me than that: I am still free. The question becomes: What then shall I do with this unavoidable and problematic freedom? But even that is wrongly put. It puts freedom outside myself. But outside what? If nothing else is so about me except freedom, then I do not possess it as an extension of myself as a power, a right, an ability, a characteristic, an attribute. I am it.

Freedom is my definition. I am free-to; I can attach thoughts and ends and acts that I am free to think about, free to do, free to aim for. Being free, however, I attach these freely too. I am free throughout, free as to means and as to ends. This takes me beyond praise or condemnation for my achievements to fear and to hope, to mood once again. I fear, for I am not only capable of the worst as of the best. I can hope for precisely the same reason. Freedom, then, catches me in the act. Authenticity names the way that I catch myself. I own my acts, own my choices. Paradoxically, even hiddenness is an act, a choice. Self-deception is to be taken literally: I deceive myself.

Inauthenticity is thus a type of authenticity too, an exercise of freedom. I mask—*I* mask!—by agreeing to the choice of custom, language, tradition, and myth made by others. I mask by choosing helplessness or denial. Above all, I mask by telling stories. But now freedom is twisted out of shape by plot and character described in the third person, as if I was not present. I am led deeper and deeper into a freedom that defeats me because I do not recognize it as my own. But I achieve failure; it does not just happen to me. I am attacking, criticizing, challenging, sneering at, and dismissing my own creation. That being so, whether successful or not, I am unsatisfied, disappointed. I do not recognize myself and feel a hidden disquiet, an inexplicable disquiet. So it is that the doctor treats the disease and not the patient. And so it is that the patient dwells on the diagnosis. Both are uncomfortable, and yet they go right on. Caught in a dance of fools—the "absurd," as the existentialist puts it—they need each other, doctor and patient, Humanist and Christian. Perhaps, even, they invent each other. Deceived about what is at stake, they neither succeed nor fail but only go through the motions. Because freedom is now reduced to going through the motions, it becomes superficial and repetitious.

With this reading of authenticity, the existential mood is revealed as an extended editorial against the domination of innerness by exteriority. To be sure, in the existential mood, I make the mistake of extending the editorial everywhere. The distinction between having and knowing is obscured or simply ignored. I must guard myself, then, against an absolutism of mood. I am tempted to forget that read as physics or sociology—which is what the existential mood invites me to do—this editorial is foolish. I would not try to follow a map or cure a patient or send a rocket to the moon when in an existential mood.

Authenticity is a protest. Hence its use of the language of heroism. It begins in the realization that unlike a thing, I can neither be deduced from premises nor predicted by empirical data. It attacks the modern effort to wash out the particulars. Of course, science has its validities. Yet when all is said and done, innerness remains unspoken, or else it is reduced to descriptive statements about electric currents or proteins or genes. I move to a different perception of myself, take a different standpoint. Now I look at myself and not at an "it"; I enter into myself. When I do, I find those various strategies with which I began my exploration of the existential mood—the strategies of deception and hiddenness. Overcoming these—"know thyself," in a modern translation of the Delphic oracle—is the success of authenticity. But it is never final. I, and not Satan, am the great deceiver, and I am the one deceived. So over and over again, I must overcome myself but, as Camus notes, I never finally do.

> All Sisyphus' silent joy is contained therein. His fate belongs to him. Likewise, the absurd man, when he contemplates his torment, silences all the idols. In the universe suddenly restored to its silence, the myriad wondering little voices of the earth rise up. Unconscious, secret calls, invitations. . . . If there is a personal fate, there is no higher destiny, or at least there is but one which he concludes is inevitable and despicable. For the rest, he knows himself to be the master of his days. At that subtle moment when man glances backward over his life, Sisyphus returning toward his rock in that slight pivoting he contemplates that series of unrelated actions which becomes his fate, created by him, combined under his memory's eye and soon sealed by his death. Thus, convinced of the wholly human origin of all that is human, a blind man eager to see who knows that the night has no end, he is still on the go. The rock is still rolling.[34]

Self-knowledge, of course, still leaves open the question: What is it that I know when I know myself? Clearly, it is not merely knowledge of my chemistry or my neurology. It is true that I fall within a class of persons who, according to an actuarial table, will die at a certain rate and within a certain span of time. But it is also true that I will die at a specific time and in a specific way. I am perceived then as both an "it" and an "I," and this double perception—unlike the perception of a thing which is only an "it"—raises the question: What distinguishes me from an "it"—what, in other words, allows me to say I am an "I"?

With that question as the climactic moment of the existential mood, I complete its editorial. I reject the compulsive attention to results that are, in the existential mood, neither predictable nor lasting. I act against exteriority itself, not against its mere symptoms. And that act, but no other, is available to me. So while "social action" is by no means ignored, its value is in the performing and not in the achieving. I attack the system, or the bad law, or the lack of charity. I subvert the bottom line and popular pragmatism. My performance, if authentic, is an inner performance, even if the stage is the world and its events. That inner performance is truly my own, while the roles I play are not mine but the world's. So at last I strip away the final self-deception. I realize that I am not summed up as father or mother, teacher or businessman, citizen or rebel. I find out that in choosing myself, I choose by myself and am not chosen by others.

Not to be chosen by others, however, can be terrifying, and in the modern world, more often than not, it is. So I worry about promotions and elections and friendships and marriages. But even more terrifying is to be chosen by others, to be at the disposal of others. I confront the overwhelming power of exteriority and the overwhelming risk of innerness. I am caught by the dangers of false choices on every side. It is no accident that Karl Jaspers could describe the existential mood as

> a terrible loneliness. . . . Kierkegaard knew that he could have no friends. Nietzsche suffered his own growing loneliness in full consciousness to the limits where he felt he could endure it no longer. Again, the same image comes to both: Nietzsche compared himself to a fir tree on the heights overlooking an abyss: "Lonely! Who dares to be a guest here? Perhaps a bird of prey, gloating in the hair of the branches. . . ." And Kierkegaard: "Like a fir tree, egotistically, isolated, looking toward something higher, I stand there, throwing no shadow, only the wood dove building its nest in my branches."[35]

Facing myself alone I am driven to the encounter with the world. But now this encounter is without illusion, is undeceived. All the busyness of exteriority drops away—or, better, I drop it away. I cease to find myself elsewhere, to measure myself by what happens elsewhere—in the office, the classroom, the voting booth. I come home to myself. My encounter is a personal encounter. But just when it is most personal, it seeks an encounter with another. So Nietzsche's Zarathustra is alone on top of a high mountain, but he comes down from the mountain to preach his new truths and to find companionship, even if the companionship is confined to being a "bridge to the overman," the companionship of disappearance. If the man of faith lives the inner life in the midst of the conventional, he nevertheless connects with his God. When I realize that I am utterly alone, I move to sociability with the other lonely ones who know they are alone too. That is risky, for there are no unambiguous signs that name them. A different society is then latent in the existential mood, a society of genuine meetings. At the same time, the danger of self-deception remains; the society may not be genuine.

NOTES

1.

> What makes self-deception possible, according to Sartre, is that the *pour-soi* differs from the *en-soi*, or to be concrete: a man is not a homosexual, a waiter, or a coward in the same way in which he is six feet tall or blond. . . . The crux of the matter is suggested by such words as possibility, choice, and decision. If I am six feet tall, that is that. It is a fact no less than that the table is, say, two feet high. Being a coward or a waiter, however, is different: it depends on ever new decisions. I may say: I must leave now—or that I am that way—because I am a waiter, or a coward, as if being a waiter or a coward were a brute fact. Actually, this apparent statement of fact veils a decision.

Walter Kaufmann, *Existentialism from Dostoyevsky to Sartre* (New York: Meridian Books, 1956), p. 44.

2. Jean-Paul Sartre notes,

> To say that I do not know is to say that I am aware that I can know, that is, the world is *already* knowable. . . . Thus, ignorance does not derive from a denial of the world which supposedly is hiding its secrets from me. Quite the contrary, all of Being is *present* to me from the moment of my surging up. . . . Human-reality can receive nothing passively: it must always conquer, not by virtue of some ruse but by virtue of its manner of being.

Truth and Existence (1948), trans. Adrian Van Den Hoven, ed. Ronald Aronson, ann. Arlette Elkaim-Sartre (Chicago: University of Chicago Press, 1992), pp. 19–20.

3. Ibid., pp. 57–58.

4. This is the point of Hannah Ahrendt's *Eichmann in Jerusalem*, which is subtitled, *A Report on the Banality of Evil* (New York: Viking, 1963).

5. Edward O. Wilson, "Is Humanity Suicidal?" *New York Times Magazine*, May 30, 1994, pp. 24, 26.

6. Walter Kaufmann, "Introduction" to *Existentialism*, pp. 46–47.

7. For a relevant discussion of this running away, see Erich Fromm, *Escape from Freedom* (New York: Rinehart and Company, 1941).

8. See, by way of example, Thomas Paine's *The Age of Reason* (Paris, 1794).

9. Friedrich Nietzsche, *The Geneology of Morals* (1887), trans. Francis Golffing (Garden City, N.Y.: Doubleday Anchor Books, 1956), pp. 226–227.

10. In this connection, see James Madison on faction in the Federalist Papers, Number 10.

11. Fyodor Dostoyevsky, *Notes from Underground*, trans. Andrew R. MacAndrew (New York: New American Library, 1961), pp. 108–109.

12. Walter Kaufmann, *Nietzsche: Philosopher, Psychologist, Antichrist* (Princeton, N.J.: Princeton University Press, 1950), p. 200.

13. Paul Tillich, "The Effects of Space Exploration on Man's Condition and Stature," in *The Future of Religions*, ed. Jerald C. Brauer (New York: Harper & Row, 1966), p. 45.

14. As Karl Jaspers points out,

> Enemies of the Enlightenment have said that it destroyed the tradition upon which all life rested; that it dissolved faith and led to nihilism. . . .
>
> These accusations apply to a false enlightenment which itself has ceased to understand the nature of true enlightenment. False enlightenment . . . absolutizes the insights of the understanding, which are always particular . . . ; it misleads the individual into asserting that he can know by himself alone and that he can act on the basis of his knowledge alone, as though the individual were everything. . . . It strives only to know and not to believe.

Way to Wisdom, trans. Ralph Mannheim (New Haven: Yale University Press, 1954), p. 89.

15. Friedrich Nietzsche, "The Will to Power," in Kaufmann, *Existentialism*, p. 110.

16. Friedrich Nietzsche, "The Gay Science," in Kaufmann, *Existentialism*, p. 105.

17. For a time in the 1960s, and following the Protestant theologian, Dietrich Bonhoeffer, there was a good deal of talk about the "death of God." In particular, this was an effort to respond to the Holocaust, to the concentration camp, and, too, to the felt threat of global nuclear destruction. See, by way of example, John A. T. Robinson, *Honest to God* (Philadelphia: Westminster Press, 1963).

18. Martin Heidegger, "Letter on Humanism," *Basic Writings, From Being And Time (1927) to The Task of Thinking (1964)*, ed. David Farrell Krell (New York: Harper & Row, 1977), p. 219.

19. Soren Kierkegaard, "The Attack upon 'Christendom,'" trans. Walter Lowrie, in *A Kierkegaard Anthology*, ed. Robert Bretall (Princeton, N.J.: Princeton University Press, 1947), p. 437.

20. Paul Tillich, *The Shaking of the Foundations* (New York: Charles Scribner's Sons, 1948), p. 75.

21. William Dean, *The Religious Critic in American Culture* (Albany: State University of New York Press, 1994), p. 115.

22. I know that there are some of my colleagues who speak of a "religious" Humanism and John Dewey even used the word *God* in *A Common Faith* (New Haven: Yale University Press, 1934), although, when later challenged by Sidney Hook, he admitted he should not have done so. But in the above context, the religious response more aptly attaches to the main lines of Western religious

development and would be confused if generalized to cover the Humanist effort to deal with "wholeness," "meaning," and "spiritedness."

23. Pascal was a great mathematician as well as a believing Christian. He challenged the rationality of atheism by pointing out that the atheist was irrational. If there was a God, then the failure of the atheist to believe, attend worship, and so forth, ensured eternal damnation. If there was no God, then the atheist risks only a few hours in church. Rejecting this win-win situation, the atheist risks everything on a conclusion that cannot be verified until it is too late—until death. For all his rationalism, then, the atheist is behaving irrationally by failing to make a minor investment for a major gain. Of course, the atheist replies that if God is as the Christian describes him to be, then he would know that the atheist is not serious about worship and faith and all the rest. So, replies the atheist, the gamble, on the Christian's own grounds, does not make sense.

24. Of course, Kierkegaard is anxious to refute Hegel at every turn and so cannot resist even the most extreme and outrageous anti-Hegelianism. If for Hegel, "whatever is is right" and world history is ultimately to be described as things "as they really are" and history's end is the realization of the Ideal, then an antiobjectivity and an anti-idealism become tactically and emotionally necessary.

25. Soren Kierkegaard, "Fear and Trembling: A Dialectical Lyric," in *A Kierkegaard Anthology*, pp. 131–134 passim.

26. John Rawls, *A Theory of Justice* (Cambridge, Mass.: Harvard University Press, 1971), p. 60.

27. For a statistical treatment of dependability, see, for example, James Gleick, *Chaos, Making a New Science* (New York: Viking, 1987).

28. Alfred North Whitehead in his criticism of the empiricist tradition pointed out, however, that this isolation of cause and consequent was an instance of the "fallacy of misplaced concreteness" and was the general error that produced the paradoxes of "inner" and "outer" that plague modern philosophy.

29. This struggle for naturalization is perfectly exemplified in the work of Immanuel Kant who opted, finally, for a distinction between the phenomenal and the noumenal: the world that could be known scientifically and the world in which moral action (actions guided by reason and freedom) was possible. Of course, this still invited a dualism although not a supernaturalism. And with that, the separation of fact and value, matter and spirit, continued, although now on naturalist grounds.

30. See William James, "The Dilemma of Determinism," in *Essays on Faith and Morals* (New York: Meridian Books, 1962), p. 166.

31. Jean-Paul Sartre, "Existentialism Is a Humanism," in *Existentialism*, p. 195.

32. Albert Camus, *The Fall*, trans. Justin O'Brien (New York: Alfred A. Knopf, 1956), pp. 11–12.

33. Jean-Paul Sartre, *Existentialism and Human Emotions*, trans. Bernard Frechtman (New York: Philosophical Library, 1957), p. 23.

34. Albert Camus, *The Myth of Sisyphus and Other Essays*, trans. Justin O'Brien (New York: Vintage Books, 1955), p. 91.

35. Karl Jaspers, "Existenzphilosophie," in *Existentialism*, p. 177.

5

THE TRANSCENDENTAL OPPORTUNITY

THE OTHER ROOT OF HUMANISM

Modern Humanism owes its existence to the "sentiment of reason" as much as to rationality. In other words, much as Humanism is a child of the Enlightenment, its other parent is transcendentalism.[1] Thus, a Rousseauian sense of the goodness of natural man shaped Humanism's view of the person. It gave birth to progressive educational ventures like the kindergarten movement and the Ethical Culture Schools. The sources of Unitarian Humanism were to be found in the thought of ministers like Theodore Parker and William Ellery Channing. Similarly, the Humanism of Ethical Culture was embedded in the neo-Kantian idealism of Felix Adler. August Comte's "religion of humanity" drew upon both rationalist and romantic sources, as did many of the nineteenth century's experiments with "ethical" religion and utopian community.[2] Yet I find myself reluctant to deal with transcendentalism. Perhaps a glance at the reasons for my resistance will explain why Humanists seem deliberately ignorant of transcendentalism or else sharply critical of it.[3]

There is something attractively undisciplined about transcendentalism with its talk of spirituality and with its adoration of the passions. For example, Joseph L. Blau called his essay on transcendentalism, "New England's Wild Oats."[4] For a transcendentalist, rebellion is possible without the murmur of conspiracy and without the bloodshed of civil war. As a transcendentalist, I can be a radical inside myself, although many transcendentalists were in the forefront of the antislavery movement. I can be an effective person without worrying about politics or economics or armaments. Even the passions are somehow made unthreatening, sublimated into a poetry of personal expressiveness. The temptations of ego are legitimized because ego is representative as well as unique. It is the universe expressing itself in me and thereby in all humanity. Thus, I can know the universe in self-reflection and without the pain of error. It is, above all, a friendly place.

I am not alone in responding to the transcendental call to my desire to be my own person against the world with its conventions and structures and limitations. Large audiences, here and abroad, read and heard Emerson with appreciation. Whitman's poetry was widely published. Radical preachers, a minority to be sure, sermonized their congregants. As Felix Adler, the founder of Ethical Culture noted,

> I made Emerson's acquaintance in 1875. I came into touch with the Emerson circle and read and re-read the *Essays.* The value of Emerson's teaching to me at that time consisted in the exalted view he takes of the self. Divinity as an object of extraneous worship for me had vanished. Emerson taught that immediate experience of the divine power in self may take the place of worship. His doctrine of self-reliance also was bracing to a youth just setting out to challenge prevailing opinions and to urge plans of transformation upon the community in which he worked. . . . So, for a time, I continued to walk on air with Emerson, and had my head in the clouds—the clouds in which Emerson enveloped me.[5]

Yet I still remain hesitant and suspicious. If ego, even when tamed, is a temptation of transcendentalism, spirituality is even more tempting. Already visible then, but even more blatant today in the vagaries of new age and sentimental religiosity, spirituality easily allows us to confuse obscurity with profundity and to use the vagueness of its reference as a cover for just about any reference at all. It can be an invitation to ignorance all the while masking as the discovery of meaning. It can be, too, as we have seen in our time, a road to victimization and religious racketeering. Philosophically, spirituality allows us to demean the world because of its roots in a dualism that counters body with soul, flesh with spirit, and earth with heaven.[6]

In its reliance on intuition, on a direct knowledge of what is really real, transcendentalism grants me an ability I am not sure I possess, so I worry about falling victim to the warmth and coziness of this near-effortless connection between me and the universe. I become doubtful of my own credentials, seeming to hear the transcendentalist call to know the universe directly and yet aware too that direct knowledge of this sort is simultaneously most secure—I know what I know and do not need the testimony of others—and most misleading. I am self-deluded by wishful thinking. I am caught in a merry-go-round of acquiescence and denial as its stylists like Emerson, Whitman, and Thoreau beguile me with their words and tonalities. I enjoy their beautiful assurances and yet worry as much about their lack of skepticism. In a like mood, Paul Kurtz wrote,

> Is mysticism . . . a kind of madness? And is this a form of truth? Is this religious virtue—madness—justifiable? There is a great danger that the skeptic will simply dismiss his religious opposite on ad hominem grounds. . . . Perhaps it is the skeptic who is blind and ignorant. I have wondered at times: Is it I who lack a religious sense, and is this due to a defect of character? The tone-deaf are unable to fully appreciate the intensity of music, and the color-blind live in a world denuded of brightness and hue. Is mysticism . . . a special kind of experience that enables a person to break out of a limited perceptual and conceptual world? Perhaps. One leaves the possibility open.[7]

Transcendentalism introduces me to a Humanism that does not use the needs of the public life as an excuse for the denial of intimacy. The transcendental opportunity is thus a psychological and ontological relative of the existential mood with its concern for subjectivity and its criticism of exteriority. Typically, solitude becomes a category of experience for both. Kierkegaard called it a "vital necessity," Nietzsche's hero lived on the mountaintop, and Emerson would "go into solitude." With transcendentalism, however, we are in a different world and a different time. The mood is exuberant and unanxious, so its recurring themes are the accessibility of my self to other selves and the accessibility of my self to the universe and of it to me. Absent is that dark cloud of defeat and anguish that shapes the existential mood. Of course, the transcendentalist was sensitive to failure and sadness and death. I need only read Emerson's journal entries on the occasion of his son's death or catch Whitman upon the assassination of Lincoln. But the shadows that shape the existential mood were simply not present.

For the transcendentalist, the universe opens up joyously. "Nature," said Emerson, "never wears a mean appearance." And Thoreau wrote from Walden Pond,

> There can be no very black melancholy to him who lives in the midst of Nature and has his senses still. . . . The gentle rain which waters my beans and keeps me in the house today is not drear and melancholy but good for me too. . . . In the midst of a gentle rain . . . I was suddenly sensible of such sweet and beneficent society in Nature . . . an infinite and unaccountable friendliness all at once like

an atmosphere sustaining me, as made the fancied advantages of human neighbourhood insignificant.[8]

Transcendentalism thus reshaped the optimism and the naturalism of the Enlightenment project, shifting the emphasis from politics to psychology and embedding it in autobiography. With this, it offered a corrective to the rationalism and individualism that in our own time leads to the shadow enlightenment. However, in its reaction to the coming of industrial society, it could be as one-sided in its personalism for all that it attended to issues of social justice, as with the labor question, the slavery question, and the rights of women and children. Moreover, transcendentalism could not really speak in a universal voice. It lacked the ability to transcend the very differences of personality it celebrated. Enamored of intuition, it could not account for those who had different intuitions or who suspected intuition's claims to direct knowledge of the truth of the matter. As with existentialism, we are dealing with a mood and not a metaphysics.

Transcendentalism was, in short, an enthusiasm—both a religious philosophy, although an unconventional one, and a religious criticism. As Joseph Blau wrote,

> It was born in dissatisfaction with the then-current opinions in liberal theology and the philosophic views on which these theological opinions were based. Its earliest advocates were convinced that Unitarian theology was unsatisfactory because of its dependence on the "reigning sensuous philosophy, dating from Locke." . . . What the transcendentalists wanted to achieve and thought that they could achieve by a discipline of their intuitions was . . . not only to transcend the senses, but also to transcend churches, clergy, and scriptures. Transcendentalism was the assertion that man has an intuitive capacity for grasping ultimate truth and thus achieving a sure knowledge of a supernatural order, beyond the reach of the senses.[9]

Transcendentalist religion reached out from within the self to the universe without the intervention of texts, functionaries, or institutions. As Emerson advised in his address to the students of the Harvard Divinity School, "Go alone; . . . refuse [even] the good models, even those which are sacred in the imagination of men, and dare to love God without mediator or veil."[10] Tracing back to natural religion and Jefferson's "ethicizing" of Jesus, religious models were reconceived as well, much to the dismay and anger of most of the religious leadership of the day. Characteristic was Theodore Parker's "A Discourse of the Transient and Permanent in Christianity," for which "only eight or nine of the Unitarian ministers would refuse to condemn him, and he was everywhere excoriated by respectable Boston."[11]

The transcendental story also leads to its nineteenth-century relatives. Emerson had announced that "truth is on the highway." With the coming of American pragmatism, William James, John Dewey, and Charles Peirce would bring that notion to life. Thus, in breaking the boundaries of the conventional, transcendentalism also opened the way for a radical reformulation of the problems of knowing and doing. With pragmatism, the activity of a community of inquirers became a relevant feature of cognition that was no longer the passive observation of an alien reality. "Truth," as William James put it, "happens to an idea." Human insight and imagination took a rightful place in the processes of inquiry:

> Peirce wanted to understand the habit of generalization, the habit of forming general ideas. The traditional logical processes of induction and deduction . . . seemed to him not to lead to new ideas. But he distinguished and named a third logical process, which he called "abduction." He insisted that "the abductive suggestion comes to us like a flash. It is an act of insight." . . . It is merely suggestive of a possibility. . . . Like William James' "will to believe," . . . abduction is entered upon in pragmatic desperation, "its justification being that it is the only possible hope of regulating our future conduct rationally."[12]

The nineteenth-century Humanist neighborhood housed a reconstruction of the main themes of the Enlightenment project. It was guided by a renewed sensitivity to the subject and the subjective and, not incidentally, was stimulated by a cultural shift from physics to biology.[13] Unlike today's postmodern dismissal of the Enlightenment project, in that neighborhood, subject and object did not need to be at war with each other. As William James wrote,

> In spite of the appeal which this impersonality of the scientific attitude makes to a certain magnanimity of temper, I believe it to be shallow and can now state my reason in comparatively few words. That reason is that, so long as we deal with the cosmic and the general, we deal only with the symbols of reality, but as soon as we deal with private and personal phenomena as such, we deal with realities in the completest sense of the term.[14]

Not just human nature but nature itself was reconceived. Taking a transcendental cue, human beings and other natural beings were inherently in touch with each other. However, it was the Enlightenment project that offered the starting point. Illustrative is the development of the idea of the sublime from its classical to its romantic form. With the sublime—that is, with the sense of proportionality, responsiveness, and awe with which the human being stood in relation to the rest of the universe—the Enlightenment opened the way to appreciation. To the leaders of the Enlightenment project, experience was richer than knowledge. Jefferson had offered images of the sublime in his *Notes on Virginia* and his descriptions of the vistas to be seen from Monticello. Kant had written, "the sublime is that in comparison with which everything else is small . . . there is in our imagination a striving toward infinite progress and in our reason a claim for absolute totality . . . therefore this very inadequateness for that idea in our faculty for estimating the magnitude of things of sense excites in us the feeling of a supersensible faculty."[15] For the eighteenth century, the sublime was to be found in the awe-provoking grandeur of natural things and events; a massive river, a waterfall, a hurricane, a volcano, a thunderstorm were typical images. With Kant, however, the sublime shifted from external event to internal activity, to the sensibilities of the responsive being in touch with the world. Finally,

> The older sublime was a gentleman's preserve. . . . The Christianized sublime, more accessible to everyone, was more democratic, even bourgeois. . . . The change in the meaning of the sublime then, was intimately connected with the power the landscape exerted over the American mind. . . .
>
> With a sublime discovered, not in sound, but in silence (in what Emerson called "the wise silence" of the Over-Soul), we move into another philosophical region. . . .
>
> Silence in the older sublime was unsettling, even awesome. The element of peace and tranquility in the later sense of the sublime is in opposition to the earlier concept.[16]

In the nineteenth-century neighborhood, then, I find both the inspiration of the Enlightenment and the corrective of subjectivity. The setting for this development—particularly in America—was hopeful and friendly. The New World was spacious and despite its failures allowed for new beginning and new adventures. In it, progress was made tangible and visible, and hope seemed a fact of life, not a dream of some other place and time. A certain *élan* characterized the Humanist neighborhood, and this permitted a temperamental indifference to the oppositions of object and subject, of city and country, of industry and craft. Even great injustices like slavery and great moral disasters like the urban slum and the exploitation of labor were but a momentary aberration. Renewal was all, and so Humanism drew, for a time at least, on the permutations of the transcendental neighborhood.

Nor was this an experience reserved for Americans. Symbolically, America was a world possession—or, more accurately, a European and British possession. It was quite literally civilization's new world and as such a point of ideal reference. To be sure, America still lacked its own academic and scholarly establishment, and the American university was still pretty much a training ground for ministers and lawyers. But Emerson's call for an American originality was heard everywhere too:

> Perhaps the time is already come when it ought to be, and will be, something else; when the sluggard intellect of this continent will look from under its iron lids and fill the postponed expectation of the world with something better than the exertions of mechanical skill. Our day of dependence, our long apprenticeship to the learning of other lands draws to a close.[17]

A new beginning was the metaphor of the American narrative. It had been forecast with the eighteenth century's Enlightenment project, and now, a hundred years later, it was felt as real with the nineteenth century's mixture of personalism and industrialism.

WILDERNESS

Nothing exemplified America's promise more than the wilderness itself. Unlike the eighteenth-century garden, such as at Versailles, wilderness was untamed—the "forest primeval," as Longfellow had it. Wilderness had its mythic counterpoint in the evolving American city, which, particularly after the Civil War, was a scene of vast energies and equally vast destructiveness. Industrial production already gave promise of a world of goods and services. At the same time, the factory system filled the air with noise and smoke, and the waters with filth. If, on occasion, the transcendental mood could celebrate the machinery—the railroad and the steam engine were characteristic images—even these took on significance because of where they led and what they stood for, and not because of what they did or produced. Ordinary citizens may have celebrated industrialism as a century of progress in 1876, but it was for the romantic a call to resistance. Wilderness, as Thoreau warned, could be lost.

In a sense, then, the transcendental opportunity signified the struggle to hold on to human and natural spaces. Transcendentalists knew they were in a battle against the forces of technology and wealth. Personalism was not merely a description of the place of human beings in a welcoming nature but a rallying cry against society itself. Emerson reminded his listeners, "I believe man has been wronged; he has wronged himself. . . .

Men are become of no account. Men in history, men in the world of to-day, are bugs, are spawn, and are called 'the mass' and 'the herd.' "[18]

For all their optimism, then, the nineteenth-century romantics knew they had work to do. Yet the struggle was poetic rather than political. Seizing on an old religious image, transcendentalism repeated the lesson of the uses of solitude and silence. The traditional move into the desert, symbol of both nondistraction and temptation, was undertaken again, but now inwardly. Wilderness was the symbolic location of this move, but the city demanded return. Solitude, in other words, was still instrumental to salvation.

It is this ode to the wilderness that shaped the transcendental mood even if most of its carriers were creatures of the city. The liberal Unitarian pulpits, after all, were urban, although Unitarian radicalism found its more likely home in the American West than in the center of the Boston establishment. But it was the West of the new American city—Chicago, St. Louis, Minneapolis—and rarely of the plains, the mountains, and the forest. Emerson lived all his life in the Boston environment and was as much a world citizen as a New Englander. Thoreau, despite his Walden Pond experiment, did not remain there. And Whitman celebrated Brooklyn and Philadelphia and Manhattan as much as he sang the song of open spaces.

Wilderness, then, did service as a personal metaphor. The transcendentalist and the romantic did not settle new lands, farm open acreage, encounter the dangers of the frontier. The focus was more reflective, as if to say that the wilderness was a matter of perception and place much more than a reality of spaces and distances. The very expansiveness of the wilderness metaphor gave point to intimacy, to the discovery of self. In fact, with the American move west, the wilderness was already vanishing.

As a metaphor, wilderness fed upon the transcendentalist's idealization of intuition, and so encouraged a naturalistic and an unchurched mysticism. The "Other" to which the transcendentalist responded was immanent in everything around him or her; the transcendentalist, in other words, responded to a pluralized Other. A brief verse by Tennyson put the mix of unity and diversity:

> Flower in the crannied wall,
> I pluck you out of the crannies,
> I hold you here, root and all, in my hand,
> Little flower—but *if* I could understand
> What you are, root and all, and all in all,
> I should know what God and man is.[19]

The relationship of self and wilderness drew upon neo-Kantian idealism particularly as interpreted to Americans by Samuel Coleridge's widely distributed *Aids to Understanding*. For the idealist, a direct encounter with the "thing in itself" was not only possible but represented a genuine and, for some, *the* genuine form of knowing. At the same time, the world of appearances, which for Kant was all that we could really know, was assigned to a secondary role. Steven Rockefeller sums it up:

In German idealism, these American transcendentalists seemed to find a world-view that satisfied an intense interest in both individual self-realization and a spiritual or religious conception of human nature and the universe. Most of them were not especially interested in scientific methods of knowing, and most were not primarily concerned with cultivating the logical powers of their discursive understanding. . . . They followed Coleridge and Marsh, therefore, in making a basic distinction between the natural understanding and the higher reason or some intuitive spiritual power of direct moral and religious insight.[20]

The transcendentalist, in other words, left behind the Baconian notion of knowledge as power and Newtonian achievement of a mathematicized mechanics. Replacing these with appreciation, he attempted to distinguish "Reason" from "reason." Subjectivity was at the center not just of feeling but of knowledge, which was at the same time both self-knowledge and world knowledge. As Emerson put it,

Science was false by being unpoetical. It assumed to explain a reptile or mollusk, and isolated it—which is hunting for life in graveyards. . . . The metaphysician, the poet, only sees each animal form as an inevitable step in the path of creating mind. The Indian, the hunter, the boy with his pets, have sweeter knowledge of these than the savant. The poet knows the missing link by the joy it gives.[21]

As science, under the transcendental inspiration, was asked to rediscover its relationship to art, so wilderness, now vanishing, led to the rediscovery of nature as well as of self. William James remarked about Whitman,

Thus it has come about that many persons to-day regard Walt Whitman as the restorer of the eternal natural religion. He has infected them with his own love of comrades, with his own gladness that he and they exist.[22]

By contrast, traditional religion saw nature either as a passing moment in eternity or as an instrument for reading God's truth and will. Typical of this theological sense of things, Wilhelm Wackenroder wrote in "Outpourings of an Art-Loving Friar" (1797),

> Nature has seemed to me the fullest and clearest index to His being and character. The rustling in the trees of the forest and the rolling thunder have told me secrets about Him which I cannot put into words. A beautiful valley enclosed by bizarre rocks, a smooth-flowing river reflecting overhanging trees, a pleasant green meadow under a blue sky—all these stirred my innermost spirit more, gave me a more intense feeling of God's power and benevolence, purified and uplifted my soul more than any language of words could have done.[23]

A few decades later, with the marriage of Calvinist narrative and modern technology, nature was a "dominion" to be conquered, settled, manipulated.

For the transcendentalist, nature was a setting and a place in its own right, and in it the human being was genuinely at home. It was rich with aesthetic and moral relationships, purposes, meanings, and values. The duality that found the human being between two worlds, whether on secular or religious grounds, was dissolved. The Enlightenment project thus found a "worthy friend" in the transcendental inspiration and its naturalization of the subject.

"REPRESENTATIVE MAN"

Unlike the cosmopolitan man of the Enlightenment project and the isolated man of the existential mood, the transcendentalist man was simultaneously individual and universal. The reconception of the political individual in the direction of sociability had its nineteenth-century sources in German idealism, ideas quite familiar on the American academic scene and to the transcendentalists. Developments in American society stirred practical questions too. While wilderness was vanishing before industrialism and urbanism, people were also separating by class and caste under the pressures of the new economic system. The honest farmer of the Jeffersonian imagination was vanishing too. Responding to the tendencies of what came to be called rugged individualism, the transcendentalist insisted on relationship. In like manner, responding to the tendencies toward conventionalism, the transcendentalist insisted on the originality of each human being. "Whoso would be a man must be a non-conformist," and, "Insist on yourself, never imitate," said Emerson. Thus, the themes of self-reliance, self-appreciation, and self-discovery were accompanied by equivalent themes of representation, universality, and accessibility. And he continued, "The new virtue which constitutes a thing beautiful is a certain cosmical quality, or a power to suggest relation to the whole world and so lifts the object out of a pitiful individuality. Every natural feature—sea, sky, rainbow, flowers, musical tone—has in it somewhat which is not private but universal."[24]

Individuality was a social and not simply a contractual idea, although the elaborations on this theme by pragmatists like John Dewey and George Herbert Mead were yet to come. The idea of the soul was reconstructed in a context of a spiritualized democracy. As William Ellery Channing put it, we know God because "in ourselves are the elements of the Divinity." And Whitman could write,

> I see something of God each hour of the twenty-four, and each moment then;
> In the faces of men and women I see God and in my own face in the glass.[25]

For the transcendentalist, the soul was transformed from dependent substance into a sociable being. In "Essay on Transcendentalism," Charles Mayo Ellis, a graduate of Harvard College and a Boston lawyer, put this idea in systematic form:

> It cannot be that man is merely . . . a sort of instrument; and that the soul is merely the sound of this instrument. . . . For how has this instrument conscious life? How can it hear the sounds if the sounds make up its existence? How does it feel the pulse of life beating in its bosom? If man is but an instrument and his soul its music, why is not his soul dead when that is dumb? . . . When is he? If he is but body, how has he been produced by this mysterious association? What is he? If his body be himself, how can he use it? If he is matter, how can he know of the existence of God? How can he contemplate that which is not matter, the good, true, beautiful? He is not a book to be read, but he records and reads for himself.[26]

Moreover, the soul matures as it is nurtured and fails to mature if it is neglected. It is not then given all at once but developed; the soul was thus biologized and socialized. It was not for nothing that a reconstructed democratic education would acknowledge its debt to the transcendentalists.[27] Illustratively, Emerson wrote, "An individual man is a fruit which it cost all the foregoing ages to form and ripen. The history of the genesis of the old mythology repeats itself in the experience of every child."[28]

The transcendentalist conceived of a person who was never alone and never lonely. In himself or herself, he or she found all others. The person was already a community just by being a human being. By contrast, the crowd, the mob, the social convention, all of which seemed to promise connection, prevented it. They were distractions much as noise distracts from music, although both are forms of sound. Hence, the familiar lines from Emerson's "American Scholar":

> There is One Man,—present to all particular men only partially . . . and . . . you must take the whole society to find the whole man. Man is not a farmer, or a professor, or an engineer, but he is all. Man is priest, and scholar, and statesman, and producer, and soldier. In the *divided* or social state these functions are parcelled out to individuals, each of whom aims to do his stint of the joint work, whilst each other performs his. . . . But, unfortunately, this original unit, this fountain of power, has been so distributed to multitudes, has been so minutely subdivided and peddled out, that it is spilled into drops and cannot be gathered. The state of society is one in which the members have suffered amputation from the trunk, and strut about so many walking monsters,—a good finger, a neck, a stomach, an elbow, but never a man.
>
> Man is thus metamorphosed into a thing, into many things.[29]

In other words, transcendentalism, despite its aestheticism, was both a personal ethics and a form of social criticism, although it deliberately denied itself a politics. The transcendentalists' individual was not Sartre's heroic figure, choosing himself or herself all alone and even against the world. Authenticity was both individuated and universalized; it was found precisely where uniqueness and representation intersected. A puzzling notion, it seems nevertheless accurately to convey our experience of relationship—certainly more adequately than mere universalism, in which the ego becomes an anonymous instance of some general law, and more adequately than subjectivism, in which the ego expands to exclude all other egos. In fact, we do recognize each other and at the same time recognize the individuation of that recognition itself.

The transcendental opportunity opens us up to the continuing interplay of self and other. On the one hand, self-assertion is demanded and, indeed, I am expected to respond to whatever self-reflection reveals of me to myself. I am to hear, with Thoreau, a "different drummer." While I may be tempted not to listen—it is after all uncomfortable to stand out and stand apart—yet I must resist that temptation. Hence a transcendental ethics is centered in my attentiveness to myself. "One's Self I sing—a simple, separate Person," wrote Whitman. But then he added the second line, "Yet utter the word Democratic, the word *En-masse*."[30] Finally, then, individuality is a movement between self and other, aloneness and sociability.[31]

COMMUNITY

Bit by bit, I have tried to overcome my hesitation and to explore the transcendental opportunity. Its sense of the person suggests a corrective to narrowed readings of the Enlightenment project. Joining nature and person, the third term of this corrective is the notion of community. I am, however, mindful of the danger of confounding community with the sentimentalities of its invocation today. Community has become, paradoxically, a term of apartness and even of hostility, legitimizing a pluralism of locations between which little significant intercourse occurs. This goes so far as to deny the very possibility of understanding between members of any one community and any other. With this denial, it becomes impossible for the reform that was so much a part of nineteenth-century Humanism to exercise the good conscience and for the exploited to be helped by others. In the name of community, human solidarity and social responsibility are fragmented and ultimately vanish. Thus, the specialness of any life-world experience becomes a justification for denying relationship with and communication to any out-worlder. Society is dissolved into an incidental collection of "communities" that have less and less to do with each other except perhaps in tribal warfare and opportunistic alliance. Today's Bosnian and Rwandan situations come to mind as horrifying metaphors of community.[32] Admission to any community is by tribe or race or faith or gender or even—recalling the 1960s—age. After all as "radical" wisdom had it, "You can't trust anyone over thirty." Community becomes a narrowed destiny.

By contrast, the transcendental community was welcoming and inclusive. Access was not refused. Entry into the community of inquiry—the sciences—was available once good faith in the search for truth was demonstrated. Education therefore had to be a universal opportunity. Religious community was generously available too, not in the pains and pleadings of conversion but in the simple acknowledgment that intuition, which was everyone's possession, had led here rather than there and might someday lead elsewhere. When compared with the community of more traditional "narrative," the transcendental community was a community of "invitation," and its narrative was an unfinished and ultimately participatory story.

Nor was community a term of discourse alone. Thoreau could find communion in the silences of Walden, and he invited others to a similar communion. Brook Farm and other utopias were practical failures but as well efforts at concrete expression of an ideal of community, and they opened themselves to anyone. The liberal Unitarianism of the Western

Conference was so inclusive that any thought of a creedal requirement was anathema to its congregations because it might divide rather than unite. Adler's Ethical Culture called for "unity in the deed, diversity in the creed." And so on. Practice, to be sure, fell short of the ideal. The boundaries between communities, however, were porous, and movement across them was not merely tolerated but encouraged.

As with transcendentalism's other themes, community was a religious idea. Once again, the Enlightenment project was amended by the transcendental opportunity. Society was to be accented by spirituality. Adler, for example, called for the "ethicizing" of society, and Dewey, following Emerson, transformed democracy from a contractual into a moral ideal. In any event, the transcendentalist recognized, although not always explicitly, that a society of arrangements and functions could not by itself meet the conditions of personhood. Indeed, by itself, society developed precisely toward the very disjointed conformism that Emerson, among others, so bitterly complained about.

The puzzle of community appeared. If society led toward conventionalism, community led toward sectarianism. The accessibility of community, which implied that going out was to be as simple as coming in, seemed to subvert the purpose of community itself as a permanent and secured life-world in the midst of a dynamic, changing, and confusing social world. Moreover, the tug of society toward functionalism and of community toward personalism led to a permanent tension, if not always to a permanent warfare, between them.

It was in the context of the unresolvable push and pull between community and society that democracy served as a mediating idea. With it, the center of attention was shifted to the sociable self with the capacity to be both "one and many," and to move freely between communities and even apart from them at times. As a moral agent, the sociable self was capable, too, of resisting society for the sake of community, of challenging community for the sake of society, or of protesting both in the name of the values of sociability itself. To take a perennial instance, the struggle between church and state, which may stand for the tension between community and society, is never resolved. It illustrates the interplay of coercion and liberation that characterizes the tension between community and society. The issue becomes one of legitimacy—not all coercions are morally unacceptable, not all liberations are morally acceptable—and practice in the presence of deliberately fuzzy principle.[33] The transcendental opportunity focused this issue by its reintroduction of the subject, thus denying the domination of both secular society and traditional community in the name of the sociable individual.

With the sociable individual, the nineteenth-century Humanist neighborhood offered an image of the person quite different from both the communicant of traditionalism and the individual of the Enlightenment project. Thus,

> The hallmark of American life-philosophy is a moral and a social solution to a religious and a spiritual crisis. . . . The self is only realized according to the American tradition, in discipleship to the community. Separation of the self from the community is self-contradictory and, in a certain sense, impossible, because at least for Royce, Peirce, and Dewey, and often even for James, the separate self is an illusion. Royce's dictum that "my life means nothing, either theoretically or practically unless I am a member of a community" is the ground principle of the Puritan strand of American life-philosophy. James, in his flight from panic fear and in his effort to reduce ontological wonder-sickness, which individualizes the human being radically, . . . embraces Royce's spirit and sometimes his letter. Peirce, of course, is as severe a critic of the separate self as Royce, claiming that a human being is "essentially a possible member of society," and that "it is not 'my' experience but 'our' experience that has to be thought of." Dewey, whose thought is the culmination of the Puritan line, interprets the individual as a link in "the continuous human community."[34]

The sociable individual, then, is the transcendentalist's contribution to the reconstruction of Enlightenment democracy. The person, in virtue of the fact that he or she is a person, is already a community—in communication with, in communion with—and is already a society—in action with, in participation with.

Against the exteriorizing tendency of society and the isolating tendency of community, the transcendental opportunity sets up the independent individual who is, at the same time, not the separated individual. But it is not, because of this interiority, a prescription for passivity. The transcendental opportunity is the basis for action in the world marking a shift from tradition and contract to a moral and, even more to the point, an aesthetic sense of identity—an intimacy, if you will. Given its energies, it cannot help but be publicly expressed. For example:

> Thoreau was much less concerned than Emerson or Parker about the spread of democracy; his words "a man more right than his neighbor is a majority of one already" ring through the years with increasing intensity. To be sure, Thoreau's writings do not exhibit great compassion and empathy for fellow beings, though he does have important things to say about love in daily living. . . . Is it possible to read Thoreau's damnation of pro-slavery people in his "Slavery in Massachusetts" and "A Plea for Captain John Brown" and not be transfixed with its

emotional intensity? No. In contrast to "Civil Disobedience" he is furious with their treatment of fellow human beings, not with their interference with the spread of democracy. What slavery does to people "is offensive to all healthy nostrils."[35]

Of course, as with nature and person, community too was shaped by passion and faith. With its deep roots in a religious sense of things, it suffered the ambiguities of identification with religious traditions that the transcendentalist tried to reconstruct. In this, for all its optimism and good cheer, it was accented by a seldom-confessed tragic sense, one that flowed from its strengths and not from its weaknesses.

HOPE AND CHARACTER

The transcendental narrative took up Enlightenment themes, joining community with society, nature with wilderness, and individuality with personhood. The austere ideals of the Enlightenment project were infused with enthusiasm. The narrative was fated, however, to remain incomplete, although this did not lead to surrender or sadness. Instead, it was a way of recasting democracy in the form of personal participation rather than as a legalist contract. The tragic sense that is very much a part of the transcendental mood is, after all, focused on the heroic and powerful in the human being. Tragedy, noted Aristotle in *The Poetics*, evokes "pity and terror." For the transcendental drama, it was also exalting. Indeed, it is possible to read the incompleteness of the transcendental narrative as an invitation—again invitation, again welcome—now to the energies not merely of the present person in the present but of all future persons in the future.

No one captured this sense of things better than William James who, with his notion of the "will to believe" and even the "right to believe," offered the human being a permanent role in the continuing creation of the world itself and sometimes, it seemed, even in the creation of the deity itself. Gone was the sovereignty of the static dynamism of celestial mechanics, vanished equally with the Dantean image of a heaven of perpetual and timeless adoration. An unfinished world asked for the energies of its participants. As Joseph Blau puts it, James "once described the world, in a letter to Josiah Royce, as 'the whole paradoxical physico-moral spiritual Fatness, of which most people single out some skinny fragment.' For himself, James wanted no such slenderizing abstraction. He wanted to comprehend the world's multiplicity in his vision."[36]

With that sense of the openness of experience to all future experience, the optimism of the nineteenth-century neighborhood revealed itself.

Neither the neatness of an earlier progressivism nor the angst of a post-modern world, optimism was to be found in acts of construction by living men and women. Implicitly, of course, this attention to the present act was a criticism of the so-called materialism of America's technologized world as it was of the future directedness, the notion of "postponed living," that colored both religious and secular views. With attention to constructing rather than achieving, the inwardness of the transcendental found an entry to the world. Citing Michael Weinstein,

> In the thought of William James, a decisive shift occurs in American life-philosophy. . . . Once belief in God is made belief in "a conception of the frame of things" it is neither a rational necessity nor even a plausible hypothesis but an aid to living in the present, to feeling "the sufficiency of the present moment." If it does not embrace life, belief should be abandoned. . . . Not only is God humanized but social morality is made supreme over religion and independent of it.[37]

Under a transcendental inspiration, the American dream—which was also a world dream—could remain alive despite the vicissitudes of a new economic system and the loss of the innocence of the American revolutionary past. Progress was not read as the assured direction of history, whether with Condorcet, with Hegel, or with Comte. It was not a product but a process. Ironically, for all that pragmatism has been popularized as another name for opportunism, consequences for the transcendental opportunity had as much to do with human development as with technical, economic, political, or even scientific achievement. In that, once again, accessibility was the clue—accessibility to the human being as such, accessibility of the world as such.[38] Once again, the powers of the sociable individual are invoked, now to provide a direction and not simply an appreciation or an expression of history, nor simply a criticism of things as they are.

Thus, the transcendental opportunity challenged and amended the Enlightenment project. Progress—and so hopefulness—had been advanced after the model of a natural law of history and society. Now, tutored by a careful attention to the actual human being in actual situations, progress was transformed by notions of heroism and originality into a personal capacity—a matter of character, in a sense. In a revealing way, the nineteenth-century neighborhood was in love with "genius," for whom Goethe and even Napoleon were models. But the democratic inspiration led from the rarified air of genius to the "uncommon good in the common man." Typically, Emerson could write,

Trust thyself: every heart vibrates to that iron string. Accept the place the divine providence has found for you, the society of your contemporaries, the connection of events. Great men have always done so, and confided themselves childlike to the genius of their age. . . . And we are now men, and must accept in the highest mind the same transcendent destiny; and not minors and invalids in a protected corner, not cowards fleeing before a revolution, but guides, redeemers and benefactors, obeying the Almighty effort and advancing on Chaos And the Dark.[39]

Hope became a characteristic of person, not of event. James, for example, gave it a religious reading in his distinction between the "once" and "twice" born, the "healthy" and "sick" souls. For the Humanist neighborhood, this focus on temperament required a shift from attentiveness to social action to concern for self-development. Of course, the danger of this shift was the possible acquiescence in a public world that was, because a matter of near indifference, simply unworthy of action. In the focus on the "word" as with Emerson or Whitman and in the focus on solitude as with Thoreau, this danger was always present. It was saved from a merely precious interest in personal growth—a preciousness exhibited in our own day by those Humanisms that have been utterly psychologized—by the connectedness of the sociable individual. Or, as Felix Adler put it in trying to mediate between reform and self development, "In the attempt to change others, we must inevitably change ourselves." "So act," Adler wrote in reworking the Kantian imperative, "as to elicit the best in another and *thereby* in one's self."[40]

Gone from this nineteenth-century notion of progress was the impersonality of historical forces and the nonpersonality of the Enlightenment individual. Indeed, not identity but differentiation was the point of this alteration. Just because each person would develop uniquely, the replaceability of anyone by any other one was morally impossible. Thus, its criticism of industrial labor practices and the "division of labor": no one could legitimately be regarded as redundant. Individuation was a democratization of the religious notion of the soul; the Kingdom of God was now transformed into the Republic of God. The individuated person was portrayed in his or her relationships as necessary to the emergence of all other individuated persons. As William James put it,

Ought it to be assumed that in all men the mixture of religion with other elements should be identical? Ought it, indeed, to be assumed that the lives of all men should show identical religious elements? In other words, is the existence of so many religious types and sects and creeds regrettable?

To these questions, I answer "no" emphatically. And my reason is that I do not see how it is possible that creatures in such different positions and with such different powers as human individuals are, should have exactly the same functions and the same duties. No two of us have identical difficulties, nor should we be expected to work out identical solutions. Each from his own peculiar angle of observation, takes in a certain sphere of fact and trouble, which each must deal with in a unique manner. . . . The divine can mean no single quality, it must mean a group of qualities by being champions of which in alternation, different men may find worthy missions.[41]

Progress, optimism, and hope were features, then, of a moral psychology as well as of a personalist anthropology. It is precisely this attentiveness to the actual and unique human being that serves as the other root of modern Humanism. The person is individuated in his or her own being and is not the individual atom who instances natural law. To be sure, transcendental rhetoric, when in its most romantic mood, promised much more than biography could ever deliver. Emerson, for example, could write, "He [the transcendentalist] believes in miracle, in the perpetual openness of the human mind to new influx of light and power; he believes in inspiration, and in ecstacy."[42] William Henry Channing, a nephew of William Ellery Channing, wrote, "Amidst materialists, zealots, and sceptics, the Transcendentalist believed in perpetual inspiration. . . . His maxims were—'Trust, dare and be; infinite good is ready for your asking; seek and find. All that your fellows can claim or need is that you should become, in fact, your highest self; fulfil, then, your ideal.' "[43] Nevertheless, these flights of language might be forgiven when understood against the devaluation of persons in the emerging industrial world, a world that seemed to take its inspiration from the least lovely reading of the new economics and the new sciences.

Obviously, the transcendental opportunity, rich as it is with religious allusion, asks finally for a nontraditional and nonconventional form of faith. It was the mark of character development in a natural world and not a description of the "soul's" turn to another reality. If it had an "object," it was the reflective and active self, and its assurance was not in its achievement but in the value of its efforts:

[William] James provides us not only with a broader view of adequate reasons for believing something, but with a non-dualistic, active, and richer view of a rational believer. With the ideal of the balanced character, James gives us a clue to the right direction to be pursued in the development of our character. But something he would refuse to give us is a precise prescription for everyone to follow. . . . Each from his peculiar angle of observation, takes in a certain sphere of fact and trouble which each must deal with in a unique manner. ". . . It would be unreasonable to ask of James that he be more specific since, . . . the only thing no theory, no printed directions, can teach us is how to will. What it might do, what it might have done, we can be taught; what it shall do depends on the inalienable essence of each individual man."[44]

Of course, transcendentalism can be faulted for its political and economic naiveté. The starving man or woman, at work fifty or sixty hours a week in demeaning labor, could scarcely be expected to respond to the ethereal pronouncements of a middle-class intellectual and poetic minority. Romanticism, in that sense, was not only a luxury but a moral affront. Yet in its generous sense of the uniqueness of each person and despite its airy, even if angry, dismissal of the oppressiveness of actual social conditions, it served to refresh the idea of democracy. To be sure, left to itself, the transcendental opportunity ultimately leads nowhere. But as the other root of Humanism, it nourishes what was all too easily left to starve by the eighteenth-century effort at the Enlightenment project.

NOTES

1. I use the term *transcendentalism* to include the transcendentalists as well as those other nineteenth-century views that find their place in the Humanist neighborhood (e.g., neo-Kantian idealism, personalism, and some forms of pragmatism). The context will make clear which of these references I am using. Further, however, transcendental themes characterize all members of that neighborhood, although with differing emphasis.

2. For help in exploring these nineteenth-century religious and reform adventures, see Felix Adler, *An Ethical Philosophy of Life* (New York: Ethica Press, 1986), Corlis Lamont, *The Philosophy of Humanism* (New York: Ungar, 1982), Mason Olds, *Religious Humanism in America* (Washington, D.C.: University Press of America, 1978), Howard B. Radest, *Toward Common Ground* (New York: Ungar, 1969), and *The Devil and Secular Humanism* (New York: Praeger, 1990), and Conrad Wright, ed., *A Stream of Light* (Boston, Unitarian Universalist Association, 1975).

3. Typical in its approach but untypical in its acuteness is Paul Kurtz's *The Transcendental Temptation* (Buffalo: Prometheus Press, 1986). For Kurtz, transcendentalism is a dangerous illusion. The sins of anti-Humanism are to be located here—antiscience and anti-intelligence. My own view differs, although I am grateful for Professor Kurtz's critical assessment of the worst features of the "transcendental temptation."

4. See Joseph L. Blau, *Men and Movements in American Philosophy* (New York: Prentice-Hall, 1952), pp. 110–150.

5. Felix Adler, *An Ethical Philosophy of Life* (1918) (reprinted, New York: Ethica Press, 1986), pp. 27–28.

6. For a more extended discussion of this theme, see Radest, *The Devil and Secular Humanism*, pp. 65–80.

7. Kurtz, *Transcendental Temptation*, p. 105.

8. Henry David Thoreau, *Walden* (New York: Oxford University Press, 1906), p. 117.

9. Blau, *Men and Movements*, p. 111.

10. Emerson, "The Divinity School Address," in *Selected Essays*, ed. Larzer Ziff (New York: Penguin Books, 1982), p. 123.

11. The sermon is reprinted in Perry Miller, *The American Transcendentalists* (New York: Doubleday Anchor Books, 1957), pp. 104–136. Miller's comment is on page 106.

12. Blau, *Men and Movements*, p. 251.

13. For example, see John Dewey, "The Influence of Darwinism on Philosophy," in John J. McDermott, *The Philosophy of John Dewey* Vol. I. (Chicago: University of Chicago Press, 1981), pp. 31–41.

14. William James, *The Varieties of Religious Experience* (New York: Collier Books, 1961), pp. 386–387.

15. Immanuel Kant, *Critique of Judgement*, trans. J. H. Bernard (New York: Hafner, 1951), p. 88.

16. Barbara Novak, *Nature and Culture* (New York: Oxford University Press, 1980), pp. 38–40 passim.

17. Emerson, "The American Scholar," in *Selected Essays*, p. 83.

18. Ibid., pp. 88–89.

19. Alfred Lord Tennyson, "Flower in the Crannied Wall," available in many anthologies. See Edwin Markham, *Anthology of the World's Best Poems* (New York: Wm. H. Wise, 1948), 5: 1798.

20. Steven Rockefeller, *John Dewey—Religion, Faith and Democratic Humanism* (New York: Columbia University Press, 1991), p. 12.

21. Emerson, "Poetry and Imagination," in Miller, *The American Transcendentalists*, pp. 200–201.

22. James, *The Varieties of Religious Experience*, pp. 83–84.

23. Cited by Novak, *Nature and Culture*, p. 14.

24. Emerson, "Beauty," in Miller, *The American Transcendentalists*, p. 185.

25. Walt Whitman, *Leaves of Grass* (New York: Grosset and Dunlap, n.d.), p. 71.

26. Charles Mayo Ellis, "An Essay on Transcendentalism," in Miller, *The American Transcendentalists*, p. 24.

27. For example, see John Dewey's essay, "Ralph Waldo Emerson," in McDermott, *Philosophy of John Dewey* vol. I., pp. 24–31.

28. Ralph Waldo Emerson, "The Method of Nature," in Miller, *The American Transcendentalists*, p. 58.

29. Emerson, "The American Scholar," p. 84.

30. Walt Whitman, "One's-Self I Sing," *op cit.*, p. 427.

31. For example, see Joseph L. Blau, "Emerson's Transcendentalist Individualism As a Social Philosophy," *Review of Metaphysics* 31, no. 1 (September 1977): 82.

32. For example,

> That ethnic and tribal rivalries can backfire on those who promote them is a truism long since accepted by scholars of international affairs. "The detour towards ethnicity is totally ruinous," said Professor Fouad Ajami of Johns Hopkins University, an expert on the politics of, among other places, Lebanon. "The tribal consolation is a false consolation. It is . . . an ethnic binge you indulge and then you realize it doesn't do anything for you. But you cannot reason with these furies. The call of blood is powerful for a moment, then people will wake up in wreckage of it all."

Donatella Lorch, "Hate Returns to Haunt Those Who Cradled It," *New York Times*, July 17, 1994, p. 1.

33. The First Amendment to the Constitution exhibits that fuzziness by both calling for the free exercise and prohibiting the establishment of religion. For example, tax exemptions serve free exercise, but denial of tax exemption can lead to the disestablishment of some and the establishment of others.

34. Michael A. Weinstein, *The Wilderness and the City* (Boston: University of Massachusetts Press, 1982), p. 138.

35. Marian C. Madden and Edward H. Madden, "Buffs and Rebuffs: Emerson, Parker and Thoreau," *Transactions of the Charles S. Peirce Society* 30, no. 1 (Winter 1994): 26.

36. Blau, *Men and Movements*, p. 259.

37. Weinstein, *Wilderness and the City*, pp. 87–88.

38. In a contemporary reconception, Cornel West rehearses this nineteenth-century reformulation of the Enlightenment project and calls it "prophetic pragmatism," which

> purports to be not only an oppositional cultural criticism but also a material force for individuality and democracy. . . . The distinctive hallmarks of a prophetic pragmatist are a universal consciousness that promotes an all-embracing democratic and libertarian moral vision, a historical consciousness that acknowledges human finitude and conditionedness, and a critical consciousness which encourages relentless critique and self-criticism for the aims of social change and personal humility.

Cornel West, *The American Evasion of Philosophy* (Madison: University of Wisconsin Press, 1989), p. 232.

39. Emerson, "Self-Reliance," in *Selected Essays*, p. 177.

40. Felix Adler was given to formulating "maxims" and "mottos" of which the citations in the text are instances. His formal restatement of Kant's categorical imperative was put as follows,

A. Act as a member of the ethical manifold (the infinite spiritual universe).

B. Act so as to achieve uniqueness (complete individualization—the most completely individualized act is the most ethical).

C. Act so as to elicit in another the distinctive, unique quality characteristic of him as a fellow-member of the infinite whole.

An Ethical Philosophy of Life (1918) (New York: Ethica Press, 1986), p. 117.

41. James, *Varieties of Religious Experience*, pp. 378–379.

42. Emerson, "The Transcendentalist," in *Selected Essays*, p. 243.

43. William Henry Channing, "A Participant's Definition," in Miller *The American Transcendentalists*, p. 37.

44. Gregory Fernando Papps, "William James' Virtuous Believer," *Transactions of the Charles S. Peirce Society* 30, no. 1 (Winter 1994): 100. Citations are from James's *The Will to Believe* and *Essays in Psychology*.

6

WHAT MUST BE RESPONDED TO?

THE QUESTION

Thus far, I have tried to explore the territory of the Enlightenment project and its critics. These reveal the contrast of the rich two-ness of Humanism with the flatness of the shadow enlightenment. The popular solutions to the "failure" of the modern, like libertarianism and the free market, only expose our predilection for nostalgia and political opportunism. Like new age and postmodernism, they too are blind to the problem of connecting intimacy and sociability. The enemies of Humanism retreat before this anthropological task by calling for a restoration of a fabled past or by running away to nihilism. Finally, in the rambling adventures of the existential and transcendental moods, there are clues to Humanism's proper parentage and so clues to reconstruction.

It would be wrong to treat today's crazy-quilt of practices, movements, and philosophies as if they united around a single agenda. We find instead a randomly assembled shopping list. Nevertheless, it is possible to discover among the critics the puzzles that seem to grow more difficult and fearful for all of us: the objectification of human beings, the evolution of massive impersonal powers, the reduction of persons to "personalities," and the exploitation of inventiveness and rationality for purposes of destruction. With this, the values of the Enlightenment project are themselves deteriorated. In short, both Humanists and their critics announce a dismay at contemporary culture.

I confess that there is something deeply satisfying in the simplicities of fundamentalism, the dramatics of nihilism, and the flirtations of the new age. After all, if I can accept the isolation of life-worlds from each other, I can stay comfortably with my friends, and I need not attend to the troubles of strangers, the survival of the human species, or the preservation of the global habitat. Similarly, if I can retreat into myself, I need not suffer the difficulties of inquiry or the pains of public criticism. And if I can put salvation forward to eternity and elsewhere to another world, I can in good conscience ignore the terrors of this world. But for the Humanist, none of these options is possible.

As I see it, we are all asking whether there is very much left worth living for and talking about. This existential doubt applies to both the personal and the public life. It is clear enough that at the same time that the world out there escapes us, the personal is trivialized as the merely private. We really do live, as has been said, in the narrowing gaps of an evolving systemic environment. That environment is characterized by the resort to routines and formulas even when it comes to dealing with the good, the true, and the beautiful. I think of a legalism that characterizes so much of our behavior, of a faddism that replaces aesthetic taste with sensationalism, and of a relativism that reduces truth to opinion. Grand causes are diminished so that what was once an invitation to idealism and commitment—like social justice or a peaceful world—becomes routine too. I compare, for example, the dream that led to the United Nations in San Francisco in 1946 with the reality of the mountain of paper that now buries it.

We boast and complain of the fact that we are led by deliberately ordinary people; leadership is only the presence of someone just like me at the top. Or, as it is said, everyone can have his or her fifteen minutes of celebrity. Conversation is a lost art, although we talk a great deal about dialogue and discussion. More and more, we communicate with a minimal vocabulary of signs and grunts and pictograms. Of course, little pleasures and little joys persist, satisfactions in a minor key in a consumer society. These hardly satisfy us—the goodies available in the marketplace, the hobby, the momentary thrill, the trivial achievement, the temporary victory in politics or on the job.

Deeper human desires persist. But the loves and hopes of family and friendship are encapsulated, isolated. At the same time, the bigness and manyness of things overwhelms even these. We have a sense that our inner lives too are at the mercy of uncontrollable forces. We seem more and more like primitive ancestors, who were victims of flood, famine, earthquake, and epidemic. We might try to appease the gods with our sacrifices, but ultimately we were at the mercy of the unknowable and, above all, the arbitrary. Once, then, we searched the heavens desperately to save our souls. But in the world of the shadow enlightenment and its critics, the soul is the very thing that has become problematic.

Reading an industrial and technical society as primitive may seem fanciful until we consider the appeal to magic that accompanies it. Omens and superstitions persist in a society that is thought to be scientifically and technically sophisticated. But, of course, we are not sophisticated at all. Our science is narrowly conceived as a mere utility or as the reserve of an elite with privileged access to the truth. I think, here, of our hasty allegiance to this or that promise of successful manipulation of the world or of our lives—the prevalence of pseudopsychological and pseudoreligious fads, for example—and of our confidence in the signs and portents of astrology. I think too of our scientific illiteracy so that technology replaces the sacred fire, and the on-off switch replaces incantation.

We are not living in a scientific culture at all. Its machinery is, for most of us, a black box whose workings are known to only a select and blessed minority. But with the increase of specialization, even that minority is fragmented so that everyone faces the black box most of the time in most of his or her experience. Indeed, we have reached a point where we do not even want to open the casing that hides the machinery. "If it works," we say, "don't fix it." To this we add quietly, "If it doesn't work, replace it; and if you can't replace it, deny it." Gratefully, we obey the warning not to tamper with things. We move from understanding to manipulation and are successfully disarmed by our inventions themselves.

For many of us, however, modern society also works. We are better placed than our ancestors, and, indeed, our very complaints derive as much from disappointed expectations as from actual disasters. To be sure, the black box is all around us, but it is also true that we are its beneficiaries, enjoying the automobile and airplane that move us from place to place, the X-ray and MRI machine that help diagnose our illness, the chemistry that cures, and the technicized agriculture that feeds us. This is not, then, the time for a Luddite counterrevolution even if some of Humanism's critics would want to return to a simpler time where everything was supposed to be in its place and everyone was supposed to know his or her place.

There is yet a third side to our modern dismay at culture. Even as we are the beneficiaries as well as the victims of an overwhelming modern world, we find our inner lives narrowed and trivialized. Our energy is given over to the requirements of exteriority, to the need to perfect our roles. Our skill is given over to meeting its demands—to the need to provide resource and labor in order to meet systemic needs, for example—so that little is left over for the rest of what we are. Mind becomes so monomaniacally dedicated to these needs that intimacy is left unminded, becoming merely emotive.

Once the Humanist would respond to life's problems with a program of social reform and social action: the liberal agenda, as in the struggle for the rights of children and women, the civil rights movement, and, earlier, the abolition of slavery, the rights of labor, model housing, and the rest. The modern situation, however, does not benefit from these older habits. Reform is all too easily transformed into yet another exteriority and even becomes an alibi for evading the personal. Our starting point then must be the recovery of self and derivatively the changing of the world. I must, in other words, be present to the situation as an actual and particular human being, denying myself the protections of roles, agents, and surrogates. And I must become competent to undertake changing the world as a personal assignment.

The dismay of culture reduces then to a question about what it is to be human under the conditions created by the Enlightenment project. It is pointless to rehearse over and over again, as both the critics and the Humanists do, the familiar litany of the doings and disasters of exteriority. Or putting this another way, even a perfected exteriority—a utopia—would still evoke our dismay. Once again, we are in the presence of the shadow enlightenment.

Symptomatic of our need to shift attention are our linguistic habits. We search compulsively for ever more refined ways of accumulating data and try to quantify everything. Behaviorism becomes a dominant way of life as we focus on narrowly conceived notions of action and conduct. In a shrunken reading of utility, our key terms are the "bottom line," the "results," "less talk and more action," and the like, and these terms are not confined to the world of the marketplace. Even where we call for moral crusade, as conservatives do, it feeds on the competitive world and is reduced to moralism.

The marketplace becomes the model of effectiveness everywhere. For example, as a one-time schoolman, I keep up with proposals for school and business partnerships as a prescription for educational reform. Although often well intended, these do not account for the differing values that shape two quite distinctive ways of being. We also convert healing into a business, ignoring the often conflicting values that inspire medicine and market. We transform professions from callings into jobs. Less tangible matters like insight and motivation are treated as soft ideas, which are better left to poets and philosophers and to those psychologists and social scientists who have not surrendered to the prevailing measurement way of thinking.

Even where normative notions are presented, we use legalist thought structures in order to avoid accusations of sentimentality and ambiguity. "Rights talk" becomes a model for most ethics talk since it seems to permit clarity of definition, reference, and precedent. Yet by using terms of ascription—we attribute rights to persons—we reveal how far we have come from notions like inalienable rights or natural rights. These, while procedural in practice, were also anthropological and ontological; they entailed a portrait of the nature of human nature as well as of the world. Human beings were said to be capable of exercising rights, accepting responsibilities, and acting as moral and political beings; the world, in turn, was hospitable to such a being. Ascription, by contrast, is a mask for conventionality, even where universally conceived, as in the United Nations Declaration of Human Rights. Conventions are another token of exteriority.

To be sure, there are signs of discontent with the reduction of sociability to contract and of ethics to moralism. A reawakened interest in culture and community is already evident, particularly under the inspiration of modern feminism. In ethics, "virtue talk" competes with "rights talk." For example,

> Ronald Dworkin has recently argued that the central doctrine of modern liberalism is the thesis that questions about the *good life for man* or the ends of human life are to be regarded from the public standpoint as systematically unsettleable. . . . The rules of morality and law hence are not to be derived from or justified in terms of some more fundamental conception of the good for man. In arguing thus Dworkin has, I believe, identified a stance characteristic not just of liberalism but of modernity. Rules become the primary concept of the moral life. Qualities of character then generally come to be prized only because they will lead us to follow the right set of rules.[1]

While raising a necessary caution, however, these new voices tend to represent in yet another way the hope of return that is characteristic of critics of the modern. Virtue ethics, for example, takes its inspiration from Aristotle; communitarianism, from a romanticized view of America's past. For the Humanist, however, the search for intimacy cannot begin and end in nostalgia.

I do not think that the Humanist is merely stubborn. For example, a sense of fairness and of the moral necessity of disinterestedness—both instances of a "rights talk" way of ethics—are still valid, as anyone who has encountered their opposite can report. Similarly, the freedom from oppressive community and the possibility of escape even to an impersonal society can be defended too. I need only consult the relief I feel in the anonymities of the large city as against the intrusions of the small town. Finally, the critics of Enlightenment fail to account for those larger connections when communities touch on each other and when strangers discover that they inhabit the same impacted world as well as their particular life-worlds.

There is, then, persistent validity to universality, cosmopolitanism, individuality, and social justice, all much-maligned terms of the Enlightenment project. There is value too in accurate description, in a focus on actual conduct, in measurement and in convention. That side of the modern would be dismissed to our peril—something that becomes obvious once we imagine living in a world from which these were banished. So the modern question is not the either-or of subjectivity or objectivity but one of personal response: How shall I respond, and to what shall I respond? Unlike description, which invites the abstractness of talking about and talking at a distance, I understand that there is no such thing as "to respond in general," no such thing as "to be responded to in general." I am forced to the particular, to the actual, to the personal as the way of sustaining the sociable.

TRANSITIONS

We are in the habit of reading the past as if it was divisible into discrete moments. Once these divisions marked off visions of the apocalypse, of the coming of the messiah, of the flood, of the creation. Today we speak of ages of "faith" or of "reason," of "modern" or of "postmodern." We search for yet another discrete moment, a next "age," in an endless round of hope and frustration. Between such moments are said to be ambiguous periods of transition when past is not yet future. For example, Vaclav Havel writes,

> There are good reasons for suggesting that the modern age has ended. Many things indicate that we are going through a transitional period, when it seems that something is on the way out and something else is painfully being born. . . .
>
> Today, this state of mind, or of the human world, is called post-modernism. For me, a symbol of that state is a Bedouin mounted on a camel and clad in traditional robes under which he is wearing jeans, with a transistor radio in his hands and an ad for Coca-Cola on the camel's back.[2]

But we are forgetful of the fact that it is we in the present—any present—who select and name what was and what will be. We see today as transition in order to look for some new salvation. The notion of transition also conveys a comforting aesthetic premise: that history is marked by successive beginnings, middles, and endings; that history is drama. To be sure, there are genuine innovations that highlight our experience—the rights of man was one of these, the dropping of the atom bomb another—but these moments do not arise suddenly. Secular history is read as moment and transition, a struggle between myth and record. My feminist colleagues would also call it another instance of masculine rationalism. History demonstrates the whys and wherefores of things. From this, the legitimation of existing arrangements can be derived—"history tells us . . ." or "that's the way things have to be," we say. Or we can ground the future as, "That's the way it must be." The move to a politics of control is not very great.

The Enlightenment, too, read history as a record of moments of succession, in particular, of moments of progress. At the same time, the Enlightenment project legitimized self-correction in its commitment to the sciences. Error was an occasion for the increase of knowledge and not for the judgment of sin. With this, it distinguished itself from other historical projects where criticism was confined to apologetics, as in scholasticism, biblical commentary, and Leninism. It made the notion of continuity and the consequent ambivalence of change self-conscious, an ironic outcome for a messianic view of an "age of reason" with its forecast of the inevitability of progress.[3]

The distinction between Humanism and its critics rests on the choice between an open and a closed narrative. Ironically, for those accused of mere rationalism, the Humanist must rely on characteristics of personality as much as on the objective situation. As John Dewey noted,

> Old ideas give way slowly; for they are more than abstract logical forms and categories. They are habits, predispositions, deeply engrained attitudes of aversion and preference. . . . In fact intellectual progress usually occurs through sheer abandonment of questions together with both the alternatives they assume—an abandonment that results from their decreasing vitality and a change of urgent interest. *We do not solve them; we get over them.*[4]

It is surely possible to read the present in terms of its rejections, but that reveals, too, a matter of mood, of readiness. It is in this frame of mind that I have pointed to the shadow enlightenment as a minimization of the passions that shaped the so-called age of reason. Intimacy appears thus not as something that announces a new age or a postmodern age but as a continuing but now-muted presence. For the critic of the modern, intimacy is a lonely hiddenness, a perennial refuge from an oppressive organized life. For the Humanist, intimacy and sociability require each other.

It is precisely the not-yet that distinguishes the Humanist from the critics, who live with the once-was and the hope of a yet-again. Nietzsche's theme of the "eternal return" is indeed a talismen of the postmodern. However, the not-yet is Nietzschean too, although this is conveniently ignored. Thus, Zarathustra claims that we are to be the "bridge" to the "overman." Symptomatically, however, most of the critics fail to select this other Nietzschean theme. In other words, not-yet reconstructs the optimism of the Enlightenment project. It implies "someday" and rejects "never" and "no way."

What then, of the not-yets in the current situation? Clearly, the dismay of culture points us toward an emptiness in our experience, although it is the conservative these days who sounds the theme. For example,

> What Mr. Kristol and others see is a yawning philosophical vacuum in American life, with people urgently trying to fill it in myriad ways. "There is a transition going on—but to what, nobody knows," he says. . . . Membership in evangelical religions is growing, even as New Age philosophies proliferate. The environmental movement, the feminist movement, the rise of alternative medicine, the explosion of street gangs—each represents a hunger for something beyond scientific rationalism, beyond material progress. "People want more," Mr. Kristol says. "They want community and they want transcendence."[5]

To fill the emptiness, Humanism's critics rely on a nostalgic politics. "Community" and "transcendence" are accompanied by the suppressed adverbial phrase, "as they once were." These are not the ideals of Emersonian optimism or the dreams of moral democracy. The characteristic term is *restoration*, not *reconstruction.* The mood is to look away from and back toward.

Thus, the renewed interest in myth and story. But "narrative" need not always be backward looking. There are utopian stories, quest stories, adventure stories, victory over-evil stories, and, today, science fiction stories too. Stories, in other words, can be regenerative and not just reminiscent, sociable and not just isolationist. The contemporary rediscovery of stories, however, is driven by a passion for the imagined past as against the undesirable present. This reveals the hidden politics behind the reference. This is not only a conservative ploy. Feminists, for example, trace history back beyond patriarchy to another age,[6] and African-Americans search beyond the boundaries of the Western canon. Interestingly, for conservative and radical alike, the golden age is behind us. But tradition is not the same as the rigidities of traditionalism. It recognizes that human beings come on the scene in the midst of histories and cultures that preexist them. We develop toward the future precisely on the ground of an absorbed collective past that feeds us but that we need not replicate. It is in this sense that, Robert Bellah writes,

> People growing up in communities of memory not only hear the stories that tell how the community came to be, what its hopes and fears are, and how its ideals are exemplified in outstanding men and women; they also participate in the practices—ritual, aesthetic, ethical—that define the community as a way of life. . . . And if the language of the self-reliant individual is the first language of American moral life, the languages of tradition and commitment in communities of memory are "second languages" that most Americans know as well and which they use when the language of the radically separate self does not seem adequate.[7]

To be a story is to capture themes that are woven around tensions between the light and dark sides of experience, like love and hate, justice and vengeance, friendliness and hostility. No doubt, apart from the political agenda of conservative and radical traditionalism, this is why the appeal of stories is a permanent feature of living and why, too, today's dismay of culture pushes us to turn to stories as ways of holding on to personal life while exteriority threatens it.[8] It is story that is more convincing than argument when matters of intimacy are at stake. For example, Andrew Greeley points out that despite Roman Catholicism's authoritarianism and sexism, Catholics remain loyal "because of the stories." He writes,

> Catholicism has great stories because at the center of its heritage is "sacramentalism," the conviction that God discloses Himself in the objects and events and persons of ordinary life. Hence Catholicism is willing to risk stories about angels and saints and souls in purgatory and Mary, the Mother of Jesus, and stained glass windows and statues and stations of the cross and rosaries and medals and the whole panoply of images and devotions that were so offensive to the austere leaders of the Reformation. . . .
>
> It may seem that I am reducing religion to childishness—to stories and images and rituals and communities. In fact, it is in the poetic, the metaphorical, the experiential dimension of the personality that religion finds both its origins and raw power.[9]

Greeley describes here what Bellah calls a "community of memory." It is the Humanist's mistake to conclude from the church's social policy or from its medieval ontology that it must of necessity be dismissed by sensible men and women.

At the same time, stories that recollect particular life-worlds are not responsive to the modern situation. The modern story must be species inclusive without being homogeneous. After all, stories can transcend boundaries of time, space, and culture and have done so. That, under an Enlightenment inspiration, we have surely learned from comparative anthropologies and comparative literatures. Stories, then, are both general and particular; they touch on universal themes and ideas. They are, in a nod to Emerson, actual and representative at the same time. In a further instance of the shadow enlightenment, however, we have failed to capture the genius of the Enlightenment project in stories. This failure makes contemporary criticism more believable than it has any right to be. In short, whatever may be the need for refinement of ideas, the equal need is for an aesthetic and a myth.

In what follows, I want to try to find those thematic notions in the Enlightenment project that provide for the setting, the transmission of intimacy and sociability. Response, I have said, is the modern clue to reconstruction. It is, of course, possible to describe response, as the psychologist does, or to attribute responsiveness to human nature, as the ethicist does. But these descriptions still leave us hidden away. In other words, response entails, "I respond" and asks, "To whom?" I must find out whose voices I hear when I speak and when I listen.

FIRST-PERSON SINGULAR

"Once upon a time . . ." opens many stories. "In the beginning . . ." opens others. "I was born . . ." opens yet others. A story gets its mood and direction from its opening. The setting, action, and character are already visible. Development unfolds the opening, restates it in detail, and reveals the tensions that were only hinted at in the beginning. In the end, if it is a good story, we are left wanting more, left with bridges to other openings and to other stories yet to come.

As a Humanist, I would start with the narratives of others, for our story must be inclusive. It might begin, "It is told of old that . . ." This setting reveals the universalism and cosmopolitanism of the Humanist tradition, much as the setting for Dante's *Divine Comedy* reveals the church and politics of Renaissance Italy or the chorus in a Greek tragedy announces the *polis* and the gods. But in its eighteenth-century incarnation, the story of universalism and cosmopolitanism was likely to be introduced without apparent voice at all as in, "All men are created equal." The narrative was objectified, even hid itself as narrative in the guise of social science or a political pamphlet. For example, Voltaire's *Candide* is an inverted morality play. David Hume's *Dialogues Concerning Natural Religion* follows the model of Plato's dramatic dialogues but without the dialectic creativity of the Socratic original.

Even at its most rational, however, the Enlightenment project had its aesthetic as well as its ideas. The sculptured garden and the classic column conveyed the beauty of unadorned line and structure. For all its optimism, the Enlightenment narrative carried darker tones too. I listen to Mozart's *Don Giovanni*, *The Magic Flute*, or *The Marriage of Figaro*. Betraying the facility of the music and the libretto are the themes of class and caste, of powerful and conflicted natural energies, and of transcending human dreams. Of course, there are references of the moment too (e.g., to the free-masons in *The Magic Flute*) and challenges to the conventionalities of the day. For example, *Don Giovanni* needed a moralist's epilogue pointing out the merited punishment of its lead figure.

Unlike the gossip-filled and curio-filled histories of the past—Herodotus comes to mind—the modern aesthetic evolved by opening up to the diversity of cultures, religions, and politics forecast in the insatiable curiosity of the Renaissance and the eighteenth-century Enlightenment. To an extent, the habits of nineteenth-century Humanism, already afflicted by academicism, downplayed the drama of this opening up to the world. And yet transcendentalist enthusiasm broke through. For example, Stow Persons notes,

> A more tangible contribution of transcendentalism growing out of the same cosmopolitan awareness of contemporary European and Asiatic thought was the awakening of interest in the comparative study of religion. . . . Although all of the free religious leaders of the post-Appomattox period displayed keen interest in the study of non-Christian religions, the works that best exemplify the importance of this interest . . . are Samuel Johnson's three-volume *Oriental Religions and Their Relation to Universal Religion*, and Thomas Wentworth Higginson's tract, *The Sympathy of Religions*.[10]

Everywhere, universalism and cosmopolitanism invited the mood of opening-up-to. Further, they invited the expectation that, like the sciences that inspired its narrative, the stories to come would tell of adventure into new worlds.

The narratives of Humanist yesterdays had their heroes, to be sure, but the style even if, on occasion, biographical was not autobiographical. Only rarely do we find the "confession"—Rousseau comes to mind—and even autobiography is intellectual autobiography. For example, John Stuart Mill's *Autobiography* describes, among other things, Mill's relationship to his father, his emotional difficulties, his affair with Harriet Taylor, his marriage to her after the death of her husband, her radical feminism. However, the tone is cool, and the text is more likely to lead to an idea or political program than to a passion.

The diary, the daybook, and the journal disclosed the private feelings, dreams, and doubts that attend us all. But these self-reflections are revealed to us, an unintended audience, after their subject is long gone. Correspondence allowed an exchange of "intimacies" as in Jefferson's letters to Maria Cosway[11] or as in the letters between John and Abigail Adams. But the style was restrained, and publication in any case was the work of a subsequent scholarship. Excepting Whitman and, on occasion, Emerson, even love poetry and romantic novels tended to be discrete and indirect, using metaphor as much to conceal as to reveal. With obvious exceptions like Dostoyevsky or Kierkegaard, who in any event were not Humanists, the novel told a story about someone else. In short, the subject was present, but at a distance and masked.

The drama of ideas, the utopian story, the myth of Everyman, the realistic novel, all of which appeared as the Humanist aesthetic emerged, do not reach to the need of the present. A modern aesthetic must begin with the subject in order to make an authentic move into expression. In other words, the opening of today's Humanist story needs to be announced by the first-person singular, although it cannot remain there. Unlike the contemplative, for example, Humanist subjectivity is not closed away into itself. The intimate reveals itself in the presence of others.

This self-revelation is quite different from the fashionable compulsion to "let it all hang out," as my California friends used to say in the 1960s. I am not suggesting that the Humanist is interested in true confessions or needs to indulge in mere gossip. Indeed, it sometimes seems as if nothing can remain personal at all. Confidences are published routinely and not just by political opponents. Intimacy itself has become a marketable commodity; witness the explosion of TV talk shows and their exploitation of the foibles and disasters of human relationships. A moral imperative is even attached to self-revelation. We have, as we say, a "right to know" just about everything about everybody. Nothing is hidden, but the consequence is that nothing much is worth hiding.

This interest in self-revelation is not really concerned with another human being at all but with a momentarily fascinating object. In fact, we quickly grow jaded by revelation. Intimacy so conceived becomes boring, and we look for the latest and most extreme expression of it in order to stay interested. Nor should this transformation of intimacy into a commodity come as a surprise. It is forecast by the ways in which exteriority intrudes everywhere, appears everywhere. Pseudointimacy becomes an inevitable corollary of the move toward depersonalization. As Jurgen Habermas puts it,

> To the degree that the economic system subjects the life-forms of private households and the life conduct of consumers and employees to its imperatives, consumerism and possessive individualism, motives of performance and competition gain the force to shape behavior. . . . As the private sphere is undermined and eroded by the economic system, so too is the public sphere by the administrative system.[12]

Intimacy is everywhere advertised and everywhere eludes us. By contrast, a Humanist concern for intimacy does not arise from a prurient interest in human perversities. The Humanist story is to be written in the first-person singular in order to acknowledge the urgency of the personal: I respond to and am responded to. Indeed, because of this, I find myself resenting all the more the conversion of "I" into yet another "it." Pseudointimacy increases what can only be called exhibitionism.

Searching out the who I am and the why I am is made more difficult by the tension between my hidden self and what I do and what is done to me under systemic conditions. At the same time, the very utilitarianism that turns intimacy into commodity also generates the discomforts that lead us toward the rediscovery of personality. Thus, the use of the first-person singular that is to open the modern story is not only another stylistic device but a challenge to the present. The story is, quite literally, to be my story in a world where personal stories are disvalued.

It is possible to glimpse the actual tensions that, in greater or lesser degree, arise from the retreat into a corporate culture. But tension and retreat, anger and anxiety are hidden behind a veil of objectivity. There is no Lear wandering madly over the moors, no Oedipus with bleeding eyes. Although these tensions may be suppressed and sublimated, they do not disappear but take form as a radical separation of "I" and "it," a separation that occurs within. The person who struggles to find a hidden innerness is the same one who acts out the role of exteriority. The first-person singular is therefore problematic from the outset.

From classic times onward, "know thyself" has been a Humanist directive. In the present, however, this finding out is more difficult than it once was. It is hidden by the ready availability of answers that look like and even feel like personal answers but are not personal answers at all. Social roles like parent, child, warrior, and priest have been characteristic of all societies and cultures. But for us, these roles have been objectified, presented as job descriptions and measured by criteria of efficiency. Convention has been stripped of tradition, and this differentiates our role playing from what has gone before. Even nonconformity is conventionalized in a new way. For example, when we explore the fascinating jumble of fashion or the strange noisiness of popular music, we notice that convention has also been exteriorized. Formula and routine dominate. The so-called personal answers—personalize your costume, your car, your apartment—are not really personal. Consequently, inner life is troubled, and sociability is accented by cynicism. The line between gossip and self-discovery is marked by this distinction between the personal and personalizing.

"Know thyself" was, of course, always a harsh directive. Our increase of psychological knowledge and our anthropological awareness of others have made self-reflection even more problematic. Earlier, I remarked that we had learned the lessons of self-concealment long ago, not as an act of choice ("I want to hide") but as a defense against intrusion. But now we have also learned to mistrust reflection itself. Hans-Georg Gadamer points out,

> Psychoanalysis, for instance, is scarcely imaginable without Nietzsche's radical calling into doubt the testimony of human reflective self-consciousness. Nietzsche set the demand that one doubt more profoundly and fundamentally than Descartes, who had considered the ultimate unshakable foundation of all certitude to be explicit self-consciousness.[13]

Self-reflection arises in the situation of the critique of the modern and of the shadow enlightenment all at once. The Humanist narrative in the first person will find hard going.

It is little wonder that the second-person singular is problematic too. We convert the other into an object, are unsure of what the other really is, and transform the other into an abstraction without personhood. After all, I select the world I inhabit from among the worlds that I could inhabit, and as I do, I select my fellow inhabitants too. I am not necessarily aware of what I am doing. My selection is already prefigured in my development, my presence in world and life-world, my illusions. Indeed, the very way in which I pose the problem is already caught in a situation not of my making. Comparative culture studies make this very clear. For example, anthropologist Robert Carter says,

The Japanese make a less than sharp distinction between subject and object. . . . The Western traditions instinctively distinguish *me*, as subject, from the tree which I look at, and scientific objectivity has to depend on being able to isolate those properties which belong to the object under investigation from those subjective properties of the investigator. By contrast, the Japanese emphasize immediate experience itself, and even as (supposedly) prior to the subject-object distinction. . . . A Japanese walking in the woods may say, "lonesome." It is not said that she or he is lonely, or that one is lonely while walking in these woods, or that he or she is feeling lonely. It is neither an objective nor a subjective experience, but both, or perhaps something in between. . . . Perhaps it is a more primal drinking in of the whole as one's entire world of the moment.[14]

Yet for all my "science," it is still "my" world. As William James put it,

Out of this aboriginal sensible muchness attention carves out objects, which conception then names and identifies forever—in the sky, "constellations," on the earth, "beach," "sea," "cliff," "bushes," "grass." Out of time we cut "days" and "nights," "summers" and "winters."[15]

At the same time, self-reflection tells me that I am an other for someone else. I too am selected and, no doubt, not as I would wish to be and not as I would do it for myself. I understand then that no matter how near or far some other is to me, he or she is inevitably a stranger—not because I do not know him or her but because the encounter between us is shaped by selections that are hardly available to reflection itself. Not least of the difficulties is that the other that I am for another person is not the other that I am for myself. The first-person singular, then, announces a journey. The Humanist narrative is an adventure story, even a mystery story.

BETWEEN

As with any mystery story, I try to uncover what was done and who did it and why. The mystery, I think, is solvable. And that, of course, is just the way the Enlightenment project approaches the world: as solvable. But now, intelligibility becomes a metaphor for human action and not a description of the way the world is or a prediction about the future of the sciences. In other words, we have again moved to characteristics of the subject. We catch hints of this move in Nietzsche's description:

Socrates represents the archetype of the theoretical optimist, who, strong in the belief that nature can be fathomed, considers knowledge to be the true panacea and error to be radical evil. To Socratic man, the one noble and truly human occupation was that of laying bare the workings of nature, of separating true knowledge from illusion and error. So it happened that ever since Socrates the mechanism of concepts, judgments and syllogisms has come to be regarded as the highest exercise of man's powers, nature's most admirable gift.[16]

When intimacy becomes a commodity, however, subjectivity becomes a commodity too. I experience the modern version of distance and come to believe that I am isolated from the world not only as observer and object are isolated but as consumer and consumer good are isolated. This relationship of isolations has the advantage of allowing me to engage in certain standard behaviors: description, measurement, manipulation. But the very success of treating persons as objects of nosiness encourages the illusion that what I actually find is real and above all titillating. Furthermore, with the ready availability of standard behaviors, I have no work to do; intimacy becomes only another skill. So it is that we talk about "office friendships," "business acquaintances," "significant others," "partnerships," "family structures," and all the rest of a vocabulary of distant intimacy—an intimacy without persons.

At the same time, intimacy remains a feature of actual relationships—the mystic and the Other, the lover and the beloved, the parent and the child—but we lack a language for expressing it. Without language, experience sooner or later is recast in the form that language permits. For this reason, we experiment with the outrageous in drama, poetry, novel, painting, sculpture, and music in a desperate effort to break into an intimacy without persons. Hence, too, the wild and confusing arts of the modern age make a point even as they stir our impatience. At the same time, language goes on shaping our reality, and so distant intimacy comes to be what we take for intimacy. We struggle against this inarticulate situation in which we find ourselves, but our dumbness develops into a process of substitution. Exhausted, we give it up as a bad job.

Always problematic, today it is all the more difficult to become a person. I always had to find out how to live in a world of strangers and in a world where I was even a stranger to myself. And I understood that I would never really succeed in either task, so the Humanist story was always a tragedy. Birth opens my story, and death ends it, but these are accidents. "Call no man happy until he is dead," said the Greeks, who caught on very early. Living is interruption, happening. Connection, too, is arbitrary, unplanned. But given our compulsion for control, the accidental is anathema. The world of strangers expands; the complexities of self grow; the masks that must be penetrated prevail. At the same time, our disquiet grows too, particularly as ways of connection become, paradoxically, both easier and more mysterious. So, for example, I have little trouble fitting in to this or that situation—on the job, in school, in the club—and yet I fit in by fitting into. Traditional ways of connecting are themselves brought within the process of fitting in. Friendliness, love and caring are transformed into modern technologies. "How-to-do-it" is the modern genre.

The media are filled with reports of the penetration of technique everywhere. Offers to sell technical skill abound, whether to "improve your love life" or "win friends and influence people." Assumed is the notion that technique is indifferently applicable to business or classroom or family. The outcome of such technologies is the transformation of personal relationships into object relationships. Early in our century, John Dewey called attention to this emerging phenomenon:

> The "joining" habit of the average American, and his excessive sociability, may well have an explanation like that of conformity. . . . We should not be so averse to solitude if we had, when we were alone, the companionship of communal thought built into our mental habits. In the absence of this communion, there is the need for reinforcement by external contact. Our sociability is largely an effort to find substitutes for the normal consciousness of connection and union that proceeds from being a sustained and sustaining member of a social whole.[17]

Increasingly absent is the availability of persons to and for each other. For example, I work with several hospitals on medical ethics. We meet the problems posed by a medical technicism. We try to restore human presence so that we can move from what is treated—a hand or brain or eye or liver—to who is treated and who treats, that is, a person. Pressed by exteriority well beyond the boundaries imposed by the economics of the situation, however, we exclude the personal through an excessive growth of standard procedures, policies, rules, and structures. Presence is undervalued, even repressed. Specialization dissects the patient into organs, even parts of organs. Expert claims build walls around the sick. For example, a doctor writes,

> Their variegated forms notwithstanding, familial and other intimate relationships are typically crucial for attaining or protecting much of what is widely valued about human beings and their projects. . . . Families aren't simply more or less efficient means to some independently specifiable good ends; they are also (at least oftentimes) valuable in themselves. On this point we have the testimony not only of our intuitions, which is not altogether to be despised, but also of reflection, which reveals something uncomfortably close to a paradox; if we think of families *exclusively* as *instrumental values* we greatly attenuate their ability to produce that instrumental value.[18]

The medical experience is not unique. I think of teachers struggling to get past the abstractions of grades, test results, and standardized descriptions. In describing a nontraditional classroom for children, a teacher reports,

> Candice knows that the challenge of teaching does not involve finding the "right" practice to apply to all situations, but finding ways to challenge the multiple views of her students. Our experiment, of course, proved to be a reminder of that and Candice found herself returning to personal and particular ways to help students collaborate. She does not passively stand by and let students "do their own thing," or coerce them into behaving as if they see the world as she does. She knows her job is to help students open the doors of learning and to do that she must find, for each student, the right keys that will unlock them.[19]

Surely any story must also be a love story. Yet it cannot be told in the old way—Dante and Beatrice, Romeo and Juliet. Love is always erotic and bodily. Even acts of charity have their sensualities as we are actually present with and to the person in need. But as Allan Bloom writes,

> Isolation, a sense of a lack of profound contact with other human beings, seems to be the disease of our time. There are great industries of psychotherapy addressing our difficulties in "relationships"—that pallid word the very timidity of which makes substantial attachments impossible. One has to have a tin ear to describe one's great love as a relationship. Did Romeo and Juliet have a relationship? . . . It is a term empty of content, implying that human connectedness can arise only out of a motiveless act of freedom. It is this contemporary condition that led me once to describe us as social solitaries. I meant by this . . . that we are lonely while living in society, with all the social needs for others yet lacking the ability to satisfy them.[20]

If feminism and gay rights have taught us anything, however, it is that loving is, even more than it once was, a coat of many colors. Despite our temptation to moralism, we have even gone a long way toward legitimizing love's variety. Less hopeful, however, is the transmutation of loving into technique—psychological technique, sexual technique. A strange dualism appears. On one side is an idea of technique that, indifferently, applies between any human beings in a relationship. In reaction, however, a superficial passionateness becomes the partner of technique. Against this cultural pattern—which does not ring true to us but in which we are trapped—loving loses its painful joys and is neutralized.

When we reduce loving to moments of sensuality and sensuality to technique, we lose those other feelings—for ourselves, for others—that loving in its more generous incarnations affords us. Thus, Nel Noddings reminds us,

> There is the joy that unaccountably floods over me as I walk into the house and see my daughter asleep on the sofa. . . . The joy I feel is immediate. . . . [But] it is something beyond the moment—a recognition of fulfillment of relatedness—that induces this joy.
>
> Must there be an object of joy? Suppose I am working in my garden or lying on the beach under a starry sky. A seedling uncovered beneath the mulch may trigger joy . . . or a shooting star may induce the feeling; but, then again, there may be no particular object of my joy. There is a sense of well-being, but more than that. I am not focusing consciousness on myself, but am aware peripherally of myself-perceiving. There is joy experienced as a real quality of the world—not as a state resulting from an appraisal of my situation in the world.[21]

Loving all too often means that we go through the motions. As a counselor, I can recall many conversations where I had the impression that my partners in the discussion were "counting coup" as a teenage boy might in a bull session with his peers or that we were going down a checklist of technical moves as an airline pilot might when taking off or landing. Uncertainty, always a fact of loving, shifts to assessments of technical effectiveness, such as the achievement of mutual orgasm and the play acting that tries to reassure the partner that he or she was indeed effective.

Caring, concerning, taking the part of, respecting, accepting, conversing, being with are technicized as well. Nothing reveals this more than the decay of the idea of friendship. We regard each other with the skeptic's eye, even the cynic's eye. A vocabulary of manipulation marks that decay. Friendships are identified with utility, as in political friendships and business friendships. When friendship is unconditioned, as some relationships can still be, there lurks in the background a question: "Am I being fooled? Is this real? Is there a hidden agenda?" Even friendships that do not look to utility become superficial or anxious. We teach the lessons of this transformation of friendship very early. I think of the deep, if not abiding, friendships made by the teenagers I have known. Yet we manage to corrupt these as well by advising the young to make the "right" connections, which will "pay off" later in life. School and university alumni industries exploit this transformation as forms of academic marketing. As we say, "It's who you know" that makes all the difference.

The world of routines is not a friendly place. Indeed, such a world cannot abide a friendly place, ought not to be a friendly place. The market values competition, ambition, advancement. Self-interest and mobility are the key. Time, a requirement of friendship, is filled with busyness, distractions, and the common complaint is "I don't have time." Space is moved through, moved to and from, is not lived in or enjoyed as. The tyranny of the clock and the schedule is omnipresent. Sacrificed are those connections that do not pretend to utility. At last, the telephone becomes a strained way of sustaining friendship at a distance. Distant intimacy has reached its end. The Humanist story has its villain.

CHARACTER

The characters in the Humanist story go up against the world as it actually is. In that going-against, it becomes a story of heroism, even of rebellion. Of course, the older and nearly forgotten Humanist narratives were stories of heroism too. Prometheus stole the fire of the gods. The revolutionary and the reformer stood against the world as it was. But the modern hero or heroine finds a more insidious enemy. The more obvious enemies of the modern age are only reminders of past struggles once more renewed. Thus, the battle with fundamentalism and nihilism is familiar, almost ritualistic. But the modern battle is ultimately located in the struggle against exteriority. But since exteriority is within me, the battlefield is within me too.

In exploring the character of the Humanist hero or heroine, the modern narrative becomes a story of ways of being for oneself and with another in a world of pseudointimacies. The ethical center of Humanism is reincarnated as a response to the way the world works against the ethical in the name of the efficient.[22] The terms of moral character are familiar enough—terms like *dignity, responsibility, magnanimity*. Each is a mode of innerness, a way of being in oneself. At the same time each is a mode of connection, a way of being with another. Finally, each is a mode of existence, a way of being in the world.

Fear and doubt are unavoidable, as are disappointment, failure, and defeat. Experience is shaped, too, by unexpected opportunity, although this is too easily forgotten in the face of overwhelming sadness or horror. A sense of humor, then, is a requirement for the humanist hero or heroine. It is ontological and not only historical or situational. Finally, the very notion of heroism entails a certain freedom. Neither a puppet nor a stone can be heroic, can go against.

In facing against exteriority, dignity becomes a central theme. But now it is transformed from a moral directive into a feature of intimacy. It is in this sense that

> worth is a correlate of dignity. It delivers the message of self respect. . . . When I conceive myself as a being of whom worth can be predicated, then through my motives, choices, and actions I am uniquely presented to the world. This presence is active, a presentation and not merely another name for the existence of an object. . . . Worth signals a special claim on my attention as dignity signals a special limitation on my action. Things may be treated as instances of categories, e.g. chairs, clouds, stars. We can even pretend a momentary blindness when we subsume persons under functional heading as when we deal with store clerks, toll takers, bus drivers, voters. But the attribution of dignity and worth tells us that we are using a "convenient fiction" and we forget that to our peril. We may treat persons statistically as if they were objects, but only temporarily and in "fear and trembling."[23]

Dignity is a demand for respect. A failure of respect works to convince me of my unworthiness, that being dealt with as lacking dignity is justified. I am taught the lessons of obedience to my betters. On a theological scale, for example, I was legitimately humbled. My freedom—a correlate of dignity—was an invitation to sin. Indeed, the misfortunes that attended my life were justified as "God's plan" even where, as often happened, that plan was unknowable. The Book of Job might well be its metaphor as God and Satan gamble cynically over Job's piety, although the game is fixed on all sides. Satan must lose, and Job cannot do anything to change the situation of which he must be ignorant in any case. Even where, in a final trial of his dignity, Job dares to challenge the universe itself for its injustice, the reply is demeaning. Out of the whirlwind, God answers Job with a naked assertion of power. In the end, Job accepts his situation and in that acceptance is "saved."

To the struggle for dignity, however, we now add the subversion within. Dignity, after all, presumes personal identity, and this is precisely what is problematic in a world marked by intimacy at a distance. As I am absorbed in roles and routines, I cease to be for myself, and I cease to be with others. Much as I struggle against this nonbeing, I always lose. I am indeed Sisyphus; there is always that same mountain to climb. At the same time—and this is the terrifying irony of the modern situation—I learn the rewards of surrender. Sisyphus, as Camus remarks ironically, is "happy." The modern world is an increasingly comfortable place to be. I am, as it were, invited to live in a cushioned slavery. To insist on my dignity, then, is to be ungrateful, and the struggle sooner or later seems to me to be not only pointless but a social, political, and economic impertinence. As we say, we "get along" by "going along" as citizens, workers, parents, students.

The temptation of the "it" is the obstacle encountered by the Humanist hero or heroine. The battle, then, is felt as resistance within, as overcoming, as asserting, as insisting. It is the inner life that is at stake, and the real enemy is to be found there. Exteriority, in other words, has been "internalized," and so the struggle to expel it is "internalized" too as a personal struggle.

Of course, there are public conditions that feed indignity, and these must still be combated: the struggle for human rights, for a decent public welfare, for a good education. Intimacy does not call for me to close myself away inside myself. But I cannot forget the fact that these conditions and relationships are implanted within and so cannot be exorcised by a merely public victory.

The question becomes, then, How shall I live as a dignified human being? Fortunately, although a cushioned slavery appeals to me, I am stubborn and contrary. For all that my inner life is shaped by powers not my own, it is never entirely captured by them. I break through, often without wanting to, which is both exhilarating and frightening. The human being resists, and it is with this resistance that the Humanist hero or heroine of our narrative is armed. There are limits, then, to violation, no matter how skilled, comfortable, and alluring violation may be. In fact, the very things we despair of in each other—our contrariness, our refusal to agree, our annoying habit of doing the "wrong" thing, our "irrational" willingness to go against our interests—is precisely the locus of dignity in the modern condition. In a strange way, therefore, terrorism, crime, and insanity exhibit the darker sides of dignity. Thus, dignity becomes dangerous in the contemporary condition. The world has equipped us with destructiveness, and so my stubbornness becomes a weapon of armageddon. The Humanist narrative tells a story of the competing moral dangers embedded in the demand for dignity itself. Dignity has become ambivalent as well.

Dignity left to itself would produce a kind of Humanist insanity. Not for nothing is the rebel a figure of both adoration and anxiety. And not for nothing is nihilism welcomed as an invitation to an adventurism of egos run wild. Nor is this merely some literary game. Its model is the urban rioter who destroys his or her neighbors and himself or herself too in a deadly demand for dignity.

The struggle for dignity is balanced by the assumption of responsibility. Typically, responsibility has been understood as a relationship of duty between persons or between persons and some collective like the church, the state, the corporation, or the family. I am responsible if I do my duty. It is a feature of moral agency in which "I" act out moral relationships in accordance with some directive and in some kind of arena. At its most austere, obligation has been understood as willing to do one's duty for the sake of duty alone. As Immanuel Kant put it,

> [Thus the first proposition of morality is that to have moral worth an action must be done from duty.] The second proposition is: An action done from duty does not have its moral worth in the purpose which is to be achieved through it. . . . Its moral value, therefore, does not depend on the reality of the object of the action but merely on the principle of volition by which the action is done without any regard to the objects of the faculty of desire. . . . The third principle, as a consequence of the two preceding, I would express as follows: Duty is the necessity of an action done from respect for the law.[24]

The nonpersonality of the Kantian goodwill, however, deteriorates under modern conditions into a going through the motions, even if they are morally good motions. Duty today is not defined by Kant's "law," which is the law the moral person gives to himself or herself and which the moral person discovers in consequence of the fact that he or she is rational. Typically, then, what began with the Enlightenment project as an effort to democratize morality now becomes another feature of exteriority. We tend to look outside ourselves to rules of conduct, which are by no means equivalent to moral law. For example, professional ethics is identified with agreed-to codes of professional conduct. Enforcement, where available at all, is a matter of punishment. Responsibility, then, is transformed into prudence—not to be caught, not to be sanctioned—which was precisely what Kant was trying to avoid by excluding consequences from moral assessment. To be sure, the resort to the impersonal "will" and to the moral "law" invited this modern transmutation.

For the modern hero or heroine, then, responsibility must be returned to the self, must be a felt responsibility, a "sense" of responsibility as we sometimes put it. To be sure, this makes responsibility less dependable than either the outcome of obeying the maxims of a rational will or avoiding violations of a code of conduct. Yet as our litigiousness surely tells us, neither maxim nor code works very well. Typically, a "scandal"—

say, students' cheating on examinations or lawyers admitting to perjury—stirs our ethical interest. We respond by strengthening the code, passing another law, increasing the punishments, even adding an ethics course to professional training. When our interests shift, a new scandal waits in the wings. The process is repeated.

A turn to innerness relocates responsibility within character, and this forces an unintended tension. The hero or heroine of our narrative exhibits a sensibility in which dignity and responsibility conflict not simply with indignity and irresponsibility but with each other. To the stubbornness that exhibits my dignity, I counterpose the responsibility that recognizes the stubbornness of others. The encounter is imagined in self-reflection and felt as genuinely interpersonal. Obedience, even to my own law-giving capacity, is replaced by accounting for as well as accounting to myself. Put another way, responsibility means that I must take account of my presence in the presence of other presences. I cannot assert myself as if I lived by myself. Responsibility then reveals sociability, which shapes who I am and what I must do.

Unfortunately, dignity and responsibility, left in uneasy conflict with each other, turn character into a battleground of ambiguities. The past took these as unalloyed moral goods. Their expression under modern conditions appears as the threat of rebellion and the conventionality of duty. Moral failure is inevitable too, and this is not so much a fact of the confrontation of good and evil but of the confrontation of good with good, of virtue with virtue. Always a difficulty of the moral life, that confrontation has now become typical. It is the moral dilemma that is more likely to be met than the moral crusade. Indeed, the effort to become crusaders again, the fundamentalist temptation on all sides, becomes understandable precisely as a response to the pains of the moral dilemma. Hence, too, the surrender of efforts to make moral sense when the choice between goods must force us to deny some good, in other words, to do evil.

Faced with the inevitability of moral failure, the narrative of innerness calls for magnanimity. C. P. Snow wrote:

> I said previously that magnanimity is in action a simple virtue, but that its roots are complicated. One of those roots is love, or compassion, or charity, or brotherhood, whatever one likes to call the glue which binds us together. Another is that sense of reality which is also part of humor. And another, I think, is a special sort of vanity: the vanity that makes us want to behave better than we naturally should. Don't be frightened of the word. We come from the earth, and the origins of human excellence are often a bit murkier than we expect. There are two opposing vanities which we have all noticed in ourselves: one is the vanity

of self-regard—when we look into ourselves, fall in love with our own guilt and squalor, and are satisfied to stay in it. The other is the vanity which tries to make us better. In a book of mine, a character speaking for me, says: "I want a man who knows something about himself. And is appalled. And has to forgive himself to get along."[25]

So much is conflicted, ambiguous, hidden. A certain gentleness and generosity of spirit is therefore called for. But as we know, to our sadness, we are hardly generous with each other. Of course, we may be overly generous to ourselves except that anxiety, guilt, and superficiality suggest that this generosity does not serve. We "forgive" neither others nor ourselves. Not least of all, moral blindness serves as our defense, and we demonstrate this blindness by our conversion of the moral into the prudential, the operational, the legal, and the technical. If, under a secular inspiration, failure is no longer equivalent to sin, it still remains the fault least forgiven among us. Not to succeed—at whatever task is imposed—is to warrant dismissal, whether in classroom or in politics or in business, or in family and friendship. Again, our cushioned slavery makes failure—not to be "with it," not to "make it"—tolerable only in the sense that dismissal does not entail the actual exile of being marooned, starved. But not to succeed morally is to be exiled in another way. It is to be thrust out of one's self and to make the final surrender to exteriority.

NOTES

1. Alisdair MacIntyre, *After Virtue* (Notre Dame, Ind.: University of Notre Dame Press, 1981), p. 112.

2. Vaclav Havel, "The New Measure of Man," *New York Times*, July 8, 1994.

3. It was Hegel, of course, who seized upon this Enlightenment theme and took it to the extreme of "objective idealism," that is, the working out of Reason through history. Marx took the Hegelian recommendation and reworked it as a theory of political economy and social revolution.

4. John Dewey, *The Influence of Darwin on Philosophy and Other Essays in Contemporary Thought* (New York: Holt, Rinehart and Winston, 1910), p. 19 (italics added).

5. Dennis Farney, "Natural Questions: Chaos Theory Seeps into Ecology Debate Stirring up a Tempest," *Wall Street Journal*, July 11, 1994, p. A8.

6. For example, see Riane Eisler, *The Chalice and the Blade* (New York: HarperCollins, 1989).

7. Robert Bellah et. al., *Habits of the Heart* (New York: Harper & Row, 1985), p. 38.

8. It is not necessary to follow Jungian psychology (and metaphysics) (e.g., ideas of "race memory") in order to appreciate the continuing and the permanent call of myth and story. Nor need we grow mysterious about the reasons. For an insightful, readable, and unpretentiously sophisticated view of the matter, see Robert Coles, *The Call of Stories* (Boston: Houghton Mifflin, 1989).

9. Andrew Greeley, "Because of the Stories," *New York Times Magazine*, July 10, 1994, p. 40.

10. Stow Persons, *Free Religion* (New Haven, Conn.: Yale University Press, 1947), pp. 22–23.

11. In the most interesting of these letters Jefferson creates an imagined dialogue between the "head" and the "heart," the struggle of the lover to deal with reason's judgment and passion's drive. See *The Portable Jefferson*, ed. Merrill D. Peterson (New York: Penguin, 1975), pp. 400–412.

12. Jurgen Habermas, *The Theory of Communicative Action*, vol. 2: *Lifeworld and System: A Critique of Functionalist Reason*, trans. Thomas McCarthy (Boston: Beacon Press, 1987), p. 325.

13. Hans-Georg Gadamer, *Reason in the Age of Science*, trans. Frederick G. Lawrence (Cambridge, Mass.: MIT Press, 1990), pp. 100–101.

14. Robert Carter, "Becoming Bamboo: Languages of Diversity" (paper presented at the Conference of the Association for Moral Education, Toronto, Canada, November 1992), pp. 3–4.

15. William James, *Some Problems of Philosophy* (London: Longmans, Green and Co., 1948), p. 50.

16. Nietzsche, *The Birth of Tragedy*, trans. Francis Golffing (Garden City, N.Y.: Doubleday Anchor Books, 1956), p. 94.

17. John Dewey, *Individualism Old and New* (New York: Capicorn, 1962), pp. 67–68.

18. James Lindemann Nelson, "Taking Families Seriously," *Hastings Center Report* 22, no. 4 (July–August, 1992): 7.

19. Theresa A. Thorkildsen, "Establishing a Moral Atmosphere in School: Don't Forget to Listen!" (paper presented at the Conference of the Association for Moral Education, Toronto, Canada, November 1992), p. 13.

20. Alan Bloom, "The Death of Eros," N*ew York Times Magazine*, May 23, 1993, p. 27.

21. Nel Noddings, *Caring: A Feminine Approach to Ethics and Moral Education* (Berkeley: University of California Press, 1984), pp. 137–138.

22. Modern moral theory, victimized by analytic dogma, has denied itself the benefits of experience, focusing instead on the uses of moral language and the logic of alternative meta-ethical groundings. There were, to be sure, advantages to be gained from this turn of ethical thought. We are more careful about our assumptions and communications than we once were, although at times an overscrupulous concern for precision blocks the hunch, the intuition, the vaguer intimations of possible insights from which ethical thinking has always benefited.

With the development of what is called applied ethics—in business, medicine, the law, moral education—a healthy relationship between ethics and actual practice appears. Substantive moral discussion is now permissible in a way that it was not for a long long time. A new moral literature is beginning to appear, of which "virtue ethics" is but one example.

23. Howard B. Radest, "Companionship (A Metaphor for Humanism)," *Humanism Today*, no. 4 (1988): 69.

24. Kant, *Critique of Practical Reason*, trans. and ed. Lewis White Beck (Chicago: University of Chicago Press, 1949), p. 61.

25. C. P. Snow, "On Magnanimity," *Harper's Magazine* 225, no. 1346 (July 1962): 41.

7

THE POLITICS OF SOCIABILITY

WORDS AND ACTS

To recapture the Enlightenment project is to restore intimacy to sociability, to have "bifocal" vision, as my teacher and colleague Joseph Blau once remarked. Personal presence is essential in order to establish the Enlightenment against its enemies, so I have explored the various ways of attending to the subject. This is not just a matter of increasing our accuracy in describing the particulars. Our technology makes detail accessible and comprehensive but still impersonal. The mood of attention must shift. *I* must attend.

A passion for subjectivity is typical of twentieth-century art and literature, philosophy and religion. But much of that passion reduces subjectivity to "canned" performances and the relativism of "it's all a matter of taste." This exposes the danger of our strategies for combating exteriority: the public life will be neglected. Anxiously, I reduce what counts to the merely personal or else surround myself with a barrier that keeps out the rest of the world. Since I cannot really live alone, however, I turn sociability into a "bounded mutuality."[1] The person who is beyond the boundary remains utterly alien and apart. I neither understand him or her nor want to. If he or she approaches me, I grow suspicious, even hostile. At the extreme, I develop an absolutist "multiculturalism." Respectfulness for persons as such—the genius of the Enlightenment's egalitarianism—surrenders to intimate connections narrowly conceived and human solidarity vanishes. Life-worlds become fortresses.

This development of separated life-worlds and a fragmented common world has disastrous results: the personal turns into self-defeating egoism; the public becomes an arena of corruptions and manipulations. In between, resurrected clans and tribes build the illusion of safety by encasement. The ordinary villainies of the public life—violence, bribery, thievery, and the like—are by no means absent in the modern age. Corruptions of a different kind develop too; they appear as insidious corruptions. For example, we come to believe that the system has its own imperatives, which are thought to be morally neutral (as gravitation is morally neutral). In the name of technicism—efficiencies and the like—we are prepared to perform and to tolerate behaviors that under other conditions would be abhorrent. Speaking at the World Economic Forum in February 1992, Vaclav Havel, president of Czechoslovakia, warned:

> We have to abandon the arrogant belief that the world is merely a puzzle to be solved. . . .
>
> . . . The way forward is not in the mere construction of universal systemic solutions to be applied to reality from the outside; it is also in seeking to get to the heart of reality through personal experience.[2]

Our language is neutralized too. For example, we talk of corporate downsizing, and so blind ourselves to the fact that this means the unemployment of thousands of people. Indeed, to call attention to the fact behind the word is to invite the sneering accusation of being a "kneejerk" liberal or "do-gooder" or, more charitably, an "economic illiterate." A paraphernalia of "scientific" language masks the interests at work. As John Kenneth Galbraith writes,

> Reputable or, as it is often called, mainstream economics has for some centuries given grace and acceptability to convenient belief—to what the socially and economically favored most wish or need to have believed. . . .
>
> There were and are three basic requirements. One is the need to defend the general limitation on government as regards the economy; there must be a doctrine that offers a feasible presumption against government intervention. . . .
>
> The second . . . is to find social justification for the untrammeled uninhibited pursuit and possession of wealth. . . . There is need for demonstration that the pursuit of wealth or even less spectacular well-being serves a serious, even grave social purpose. . . .
>
> The third need is to justify a reduced sense of public responsibility for the poor. Those so situated . . . must, in some very real way, be seen as the architects of their own fate.[3]

We grow used to advancing nonmoral reasons for our conduct even where that conduct might be morally praiseworthy. In fact, we are cultural cynics, suspicious of any effort to assign a moral motivation to a public act. We find in our roles reasons for acting as objects toward other objects. This abdication of the personal also opens the door to the unscrupulous who are defined as those who know how to work the system. They use moral neutralization to perfect old villainies and invent new ones.

Intimacy becomes a shriveled intimacy. I learn to live two lives. But even as I leave the public space behind—the workplace, the polling booth, the market—I carry it with me into home and friendship. The habits of manipulation, busyness and role playing are internalized. Even my "leisure" becomes organized, frantic, and busy.[4] To be sure, the antique languages of intimacy (e.g., tradition and myth) include moral values. But these languages become simply moralistic and ineffective in meeting the world as it is.

Not for nothing, then, is there a widely shared cultural dismay. It arises not only from the apparent disasters of modern experience but also from the frustration of moral helplessness. For example, "family values" are "rediscovered" by public figures on all sides, and draconian measures are proposed in order to impose those values. Yet juvenile crime increases. The number of one-parent families rises, and a majority of our children will, at some time or other, live in such families. Births to unwed teenagers are epidemic. And a pattern of welfare dependency now reaches across the generations. Solutions drawn on the basis of moralistic judgments, however, scarcely touch these problems. Indeed, they cannot, for the public world marches to its own operational and functional tune. Little wonder, then, that moralism finally invites us to enter saved enclaves that pretend to be immune to the immoralities of the world.

Fundamentalists, however, are not the only ones who withdraw into the secured past or the hidden-away enclave. The "liberal" pulpit, like its conservative partner, abdicates its prophetic role. I need only recall the voices of the 1930s or the 1960s with their passion for social justice in order to establish the comparison. Indeed, today's pulpit is more likely to concern itself with a "saved" community and a psychologized self. I recall the condemnation of Vice President Quayle's invocation of family values when he criticized TV's single mother, Murphy Brown, during the 1992 presidential campaign. But to the amusement of the right, liberals soon discovered family values too. Forgotten was the fact that the family of American nostalgia was not necessarily a good family in which to live—at least not for many women and children.[5]

It is clear enough that moralism is satisfying. It feels good to condemn the unrighteous. Thus, the religious right—which may be said to have the only viable politics around—has, in its own uncharitable terms, evolved a politics that surrenders sociability to exclusiveness. It is erected on the narrowed grounds of a life-world that has as its mission the conversion of the rest of us to its specifications or, failing that, the exclusion of the rest of us from civil and not just cosmic society. To be sure, in meeting the needs for electoral success, the religious right occasionally mutes its theological message. For example, Jews and others are invited to join the Christian Coalition as it seeks the allegiance of "40 million evangelicals."[6] Leaving the safety of the pulpit and the pew, fundamentalist candidates are elected to school boards, local government offices, and the like in growing numbers. Once they are in power, the message—"pro-life," "creationism," prayer in the schools, a "Christian nation"—rediscovers its faith.

The Humanist response is a call for insulating religion from politics, thus confusing the institutional issue of the separation of church and state with the legitimate use of religious (and other) values in the public arena. The problem is the absence of countervailing faith. At the same time, it is predictable that we will witness a growing conflict between life-worlds as others discover the benefits of sectarianism or else have to defend themselves against its invasion. Holy war in modern guise is not unthinkable, although, initially at least, it is more likely to be waged in the media and the courts than in the streets. As is already evident in the bombing of the World Trade Center and the abortion controversy, however, holy war is on the streets too. Toleration is a dying art. That is to be expected in an environment of life-world apartness and fundamentalist nostalgia.

To be sure, we seem to participate in what looks like a politics. We are urged to vote, to contribute to the candidates of our choice, to offer our opinions on this or that proposed policy, to write letters to legislators and newspapers. It would seem that we have politics enough. Yet our behaviors reveal that we do not have a politics at all, only a rather poorly played political theater.[7] The politician is an object of humor and scorn—which is traditional enough—and more and more of cynicism. Ever hopeful, we greet the latest candidate as new and different, only to find out very quickly that he or she is only more of the same. The party platform, so earnestly debated every four years, is known to be a charade. Its grand promises turn into the backroom deal, in which enough must be seen to be done—but only *seen* to be done—to keep things quiet through election time. Little wonder that the outsider is by that fact alone greeted with hope and that even insiders play the outsider game. Our recent national elections are in this sense revealing. Candidates in the past two decades from Mr. Carter to Mr. Reagan, Mr. Bush, and Mr. Clinton have worked very hard to convince a majority of us to "vote against Washington." And in a paradigmatic instance of the strange contradictions this outsider game produces, a billionaire, Ross Perot, becomes a populist hero.

Government itself becomes the villain. Compromise is reduced to a balancing act between self-centered interests. The give and get of clearly defined but partial positions to meet a common problem is forgotten. Compromise, in this constructive sense, is the political translation of the philosopher's dialectic and is, in fact, the art of democracy. Instead, dogmatism becomes our political style. It may, on occasion, be softened in the name of temporary accommodation, but the positions remain fixed and only wait their moment for capturing the public life. By now, however, this show fools no one for very long.

A sense of the deterioration of politics into the alliances and confrontations of exclusive rigidities must inform our efforts to reconstruct the Enlightenment project. Its democratic radicalism shaped politics as a bridge between intimacy and sociability. The rights of man was not merely a derivation of natural law but an invitation to everyone to enjoy the personal experience of public participation. The struggle against the tradition of exclusion was fought in flesh and blood and passion. Declarations and documents only put the period to revolution and gave it voice. In our current usage, the American Revolution has become a respectable and a conservative symbol. By skeptics it is interpreted as only another instance of interest group politics—as the interest of the colonists in competing with the British for economic success. It was, as the critic of right or left says, in praise or complaint, a "bourgeois revolution."

We use traditional myth in order to forget. Ritualistic reference to the American Revolution remains, but loyalty to its content is missing. Indeed, those who take its message of liberty and equality seriously are unwelcome. For example, in current popular discourse, a defense of civil liberties is somehow taken for socialism by the right and sexism or racism by the left. The Bill of Rights would have hard going in a popular referendum.

A politics of sociability is an inclusive, participatory, and personal activity. The emphasis of such a politics is on personal action against a world where action is channeled into nonpersonal functions. In this way, participation is recovered from a reality that has reduced it to programmed gestures like financial contributions, the employment of surrogates, and the ritual of watching things happen at a distance. Only derivatively is this personal participation in the public life a confrontation with the enemies of the Enlightenment. The political task is essentially cultural, the incarnation of a generous image of human beings and their capacities, and is not merely partisan or activist.

The "children" of the Enlightenment seem to take the Gospel according to John almost literally. "In the beginning," he said, "was the word." Today we would no doubt substitute the "media," but the point is the same. Of course, there are explanations for our logophilia. We have been tutored by declarations and manifestos, so much so that we seem to believe that saying makes it so and that a good argument is a sufficient cause. We have been taught as well by our contractual democracy to believe that passing a law ends the matter. And now, invited to be eyewitness to reality without pain or fear—the war in Vietnam or TV taught us that—we have also learned that even the bloodiest of actions can be abstract and safe. But words are not deeds, laws are not self-enforcing, and what we see on TV is not safe for those who are actually present. The "word" thus reinforces both our ambivalence and our anxiety.

The reality of politics is doing and making—being an actor and not an observer. Promises, speeches, and platforms can be instruments of action. Today, however, political language only sounds as if it means something but is more like noise or static. Only rarely do we pay attention to the language of politics. I think of exceptions like Lincoln's Gettysburg Address, Roosevelt's First Inaugural, Kennedy's Inaugural. But on the whole, we have learned to be deaf to the political message that seems to come at us in the same way indifferently from left and right. In turn, the message is reduced to sound bites and photo opportunities—minimal imagist signals. This both serves the needs of exteriority and justifies us in using the dumbness of politics as another defense against it. Most of us retreat into a-politicality. But politics—even in its truncated existence today—is still a form of power. It still gets in the way of the value-neutral ideal of technicism and even exposes its pretense. This increases our anxiety even more. After all, we buy into the benefits of the value-neutral arena and have been taught the risks of subverting it.

To achieve a politics of sociability, we need to reconstruct our habits; the political task remains educational. Once again, we arrive at the need to subvert what we have learned from the shadow enlightenment. It has taught us to move from the general to the particular, the theory to the event, the collectivity to the person. More disastrously, it has taught us to substitute the former for the latter. By contrast, intimacy inheres in sociability. The personal act becomes the ground of a renewed politics. In Goethe's words,

'Tis writ: In the Beginning was the word.
Right here I'm blocked! Who now will help afford?
A Word can't possibly so high be rated;
This must be differently translated.
If by the spirit I am rightly taught,
'Tis writ: In the Beginning was the Thought!
Consider well the first line's ending,
Let not your pen to undue haste be tending!
Does Thought create and shape things hour by hour?
I read: In the Beginning was the Power!
Yet even while I write I'm warned and falter,
That even this I must in some way alter.
—This spirit aids! Illumined, I proceed
And write, "In the Beginning was the Deed![8]

Of course, words have their uses. I am not counseling a reduction of intelligence to grunts and gestures. When I "act," I am a minded and mindful being. I weave ideas, judgments, choices, responses, sensitivities, and connections into my biography. In doing this, I mark myself off from objects and things that have a record but not a story. And as a "rational" animal—for I do not surrender my love of reason—I take the "act" seriously when I embed thinking itself in the complicated business of thinking-doing-feeling.

Unfortunately, however, when I hear the word *act*, my attention turns only outward. Acts deteriorate into activism. I mobilize a machinery of cause and effect, look for results and efficiencies. I think of social action, of reform, above all, of organization. I remember the causes I embraced—so many causes in a lifetime. I dance a minuet of left and right. An army of habits is triggered by the word *act*. In the mind's eye, I see petitions and votes and resolutions and debates. I remember marches and demonstrations and all the paraphernalia attendant upon the powers of the world. Yet these tangibilities all too easily turn me into a creature of collectivities and anonymities. Typically, then, I am captured by the "we" and the "they." All of this action is apart from me even when I am present. But then, "I" am not expected to be present. My "private" person—I easily fall into the habit of thinking of myself as a private person playing a public role—is insulated, untouched. So I do what I must do—or better, what it is said that I must do—and go home still disconnected. Even as I debate, argue, attack, defend, I hold aloof. I discover that social action can as easily be a hiding place as a commitment.

So I have to start further back in order to reconnect intimacy and society. I must "own" and own up to my public conduct. In saying this, I am also saying that, for a Humanist, intimacy cannot be reduced to the merely reflective or even the merely interpersonal. A Humanism of the act grounds a politics sociability. My acts emerge from my loves and hopes and dreams and, in turn, reshape them. In that way, my acts are "authentic," as the existentialist might say. They are tokens of my character even as they shape and reshape my character. I am reminded of Felix Adler's motto, "In the attempt to change others, we must inevitably change ourselves." An act, therefore, is in its nature intimate and sociable all at once.

AN ACT IS . . .

An act is a center of personal energies that joins me to the world and the world to me. With an act, I also break into the world, but that, in turn, opens me up to the world. An act is not then simply a transfer of intention from inside to outside, not simply the execution of a plan, and not simply aimed at a product, an outcome. Much as it is aimed at changing a situation, an act is both existential and purposive. Indeed, the intention that seems to initiate the act grows and changes precisely as act turns into action. Means, in other words, penetrate ends and remake them. An act is simultaneously an exhibition, an expression, a connection, a celebration—and only finally an action. An act conveys far more than the simplicities of means and ends. It is an aesthetic, emotional, and moral event in my life. Of course, an act is also a response to the person in pain, the society in turmoil, the dream turned nightmare. Less sadly, it is also a response to the warmth of the lover, the friendliness of the colleague, the work of the creator. Above all, an act verifies my being as a subject and not an object. Even the hesitation that accompanies an act tells of my being. Things do not hesitate, do not fear, do not hope. Things behave, persons act.

Exhibition

An act exhibits me. With that, I realize that the sharp line between words and acts is blurred. I need not make an exclusive choice between them. I have remarked, however, that words in the modern condition take me away from myself and into a world of abstractions. Language, in other words, appears to us as a relatively autonomous world—a world of interactive signals where the person is only a transmitter and, as technology is perfected, a dispensable one. I watch the clerk at the supermarket checkout counter. He or she passes a computer code across a laser reading device. Item, quantity, and price are automatically printed on the receipt. At the same time, inventory, cost, and income are recorded in a central data bank for use by management. To all intents and purposes, the motion of the clerk's arm is all that is left for the person to do.

But automatism does not exhaust the possibilities of language. Language also serves as personal expression and interpersonal connection. Thus, the distinction between a set of directions and a poem, between a "standard operating procedure" and a personal response to the situation, between a memorandum and a personal letter. My speech can indeed be a transfer of meanings between us, but this can be a set of abstract signals between mechanisms or a form of reaching toward and of being reached by. Speech, in the public arena and in the personal life, can also be a "speech-act," a type of doing.[9] Whatever else speech may be, it is a type of revelation of myself to myself and to others. After all, words can hurt or help, build or destroy, teach or mislead. In this sense, "words" perform and do not only express or signify or isolate. They perform as personal commands, criticisms, insults, invitations, approvals, and they also convey moods and tonalities. My accent, my choice of words, my subject matter tell my story too, as do my movements and manipulations and silences. At the same time, personal speech is easily sublimated as in general directives, common names, job descriptions. I can tune out speech. Indeed, just because I can tune out, the modern aesthetic grows louder and more shrill in an attempt to capture attention, to break in. "Rock" becomes "hard rock" and "heavy metal." I manage, however, to raise the threshold of my indifference; my deafness grows.

In an act, I show myself to be an energetic animal. Unlike the fall of a stone or the motion of a planet, however, my act has a trajectory that is not dictated by the forces acting upon me. Indeed, aware of these forces, I resist—I am contrary—and so exhibit in yet another way that I am who I am. I do not simply go along with events and powers, even those that seem to be working on my side. Autonomy, which I demonstrate by my stubbornness, is as important to me as achievement and reward. As I say, "I'd rather do it myself." And even if I am a stoic, admitting that in some circumstances I can only be done to, this is itself a decision to acquiesce. I act upon and against. With that, I am seen to have feelings, commitments, concerns, interests, hopes. Try as I might to hide myself, I stand out like the swimmer against the current. Indeed, as a human being, I am often seen to go against, which is why Prometheus is a Humanist ideal or why talk of ends and judgments and responsibilities, none of which can be said of objects and mechanisms, makes sense. An act exhibits me as a different kind of natural being.

An act connects me to myself and to others across space and time. It arises out of what I have done and whom I have done to. As I act, I engage with myself and with others. Even in acts that seem to disconnect—as in revolution and withdrawal—I presume connection. Revolution, after all, is action against oppressive connection; isolation, after all, is action against trivializing connection. Rebel and hermit, then, depart the world that merely is, but in the departure they shape the manner of their going by their rejections and transvaluations. So, paradoxically, in their acts, rebel and hermit are exhibiting connection just by breaking it.

An act is latent with meanings. In those meanings, an act differentiates me, identifies me as I am and as I was and as I will be. An act, in other words, exhibits "me" in the making, catches me at a moment but in that catching reveals the me that is happening. When I say that I am a child of the Enlightenment, I am making a specific claim that goes backward and forward in time. I am telling you about the shape of my acts and so about their meanings and my future—unless, that is, I do not mean what I say or, more accurately, I do not "do" what I "say." In that case, my saying is really emptied of meaning, at best an exchange of words for words, and so not really a saying at all. My doing becomes only a movement among movements, at best a reaction.

What then is an example of a Humanist act? I talk about respect and concern for all human beings, including myself. Yes, I talk of *all* human beings. I use words like *dignity* and *worth*, and that is an act of calling attention to and announcing an expectation of. But when I come to give dignity its content, I find the doing of it much more difficult than the saying of it. In the act, dignity is painful. I must exhibit my acknowledgment of an actual other. I must make way for, allow space for, an actual other. That requires me to hold back, to accept restriction. Nor is this simply a matter of moral rules and lawful commands and proper arguments—like "do no harm" or "honor thy father and mother." These, after all, allow me to transfer the personal act for which I am responsible to the collective activity—of the state, the law, the society, the church—where I can be safely anonymous. These even tempt me to praise anonymity in the name of objectivity.

An act is a test of my faithfulness. Dignity, after all, asks me to respect even the unpleasant and evil other. It asks me to account for my own dignity and so to take account of my own unpleasantness and even evil. I must listen carefully to myself and another, which is never easy. Inattention, in other words, is an affront to dignity, so I perfect the appearance of attention—the social graces, as we say. I am, however, much more likely to rush to expression, which in its noisiness is a way of suppression. Feminists, for example, are right to call attention to the way boys and girls participate differently in the classroom and to judge the relative silence and lack of teacher recognition of the girls as an instance of suppression. I am much more likely to enjoy the sound of my own voice, so I do not listen as the parent does not listen to the child, the teacher to the student, the leader to the voter. I am much more likely then to surrender dignity in face of its demands and its discomforts. This surrender is quickly given its reasons: "they aren't ready" or "they don't know" or "they aren't worthy." But that betrays my claim to honor the dignity of another.

Of course, I have my likes and dislikes; I am, after all, not a saint. Deafened by my likes and dislikes, however, dismissal of another becomes easy. It is possible, then, to violate the dignity of loved one and of enemy alike and for the same reason. My child, for example, is so precious that I put myself between him or her and the world. My act is a form of protection against the world. Or my enemy is so despicable that I put myself between him or her and the world. My act is a form of protection for the world. Yet the putting myself between is an act of replacement and so an act of dismissal. The other—loved one or enemy—is not granted the stature of his or her acts, is reduced to an object.

Indeed, dismissal exhibits a greater disregard of dignity than opposition, anger, disagreement, criticism. In dismissing you, I empty you of being, literally make you ineligible for dignity or at least doubtful of your dignity. I also teach, in the act of dismissal, the legitimacy of your eventual indifference to me. I model it for you. As it were, I prepare the way for my own indignity. So,

> recognition has to be mutual. . . . One can make this clear by means of a simple example that everyone has experienced. One of the most external ways of showing honor is greeting someone. Who is not familiar with that unpleasant feeling when one greets someone and the other indifferently looks right past one, whether because of our having mistaken the person or whether it is because the other does not want to acknowledge one? To have uttered a greeting in vain is an experience in which one's sense of self momentarily breaks down.[10]

Each of us can verify this subversion of dignity, a subversion made all the more painful by the moral democracy that the Enlightenment project had promised. Each of us has been another for someone else and so has known what it was like to be ignored, dismissed. I ceased to count, which pained me far more than accusation or anger or even punishment. That ceasing to count, finally, exhibits the act of violating dignity.

Expression

I have powers that I enjoy and limitations that I admit, unwillingly to be sure, except when I need an alibi. In an act, I express those powers and limitations. I take the resistant stuff in me and around me and make it my own. Just as the engineer or craftsman reworks materials into something else, so I rework myself in the act. But the world is recalcitrant. I cannot, like Joshua, command the sun to stand still. I can, however, speak with you of the sunset or the constellation, and you can understand me. I can show these to you in painting and sculpture or sing of them in poem or symphony. So I embed my subjectivity in the world we share. The movement of star and planet is transformed into a presence for us. I write the love poem to my beloved but also to the universe. Unlike the standard namings of functionalism, I do not do this only once but over and over again, each time a bit differently. In the doing, I am expressed. I am both Prometheus and Sisyphus. I know that the stone runs inexorably down the mountain again after all my labors. And ultimately, when you and I and all the you's and I's to come are gone, I know that the movement of things will continue on indifferently, an ultimate recalcitrance. But something will have been lost to the world even if no one is around to mark the fact. Expression, then, is a confession of the tragic qualities that inhere in the act and so reveals the tragedy of human being.

In an act, I discover that I do for myself and to myself. When others try to do it for me or to me, I resent it because they silence me. They are usurpers, whether acting for my "good," as they so often say, or for their's, which is my suspicion. I am violated. My act, then, becomes a form of rebellion. That is exhilarating in its power and frightening in its responsibility. And it is comical too when I measure my hopes against my realities. An act catches this strange complexity of silliness and achievement all at once. In that catching up of myself, an act announces my freedom and my unfreedom.

I act intuitively, directly. I do not first wander the battlements, Hamlet-like, musing, "To be or not to be." Only later do I reflect and name and give reasons. Only after that do I invoke my metaphysical and moral vocabulary. Mistakenly, rationalism has it otherwise, sees an act as an outcome of assumptions and deliberations, tries to turn my experience Euclidian. Reason so performed tells a lie about experience. In schools, for example, we make an icon of this rationalism. We are thus taught backward—from abstraction to conduct, from rule to application. But we act forward, from conduct to abstraction. This is no small cause of our dismay at schooling and our mistrust of reason.

An act calls attention to who I am, to my character, which is expressed aesthetically and not just morally. I take on my duties, and I do not look for someone to take on what must be made my own. But I also take on my imaginings and shapings. I am a storyteller and not simply a reporter. In an act, in other words, I become for that moment who I say I am.

Just as I listen in order to exhibit my Humanism, so I pay attention in order to express my Humanism. By contrast, I am easily tempted to abstract a person from his or her being. I am adept at labels—believer, unbeliever, atheist, theist, liberal, conservative, and so on—which permit me to put the other person behind a curtain, even to put myself behind a curtain, as in taking roles and positions. Even more radically, I have been taught by exteriority to exploit abstraction, not simply to dismiss the person but to corrupt him or her. Personal freedom is transformed into the movement of objects and things. Expression then becomes self-expression—without a self.

With an act that is genuinely my own, I penetrate surfaces. Of course, that is never entirely successful, so I am almost grateful when the struggle to act is lost. I can relax. I know how easy it is to find reasons for not having acted (which is not the same as acting to remain aside "for a reason"). I also know how easy it is to find "reasons" for reacting to the requirements of role and command. I say to myself in mitigation, "If I don't do it, then someone will." I adopt, in other words, a pseudomoral algebra—use any "I" for *x*—and so evade myself. The idiocy of reason, as a skeptical Montaigne wrote long ago, is the power to play around with at least two arguable outcomes for any actual choice even after the choice is made, to turn dilemma itself into ontology and alibi. Reason all too easily becomes my Hamlet pose. In short, it is easy not to pay attention and so not to expose myself.

Connection

An act is an encounter with another and with the world. I never act alone despite the illusion that appears when individuality decays into egoism and subjectivity decays into subjectivism. I act on and with things and persons. In these encounters, I am also acted upon, and I also act upon myself. An act that seems so easily encapsulated in a boundaried description is a connection whose edges blur across time and geography. My act emerges from my character, to be sure, but my character emerges from my acts. I am shaped by the things I encounter, learning to make them my own or to be repelled by them or to be used by them. I am shaped in my encounters with parents, teachers, friends, and with so many unknown others. I am shaped in my encounters with so many imagined others as well—those met in literature and poetry and drama and dream. So an act implicates me in all of these too. I am a social animal as the Greeks had it, but sociability is more dimensioned than society. Connection is not just a matter of what is evident in cause and consequence or in a known circle of family and friends.

In an act, I am alerted to my sociability. Indeed, the act as an encounter will not let me live in the illusion of isolation. I am alerted as well to the pressure for disconnection, for building life-world into fortress. The unavoidable interdependency of the system encourages us to build fortresses in a frantic search for an interdependence of persons and not of things and functions. As a reporter wrote,

> The growth of the global economy and of more powerful transnational institutions is producing the opposite effect. Instead of fading away, nationalism is flourishing, and not just in the war-ravaged Balkans. Now even tiny groups of people can contemplate breaking away from the central state and plugging into the world economy on their own. Regions nursing ancient grievances are claiming independence, or at least autonomy, confident they aren't committing economic suicide. At the same time, the big corporations and institutions shaping the world economy seem so remote that many people turn to local ethnic groups and obscure languages for their identity, furthering the world's political fragmentation.[11]

I resist and am resisted. But where can this come from if not from another—indeed from many others? I cannot get away with solipsism despite my inability to demonstrate conclusively the existence of others and of the world. Connection, like expression, reveals itself in the tension between associating and breaking away. For all that an act is a point of personal focus, it is a diffusing event too. Like the diver who leaps into the lake, an act is both a point of attention and a center of distribution. I hesitate because the presence of another is encountered. I cannot help but be unsure of what my doing does to another or to unimagined others, nor can I be sure of how my act will be responded to. An act, I am made painfully aware, is never a by-itself, never an in-itself. An act challenges our assumption that the community we talk about so glibly these days is necessarily a welcoming relationship. Connection is as much a token of risk as of support. As Talmud puts it: if I destroy a life, it is as if I had destroyed a world, and if I save a life, it is as if I had saved a world. The actual connection with another carries a world burden since the other will, more often than not, be a stranger. By my act—my act!—a next-world is created between us; by my failure to act, a different next-world is created between us. In either case, although hardly aware of all that I have done, I cannot evade the responsibility of next-worlds. Little wonder then that I try to hide from an act by using the abstractions of role and function.

Connection, made real in its varied encounters, announces a caution. The danger of using the first-person singular appears. It is the illusion of the "I" all by itself. But I am a continuing outcome, a next-person. I acknowledge, therefore, my need for another and my being needed by another. My individuality—which is not the same as individualism—arises on the ground of my connections. Who I am emerges from my place and time, my actual world-space. I know that I would have been another person if I had emerged in another world-space, another time. An act as connection therefore leads me to grasp the play of fortune in my life. So an act carries its own cure for pride of achievement, pride of choosing, pride of doing. An act reminds, re-minds.

My individuality comes into being just because of my connections. I know myself just because I know you. If I were alone in the world—left on a desert island, let us say—I could not be an individual at all. Like the victim of sensory deprivation, I would have no character except for some echoes growing more and more indistinct of such character that was there before I was marooned. I would not notice its absence. It is just my difference from another and my presence to another that makes my identity. On a desert island, in other words, character is merely a game. I play all the parts, and none of them counts for very much. When our myths sing of God the creator, they remind us of our dependence, although we learn the lessons of dependency soon enough when hungry and cold and frightened. But they remind us that the gods need creation too. Without it, they too are unformed, characterless, ultimately empty.[12]

Celebration

An act is a celebration. When I act, I am alive. I feel joy, pleasure, satisfaction. I feel fear, pain, and frustration too. The tragedy and the comedy are never far from me. Doing, then, is a doorway to what I am. I learn over and over again that I am alive. With this knowing—which is now genuinely personal knowledge—I want to sing my embrace of it all. I want others to know my aliveness. I am typically anxious to tell a friend the good news; I look for comfort when in pain. I want others to know! Later I will find words like *community* and *empathy* to describe that embrace.

In an act, I confess that my experience is *my* experience—the dark tones and the light, the mountain and the abyss. In my embrace, I do not yield the glory to God, the pain to Satan—even to the God and Satan in me as if I were two persons. So as a child of the Enlightenment, I depart the myths of yesterday, not on the inane ground of truth and falsity—a myth is not a science—but on the pertinent ground of meaning and meaninglessness. The myths of yesterday do not tell the story of my world. In a Humanist narrative, I am, above all, of this world and not another. This is the unity of one and many that is pointed to in an act as exhibition; I show myself. It is sounded in an act as expression: I announce myself. And it is told in an act as connection: I evoke myself. At the same time, so that my subjectivity avoids the trap of subjectivism, an act is an encounter: I show myself to another, and I announce myself to another. And I am heard and seen.

With an act I celebrate that I am. So a celebration is always in the present whatever its content and no matter how long a time passes in the story it tells. Indeed, it is the magic of celebration that it brings past and future into the present. So I never quite sing the same song, tell the same story. Style and temperament are not trivial adornments. That is myth's renewal—it is not mere formula and recitation—and its renewing power. Time and space are, for that moment of celebration, annihilated. All is before me now. That is the mark of theater, of poetry, of music, of dance.

Celebration is presentness and presentation. I am now, and that calls attention to the deadliness of postponements. So I am led to the now of love and friendship and do not wait upon these after some prerequisites are met. Not for nothing are these described, ideally, as unconditioned. In an act as celebration, I learn that experience is a having and a being, not merely a marketplace of give and get.

From an act emerges the reenactment—the rite, the ritual.[13] The necessity and desirability of ritual is anathema to many Humanists. They mistake naturalism and secularity, themselves the seeds of myth and so of ritual, for matter-of-factness and secularism. In ritual, an act is reenacted, and with that all of its manifold richness is brought into the present, the now of the reenactment. But—and this is the miracle of ritual—the now of reenactment can occur over and over again, so I can remember over and over again and connect over and over again and dream over and over again. Thus, an act as reenactment becomes a way that I can share with another and another can share with me. In that sharing, absent others can be present too. Even when I am dead, I am still present in that sharing. The reenactment is thus an invitation to sociability across the boundaries of time and geography.

The issue is not between ritual and no ritual. That, alas, is the way modernist and traditionalist argue the matter. Rather, the issue is the integrity of the ritual. Does it sing my song; does it celebrate my meanings? The issue is also the aesthetic quality of the ritual. Is it beautiful or ugly; is it alive for me or merely a going through the motions? The issue is also the truthfulness—not the truth—of the ritual. Does it reenact my memories, provide an interpretation that leads out rather than shuts in? An act forces these questions upon me not once but many times. For as act succeeds act and as actors multiply, no single song will do. Reenactment, then, is also a renewal of sociability.

ACTS AND PRODUCTS

Only now do I come to the act as doing something. Of course an act aims at an achievement. When I act, I not only change the world by being present to it—invoke a next-world as I have said—but I intend to change the world in a direction and to introduce into the world that which was not there before. My act is personalized; it is always original. Although it may seem to duplicate the acts of others, it is not merely an echo. In that way, the personal act defies standardization. With the intention to do something, moreover, I move from the existential features of an act—as exhibition, expression, connection, celebration—to practice. Now the hesitations that appear are not only expressive happenings but are deliberated; the interruptions between intention and outcome are deliberate.[14] As the Hegelian and the Marxist might put it, the act is embedded in a *praxis*, a flow between the concrete situation of doing and achieving, its criticism in reflection, and the return to the concrete situation at a different point. The continuity of becoming, knowing, and doing challenges the view that theory is simply applied to practice.

Intimacy is thus not mindless. Once again I notice that the mechanistic presuppositions of the shadow enlightenment and the subjectivism of its critics are misleading. To be sure, I do not suggest that so-called abstract thinking is simply to be dismissed. It is, as John Dewey noted, the way in which deliberate interruptions between "problems" and "solutions" are structured and made useful. We are not left only at the mercy of accidental interruptions. Nor is meditation—listening to the silences—to be trivialized. But for the Humanist, these are anchored in the world by the act.

In my fascination with the mechanics of an act, however, I can easily forget that world changing is a dangerous undertaking. I fall victim to the urge to "do something," to yield to what has been called the technological imperative: if it can be done, it should be done. My failures, when acknowledged as my own, teach me the lesson of personal risk. My successes teach the same lesson, but perhaps not as quickly. I learn that no success is ever what it seems. Let time pass and doubt grows. Little wonder then, when I realize this, that I prefer the anonymity of collectives or the defense of busyness or the illusion of passivity. But next-worlds will arrive, and my presence, for or against or abstaining, will shape them. I am then unavoidably implicated in events by being present to the world even where I think I can refrain from intending anything, doing anything. Responsibility is not a matter of assumption, as in "I take responsibility for . . ." I am responsible simply because I am. Of course, in the act, I seem to take on some responsibilities and not others, but I learn that the edges between this responsibility and that are, as time passes, never sharply drawn. Experience is unkind to boundary lines. One thing leads to another. I find out that acting responsibly is inevitably an imperfect performance. Responsibility thus carries with it the assurance of limitation. Autobiography is tinged with sadness.

Conscience is thus always a troubled conscience. Without it, however, responsibility too readily becomes mere legalism and another abstraction. But conscience is not to be reduced to the voice within of a "superego," the interiorization of the external, whether it be parents or gods. For the children of the Enlightenment, conscience emerges with personal knowledge. It is, as it were, naturalized and democratized. As Erich Fromm put it,

> Humanistic conscience is not the internalized voice of an authority whom we are eager to please and afraid of displeasing; it is our own voice, present in every human being and independent of external sanctions and rewards. . . .
>
> . . . If love can be defined as the affirmation of the potentialities and the care for, and the respect of, the uniqueness of the loved person, humanistic conscience can be justly called *the voice of our loving care for ourselves*.[15]

I not only change the world but I change myself. This I scarcely intend because I think of myself as working on some external material but do not think of myself as either material or medium. Even so-called self-improvement programs exteriorize the self and rely on a manipulation of psychologized objects. Yet it is just the degree of continuity between self and medium that marks the difference between the novice and the master, whether in the arts, athletics, or anything else. Again, aesthetics instructs ethics and politics. I do change myself; it happens poorly or well, in awareness or blindly, but it happens. That next-self is thus an act's productivity too. I perform and generate next-selves as well as next-worlds. An act thrusts me into this maelstrom of makings and doings. With that, I acknowledge not just responsibility but all the fearful joyousness of creation. It is then not simply the product—which is an abstraction—but my product. Unlike the objects of industrial production, for example, my products have a signature.

Here and there in the chaos of the world a point of organization appears—temporarily—and that is where I find the product and the producer. An act is then also an act of construction, of structuring with. Even an act of naysaying provides a structure that was not there before. For all that an act is energies and changes, it is also stabilities. That is why an act's outcome can have a name.

Surely there have always been those geniuses of creation whose acts stand apart from the ordinary. Creation, after all, is the signal of poet and composer and sculptor as much as of reformer and revolutionary. Most of us, however, are not creative geniuses. We are simply ordinary. In a radical move, the Enlightenment project assigns creativity and not simply rights and duties to the human being as such. Of course, I know the difference between masterwork and routine. I seem then to be excluded from creativity not by birth and blood but by talent or lack of it. Enlightenment seems thus both to affirm and deny the very differences it celebrates precisely at the point where it is most important. It imports elitism without confessing its consequences to the Enlightenment project of doing so. Mr. Jefferson spoke of an "aristocracy of excellence" and the French *philosophe* sneered at *le canaille.*

But Enlightenment is a *project.* Democratic voices thus reveal the act of faith that is exhibited in producing and in its product. As John Dewey said of Emerson,

> In sorry truth, the idealist has too frequently conspired with the sensualist to deprive the pressing and so the passing Now of value which is spiritual. Through the joint work of such malign conspiracy, the common man is not, or at least does not know himself for, an idealist. It is such disinherited of the earth that Emerson summons to their own. "If man is sick, is unable, is mean-spirited and odious, it is because there is so much of his nature which is unlawfully withholden from him."
>
> Against creed and system, convention and institution, Emerson stands for restoring to the common man that which in the name of religion, of philosophy, of art and of morality, has been embezzled from the common store and appropriated to sectarian and class use.[16]

World generating is not simply found in the extraordinary efforts of genius. In fact, for the Enlightenment project, there is little point in the "work of art" in isolation. The work of genius is the end of a continuum. I think of the adventurous colors and shapes produced by the young child and, sadly, of their loss when convinced that art is the special province of artists. With this shift in perspective from the work of art to the act of participation, we rediscover the merit of the personal diary in our effort to remedy the aesthetic neglect of women and blacks and native peoples. We appreciate the tasteworthiness of folklore and folk music and the popular arts. Art acquires an enriched and enriching meaning. As we might say, I "make" a home; I am a friend; I do my job. I add, subtract, invent, remove, shift—and in all of this I generate a world. That is the grand democracy of an act. When, as is likely under modern conditions, this is repressed, whether in the name of genius or for other less worthy reasons, a chaos of movements replaces action, and we are returned again to the insidious corruptions of modern culture.

Among these corruptions is the habit of setting aside the work of genius in a protected and isolated space. Citing Dewey again,

> When artistic objects are separated from both conditions of origin and operation in experience, a wall is built around them that renders almost opaque their general significance, with which esthetic theory deals. Art is remitted to a separate realm, where it is cut off from that association with the materials and aims of every other form of human effort, undergoing, and achievement. . . . The task is to restore continuity between the refined and intensified forms of experience that are works of art and the every day events, doings, and sufferings that are universally recognized to constitute experience.[17]

The democracy of the act calls attention to the need to extend the creativity of the act everywhere and to expect the creativity of the act of every one. I leave something of myself, give something of myself by being and acting. Productivity departs the esoteric territory of genius and attaches to the personal response. Even the mundane world of the marketplace is transformable, although the habits of exteriority make the effort problematic.

Productivity expects humility. How often do I wish it had been otherwise, say that I did not mean it, express my regret. Yet an act teaches me that I cannot call things back. Responsibility is thus double sided: joyful and frightening. In recalling my acts, I explore my personal archaeology. In my acts, I see my character in formation. My achievement then has an ironic ring to it, for my achievement is both evanescent and stable, both self-revealing and self-altering. The next-self I see in the act and the next-world I see in the act are elusive. I cannot catch them, and when I do,

I am confronted by that which I would rather deny as well as that of which I am justly proud. For all its apparent simplicity—an act, after all, has a beginning, a middle, and an end, or so we think—an act reminds me that experience always outruns my grasp of it.

ACTS AND INSTITUTIONS

When I began, I did not expect the notion of an act to turn out so dimensioned. I had in mind a simple shift away from a Humanism of manifestos and arguments and "statements of principle." I had in mind a move toward Humanism as lived experience. Unfortunately, the more I pondered this shift, the more puzzling it appeared. I realized that the shift from word to act was not only an effort to evoke Humanist "witness," as our Protestant friends might say, or to "build a better world," as our reformer friends might say. Nor could I advocate a new age of activism. I realize, too, that notions like next-worlds and celebration would be uncomfortable for the children of the Enlightenment. As a Humanist, I am, after all, not given to these mythopoetic forms.

I have focused my excursion quite deliberately on the first-person singular in order to remedy the errors of the shadow enlightenment. Of course, I live with others, and we live by communal and social practices. The first-person singular is, in its own way, misleading, just as the "I and thou" of interpersonal relationship is misleading and the impersonality of "it" or "they" misleading. My act is embedded in institutions, is mediated by them and reconstructs them. If I am Prometheus, I do not face the gods alone, and if I am Sisyphus I have companions on my journey up and down the mountain.

Humanists, alas, have been careless of their companions and their institutions—a legacy of the deterioration of individuality into individualism. Consequently, a Humanism of the word is a lonely Humanism. But this loneliness is covered over by routines, busyness, and superficial associations. Indeed, it sometimes seems that we would do anything not to be by ourselves. When we are together, we argue, debate, talk endlessly. Missing, all too often, is simple companionship. Nor is this loneliness the heroic move to the top of the mountain, Zarathustra's move. Our loneliness is a type of hiding away and not a type of standing forth. It is, further, an act of disarray in which even under the best of circumstances the common world is sacrificed to the separated life-world.[18]

We have been brought up to think of institutions as mere contrivances. The social contract encourages us to believe that we bring institutions into being as mere tools for some short- or long-lived ends. This also allows us to believe that such ends are brought to the institution by disparate persons as self-interests. So my interest in an institution vanishes when my ends are achieved or when "its" ends separate from mine. We are, then, consummate proceduralists. Concretely, we reveal this when the first step—or almost the first step—of institution creation is writing bylaws (after the model of a "constitutional convention") and when the last step—or almost the last step—of institution is a legalistic quarrel.

The move from word to act carries with it the need for a shift in our way of institution too. For this, the existential features of an act are particularly significant. To invoke history, connection, celebration, and exhibition is to call for institutions that tutor us in the aesthetics of an act and not just in its ethics, politics, and mechanics. An act so conceived calls for a place to perform its reenactment. It calls, too, for the encouragement of an audience, for the pedagogy of a critic and for support of a cast of characters. The future of a Humanism of the act then carries with it the need for Humanist institutions that are not reduced to the merely instrumental. In our anxiety to overcome the oppressiveness of the sacred, we dispensed with institution as habitation, as a place for being and not just for using. Given the tragedy that inheres in the human condition too, we need to be comforted and supported. That is what institutions are all about. Not least of all, they are about helping us to be ready-for.

Finally, institutions are the locus of politics made personal. But instrumentalism misleads us into thinking of institutions only as organizations—for mobilization, for collective action, for interest-group politics. This reduces the personal character of politics to a technical machinery for winning elections, gaining special legislative benefit, or what have you. It ignores institutional *praxis* as a pedagogy so that the lessons we expect to learn from institutions are essentially technical: how to raise money, do public relations, organize campaigns. We reduce institutions to functional organizations. The postmodern criticism rightly identifies the problem, although it misses the solution with its descent into subjectivism.[19]

Absent attentiveness to inclusive, regular, and supportive practices, institutions in short, we are forced to learn only from the acts of strangers. We mimic the models of tradition without admitting it and so subvert the Enlightenment project. Because these traditions are not our own, we are trapped into uncomfortable imitation or compulsive opposition. And because both imitation and opposition are unsatisfying life diets, we find even more reason to withdraw. Humanist loneliness is reinforced. As a Humanist, I finally become passive.

The complexity of an act also describes the structure of an institution. It is a place where I exhibit, behave, celebrate, connect, and produce my

Humanism and where, in turn, I learn to act in all its dimensionality. Out of this context of energies, productivity grows—world changing, world reforming. Back into this context, celebration comes, reenactments and continuities. From this context, values and ends emerge—not just interests and goals. Creating and sustaining practices is another way of describing a Humanism of the act. Finally, as these practices are undertaken, the organizations, which are the instruments of institutions, emerge. Humanist organizations, however, all too often fail to meet the tests of practice. No small cause of this is the collapsing of organization into institution, of *praxis* into practice, and so of burdening organization with the weight of institution. A technical instrument cannot be an abode, a living space. A Humanism of the act calls attention to this reduction.

NOTES

1. See Howard B. Radest, *Community Service: Encounter with Strangers* (Westport, Conn.: Praeger, 1993), pp. 181–185.

2. Vaclav Havel, "The End of the Modern Era," *New York Times*, March 1, 1992.

3. John Kenneth Galbraith, *The Culture of Contentment* (Boston: Houghton Mifflin, 1992), pp. 95–97 passim.

4. Nearly two decades ago, many of us were exploring the reconstruction of labor, looking at the impact of automation, the need for a more flexible use of worktime, the problems for family life posed by the radical separation of and distance between workplace and home, the need to redesign jobs to reduce the mindlessness of production, and so forth. But this interest died down as the need for international competitiveness increased, as a more conservative mood captured politics and culture, and as labor lost its power. Yet the problems did not vanish, and, indeed, it is ironic to note that once again we are looking at efforts to reconstruct work and leisure, through teams, worker-management cooperation, empowerment at the lowest possible level of management, and quality circles, for example. For an instance of that 1970s exploration, see *Humanizing the Work Place*, ed. Roy P. Fairfield (Buffalo, N.Y.: Prometheus Press, 1974), and my article, "The Virtues of Wastefulness," pp. 239–256.

5. For example, see Tamara K. Hareven, "American Families in Transition: Historical Perspectives on Change," in Arlene S. Skolnick and Jerome H. Skolnick, eds., *Family in Transition*, 5th ed. (Boston: Little, Brown, 1986), pp. 40–58.

6. In September 1994, for example, I received a mailing from Pat Robertson's Christian Coalition addressed to "Christian voters" which illustrated this centrist tactic. Attention was paid to such issues as gays in the military, publicly funded abortions, high taxes, and medical care policies. There was little reference to Jesus or to Scripture.

7.

> Habermas argues that modern representation has been antithetical to the survival of a healthy public sphere for several reasons. . . . Representation becomes the "translation of interests." The legislature is transformed into a theater, offering platforms for presenting propaganda. No meaningful exchange occurs. No one changes his/her mind as a result of enlightened discussion of differing points of view.

Pauline Marie Rosenau, *Post-Modernism and the Social Sciences* (Princeton, N.J.: Princeton University Press, 1992), p. 102.

8. Goethe, *Faust*, trans. and ed. J.F.L. Raschen (Ithaca, N.Y.: Thrift Press, 1949), p. 61.

9. See, for example, John L. Austin, *How to Do Things with Words* (Oxford: Oxford University Press, 1962).

10. Hans-Georg Gadamer, *Reason in the Age of Science*, trans. Frederick G. Lawrence (Cambridge, Mass.: MIT Press, 1990), pp. 32–33.

11. Bob Davis, "Growth of Trade Binds Nations But It Also Can Spur Separatism," *Wall Street Journal*, June 20, 1994.

12. On this point, Buddhism exhibits an explicit development of the benefits of nothingness and so of the need to dispel the illusion that there are gods who judge, create, and destroy. Strange to the Western ear,

> The escape is *nibbana* (Sanskrit: *nirvana*), for the Buddhist the supreme bliss and the final liberation. This is the ceasing of suffering: the third truth. Craving and ignorance are ended. Just as when the cause of disease is removed, the state of health returns, so when the cause of suffering is removed *nibbana* ensues. The individual who reaches this final goal experiences great joy and happiness. All doubts and burdens are gone. His mind is free from prejudice and complication. He has a firm knowledge of freedom and liberation.

John R. Hinnels, ed., *A Handbook of Living Religions* (London: Penguin Books, 1984), p. 306.

13. "Ritual practice," writes Jurgen Habermas,

> is, of course, already part of a sociocultural form of life. . . . Language (in the strict sense) breaks up the unity of teleological, normative, expressive, and cognitive aspects of action. Yet, mythical thought shields ritual practice from the tendencies toward decomposition that appear at the level of language. . . . Myth holds the same aspects together on the plane of interpretation that are fused together in ritual on the plane of practice. An interpretation of the world confuses internal relations of meaning with external relations among things, validity with empirical efficacy, can protect ritual practice against rips in the fabric woven from communicative and purposive activity indistinguishably. . . . The experience gained in everyday practice is worked up in myth and connected with narrative explanations of the orders of the world and of society. In this regard myth bridges over the two domains of action.

Jurgen Habermas, *The Theory of Communicative Action*, vol. 2: *Lifeworld and System: A Critique of Functionalist Reason*, trans. Thomas McCarthy (Boston: Beacon Press, 1987), p. 193.

14. Interruption, as I use it here, adds a certain passionate spin to the notion of the process of inquiry developed in the pragmatic tradition. See, for example, John Dewey, *Logic, The Theory of Inquiry* (New York: Henry Holt and Company, 1938), pp. 101–119.

15. Erich Fromm, *Man for Himself* (New York: Rinehart, 1947), pp. 158–159.

16. John Dewey, "Ralph Waldo Emerson," *The Philosophy of John Dewey*, ed. John J. McDermott (Chicago: University of Chicago Press, 1981), p. 29.

17. John Dewey, *Art as Experience* (New York: Milton Balch and Company, 1934), p. 3.

18. As Habermas remarks,

> The growth of subjectivism of beliefs, obligations, and needs, the reflexivity of the understanding of time, and the mobilization of the consciousness of space can be read in many phenomena. Religious faith is privatized. With the bourgeois family and the decentralized religiosity of the congregation there arises a new sphere of intimacy that is expressed in a deepened culture of reflection and feeling and that alters the conditions of socialization. At the same time, a political public sphere of private persons takes shape, which, as a medium for permanent criticism, alters the conditions for the legitimation of political domination. The consequences of this rationalization of the lifeworld are ambivalent: What some celebrate as institutionalized individualism . . . others abhor as a subjectivism that undermines traditionally anchored institutions, overloads the individual's capacity for decision-making, gives rise to a consciousness of crisis, and thereby endangers social integration.

Habermas, *Theory of Communicative Action*, vol. 1: *Reason and the Rationalization of Society*, trans. Thomas McCarthy (Boston: Beacon Press, 1984), p. 341.

19.

> Post-modern political action is generally aimed at arousing aspirations, raising consciousness, exploring the politics of identity, and opening up opportunities for those who are marginal. . . . Post-modernists seek new ways of acting politically and new spaces for political action. This means less concern with the state . . . and more concern with the neighborhood, local regional, and community levels. Small is beautiful and autonomy is a prerequisite. Post-modern social movements are interpretive, connective (intertextual); they search to have an impact on seemingly remote structures of everyday life. . . . In the field of politics the specific character of the new post-modern subject takes shape; here the post-modern . . . individual has no choice but to confront modern agency and authority.

Rosenau, *Post-Modernism*, pp. 147–148.

8

THE LIFE OF REASON

THE ABUSE AND USE OF REASON

Reason is in bad repute, and naturalism is under attack.[1] Once upon a time, however, they inspired modern science, technology, politics, and economics. To be "modern" meant that we were all on the way to becoming rationalists and naturalists. Although anticlerical, this did not necessarily mean being antifaith, antireligion, or anti-God. Natural religion, rational religion, and ethical religion also reflected this turn to the world.[2] Nor did these religious ideas remain fixed in a deistic and Newtonian frame of reference. Typically, John Dewey developed a Humanistic accommodation of faith and modernism. As Steven Rockefeller described it,

> From early in Dewey's life, both aspects (faith as moral, faith as religious) are at work in his personal religious experience and both find expression in his philosophy of religion. The moral aspects tend to be dominant in both his early ethical idealism and his religious humanism, but there is also a noteworthy current in his thought that emphasizes the role of feelings of belonging, harmony, and peace.[3]

In short, for religionist and secularist alike, we were not simply passing through. At the same time and for all the Humanist's optimism, the world was, often enough, an unfriendly place. It had to be made more inhabitable. This gave rise to the efforts to create wealth, achieve social justice, and construct modern sciences and technologies. In turn, the success of these activities stirred the imagination and loyalty of those who gave themselves to the Humanist cause. The "modern" human being, then, looked to a world that had become genuinely his or her own. No longer did he or she have to look inward to the soul or outward to heaven and hell. Today, however, modernism is met with doubt and cynicism. Looking inward has become the postmodern habit—but without the grace of salvation or eternity. The outcome is the demoralization of the children of the Enlightenment by the shadow enlightenment and its critics.[4]

Reconstruction—to borrow a characteristic term used by modernizers as different as John Dewey and Felix Adler—becomes the Humanist agenda.[5] This is not simply a matter of educational or social reform or of psychotherapy. Today the situation calls for a renewed moral contest. But in the contemporary narrative, enemies and heroes are not neatly arranged on the side of virtue or vice. Contradictory impulses were always present to be sure, but they were absorbed in a myth of "good" guys and "bad" guys. These impulses are now acknowledged on all sides so that the moral struggle must confront the ambivalence of its protagonists. It is not at all clear where virtue and vice lie. The "western" film becomes the "adult" western. The "lovers of wisdom" embrace both positivism and nihilism. In this dramatic setting, the so-called death of socialism together with the flirtation with the free market on one side and the rise of fundamentalism and postmodernism on the other mark the moment when moral ambivalence becomes our milieu. This forces upon the children of the Enlightenment the search for a new self-consciousness. The modern credential cannot simply be assumed by the revolutionary hero or the adventurous entrepreneur.

The lines of the struggle once seemed clear. Typically, socialism and social democracy attracted us because of their universalism, rationality, and a sense of justice. By connecting these values to politics and economics, they joined moral ideal, idea and practice; they constructed a *praxis*. At the same time, the attractions of the free market were to be found in its celebration of freedom and human productivity. Thus, the construction of yet another *praxis*. In other words, the modernist enjoyed an affinity for both socialism and the free market. These were a climactic affirmation of Humanism, celebrating an Enlightenment that built upon the human powers that characterized the Renaissance and the rationality that shaped the high culture of fifth-century Greece and ultimately of Western civilization itself. By contrast we carry a different picture in our heads. Reason, we boast or complain, is univocal, neat, orderly, and, above all, disembodied. Something, then, is wrong with our images of reason, as ambivalence becomes a feature of knowledge as well as of virtue.

For the children of the Enlightenment, Humanism begins and ends with the dignity of the autonomous human being. Humanism is not a philosophy of postponements—either to this world in some distant future or to the next in eternity. The rights of man are written in the ever-present tense. Hence it is that neither socialism nor capitalism as they evolved could really do. Inspired by the scientific metaphors of the seventeenth and eighteenth centuries, they were modeled on the notion that there were natural laws of society, just as there were natural laws of the universe. Thus both socialism and capitalism were grounded in social mechanics. However, they departed the inclusive personalism of Enlightenment politics and sociology, the notion of a public good personally felt.[6] As social "laws" operated, specialized subpopulations would move to the top of a natural hierarchy. This was the departure from the Humanism of the Enlightenment that was forced upon both capitalism and socialism by the effort to accommodate Enlightenment values to a developing massive industrialism.[7] In consequence, both the entrepreneur and the revolutionary left the vast majority of men and women behind to await the ministrations of the market or of history. Both became antiheros. Human beings, except for a tiny minority, were left—temporarily in both cases, it was claimed—to await the long-term consequences of the acts of others better tuned to the demands of nature's law. Little wonder, then, as this truncated Humanism appeared, that critics should resist this purgatory in naturalist form—on the left in the name of freedom and on the right in the name of salvation. As Richard Tarnas put it,

> The underlying intellectual ethos is one of disassembling established structures, deflating pretensions, exploding beliefs, unmasking appearances—a "hermeneutics of suspicion" in the spirit of Marx, Nietzsche, and Freud. . . . To think well, to feel well, to act well, to read well, according to the *episteme* of unmaking, is to refuse the tyranny of wholes. . . . Grand theories and universal overviews cannot be sustained without producing empirical falsification and intellectual authoritarianism. . . . Any alleged comprehensive, coherent outlook is at best no more than a temporarily useful fiction masking chaos, at worst an oppressive fiction masking relationships of power, violence, and subordination.[8]

Democracy too becomes a puzzlement. For Humanists, it is ultimately sociable, a scene of personal connections, carings, and participations.[9] For it, universal participation and human solidarity are at once articles of faith and commitments to conduct. Above all, sociability is pervasive. It appeared in the small as in the large, in the school as in the home, in the polity as in the marketplace. Democracy is a way of living.[10] It is more complicated than Emerson's "moral" democracy or John Dewey's participatory democracy,[11] a view that was not invented by the left-romantics of the 1960s. The human being is not merely a creature of self-interest and negotiation and not merely a creature of social conscience and intelligence. He or she is an appreciating, responding, and imagining being. Sociability, moreover, calls for the inclusion of all persons in the powers and benefits of social life. In that sense, it is both a way of caring even for the stranger, as well as a way of judging and functioning.[12] With a generous sense of schooling and politics, it finds in the uses of an expanded intelligence the capacity for achieving its various ends. At root, sociable democracy is the act of confidence that makes Humanism uniquely what it is: that all human beings are qualified to be participants; they can enjoy the company they keep and the participation that company affords.

Instead of facing the modern contradiction in our images of rationality—postponement at the center of commitment, individualism and legalism in the moment of democracy—we have erected a formalist rationalism. At one and the same time, it promises more than it can deliver and impoverishes what it claims to provide. Against freedom, it demands control, containment, organization, and the minimization of human "interference." Thus, reason itself becomes the "enemy." The anthropologist Robin Horton noted,

> As a scientist it is perhaps inevitable that I should at certain points give the impression that traditional African thought is a poor shackled thing when compared with the thought of the sciences. Yet, as a man, here I am living by choice in a still heavily traditional Africa rather than in the scientifically oriented Western subculture I was brought up in. Why? Well there may be lots of queer, sinister, unacknowledged reasons. But one certain reason is the discovery of things lost at home. An intensely poetic quality in everyday life and thought, and a vivid enjoyment of the passing moment—both driven out of sophisticated Western life by the quest for purity of motive and the faith in progress.[13]

Naturally we resist a rationalism so construed and so conveyed. We grow doubtful of human powers and, more seriously, doubtful as well of the value of those powers themselves even if generally distributed among us. Our images of reason convey a picture of ineluctable moves from point to point. As Nel Noddings writes,

> Habermas criticizes Rawls for the monological nature of the conversation that goes on behind the veil of ignorance. Rawls himself admits that only one thinker is really necessary, because all thoroughly rational thinkers would have to agree. In contrast, Habermas rightly insists that conversation must be pluralistic; several

views may be put forward, and each may be free of obvious logical flaws. A competent conversational group has to assess the strength of each argument. It seems, then, that Habermas is arguing for a genuine forum—many voices dedicated to locating and accepting the argument with greatest force.[14]

When perfected, the formalist metaphor continues, reason has no need of human beings at all. Our ideal of reason is some grand computer like Hal in the film *2001*, able to integrate all the data and ultimately able to provide the "one best answer" to all questions even if that answer entails destruction.

If reason becomes a monster, too many Humanists have made it so. Reason is proceduralized, reduced to "instrumental rationality." It has encouraged us to think of ends and values, dreams and hopes as matters of mere personal or communal taste. Nature is literally devalued, and we are left to drift in an ocean of gray. Natural being is consequently to be found in "operations" and "functions," even if the human being has the illusion of valuing, choosing, and enjoying. In fact, reason conceived as technical manipulation has, as often as not, merely served the least desirable of our purposes like conquest and greed and ego.[15]

At the same time, this legitimate indictment of rationality is reinforced by less defensible arguments. Reason is a corrosive.[16] Just when I am settled, the voices of reason insist on being heard. My illusions are threatened by demands for coherence and evidence. But I love my illusions! No doubt this helps to explain our anger at reason. It can be a harsh critic of what is most dearly held, and it is never easy to surrender a dream. Yet reason insists on its vocabulary of "truth" and "falsity," of "coherent" and "incoherent." Typically I resist and grow all the stronger in my refusal to surrender, like the child who shouts, "I won't," the more insistent the parent becomes. Reason will not let me rest. I am forced, over and over again, to face a next-question.

Then, too, our image of reason promises certainty while the act of reasoning reveals doubt. But I do not doubt "in general." Charles Peirce noted that genuine doubt is not an abstract exercise but is personal, specific, and concrete. It has biographical and not merely epistemological consequences. Thus, rationalism encourages what Richard Bernstein calls a "Cartesian anxiety." Thus, too, driven by this anxiety, is the irresistible search security. The "quest for certainty" then is not reserved to the traditionalist and religionist alone. Berstein writes,

It would be a mistake to think that the Cartesian Anxiety is primarily a religious, metaphysical, epistemological or moral anxiety. These are only several of the

> many forms it may assume. . . . At the heart of the objectivist's vision, and what makes sense of his or her passion, is the belief that there are or must be some fixed, permanent constraints to which we can appeal and which are secure and stable. At its most profound level, the relativist's message is that there are no such basic constraints except those that we invent or temporally (and temporarily) accept. . . . The primary reason why the *agon* between objectivists and relativists has become so intense today is the growing apprehension that there may be nothing—not God, reason, philosophy, science, or poetry—that answers to and satisfies our longing for ultimate constraints, for a stable and reliable rock upon which we can secure our thought and action.[17]

Reason needs beginning points, assumptions, axioms, self-evident ideas, undemonstrated procedures, intuitions, and leaps of insight. These are notoriously various and, even where satisfying, logically arbitrary. Moreover, the test of the competence of reason is located in the detection of error, which is not only a technical achievement but a source of pleasure and pain. It is not unusual for me to enjoy the exposure of the mistakes of another. At the same time, it is not unusual for me to feel the pain of being exposed. Nor is it unusual when exposed for a certain blindness to afflict me: I deny that an error has been made. We claim, all too glibly, that in the presence of error, scientists simply change their theories. The fact is that we hold on to our ideas in spite of evidence of "disconfirmation," and we let go unwillingly and belatedly. The praise of the benefits of exposure—as with most pieties—is distanced from our actual feelings of disappointment, defensiveness, and resentment.

In short, the image of reason that has emerged as a rationalism of method misses out on the culture of rationality. Much as reasoning consists in assumptions, propositions, and inferences, it relies at least as much on creativity and imagination. Nor are these confined to the invention of starting points. Thus, we speak of an "elegant" proof; we refer to fittingness and harmony. We detect a mistake when we say, "Something is wrong, out of kilter, unbalanced," admitting the legitimate presence of intuition, and this well before we go to the demonstrations. We distinguish the routine performance from the clever invention. Nor is it strange to feel reason's adventurousness, reason's riskiness. We set out to reason without knowing where we will arrive. It is insufficient to dismiss all of this as merely facts of human psychology and not truthful to reasoning as such. It is claimed that the conclusions of a deductive process are, after all, "already contained" in the assumptions and rules.[18] Even if true—and this cannot be demonstrated for any interesting proposition—this is as misleading as the notion that a chess game is over once the first move is made.

Our image of reason is only a latter-day distillation of an impoverished culture of reasoning. I wrote in another context,

> The price of Enlightenment was high, but the willingness to pay it was understandable, for it reflected an accurate reading of history. Passion, sensuality, and faith had indeed been historic instruments of tyranny in politics and in religion. The claim of special truths and powers had indeed been used by the few to manipulate and oppress the many. And, more subtly but no less significantly, such claims had been used to deny at the same time the availability and the possibility of knowledge to the generality of human kind. . . . In short, the Enlightenment, looking backward, was concerned to make knowledge and thereby power available to all persons, to discover capacities that could legitimate the democratic impulse. It is not accidental that the great social struggles of Enlightenment are for a lawful participatory politics and universal literacy.[19]

Not least of all, the culture of reason can be generous and democratic. So it is that our image of reason is not merely intellectually doubtful but politically mistaken. The restriction of reasoning to a specialist population with privileged access to the new mysteries hides an unconfessed social agenda. Against it, the culture of reason presupposes a capacity that can be nurtured in just about everyone and that connects the least pretentious bit of reasoning to the flight of genius. In other words, human solidarity is entailed in it. We exhibit solidarity when, after "genius" succeeds in solving a once "insoluble" problem, access to it spreads to the rest of us. I need only compare the science textbooks of a generation ago to those of today, the science and mathematics lessons of a generation ago to those of today, or more generally the literacies of a generation ago to those of today. Our "common sense" is instructed, in ways inconceivable but a short time ago, about diet, space, and energy, about peoples, places, and products. Of course, it is popular to demean the present in favor of the past. The warfare of the "ancients and moderns" after all, is an old habit and reflects social and political prejudice.

The culture of reason is justified, finally, by the democracy of its central theme: the unfolding of an idea as a personal action that can be widely shared without loss to its originator. Typically, Thomas Jefferson illustrated this in discussing "Oliver Evans' claim for a patent on a grain elevator":

> If nature has made any one thing less susceptible than all others of exclusive property, it is the action of the thinking power called an idea, which an individual may exclusively possess as long as he keeps it to himself; but the moment it is

divulged, it forces itself into the possession of every one, and the receiver cannot dispossess himself of it. Its peculiar character, too, is that no one possesses the less, because every other possesses the whole of it. . . . That ideas should freely spread from one to another over the globe, for the moral and mutual instruction of man, and improvement of his condition, seems to have been peculiarly and benevolently designed by nature, when she made them, like fire, expansible over all space, without lessening their density in any point, and like the air in which we breathe, move, and have our physical being, incapable of confinement or exclusive appropriation.[20]

Reason appears then as a dramatic theme and not simply as a technique. For all that it is presented to us in logical formulas and mathematical propositions, it is finally paradoxical and political. Reason is embedded in persons and personalities, in histories and events and purposes.[21] The life of reason is a shared adventure. In short, we can reintroduce rationality to intimacy. To this end, I want to explore my own experience of reason. So it is that I shall advance reason's unlikely partnerships with seduction enchantment, and passion.

SEDUCTION

"Two things," says Kant, "strike me with awe: the starry heavens above and the moral law within." Thus, he reveals himself as a lover of reason even while, according to legend, he was so meticulous that the citizens of Konigsberg could set their clocks by him as he passed by on the way to the classroom. Indeed, when we discover them at work we find out that the lovers of reason are indeed passionate in their reasoning. I think of the impatience I show when meeting someone who thinks, speaks, and behaves "unreasonably." Of course, he or she feels the same way about me. We become passionate adversaries. I think of the angers so evident among the lovers of reason, which, in their vehemence, give the lie to the notion that reason is an objective encounter about abstract ideas. If reason were not a passion, then my impatience and anger while reasoning would be a mystery. But my passion extends well beyond my love affair with rationality as a performance. I think, too, of my pleasure when my reasoning is recognized by another—"that's a good idea," or "why didn't I think of that?"—best of all when my reasoning is agreed to by another. Reason is also a form of sociability. After all, if reason were simply what our modern image of reason claims it to be, then it could best be pursued by a well-instructed computer. Neither pleasure nor pain nor hope nor disappointment would be in point.

I have my desires, hopes, motives, dreams, ideals. I have, as we say, my "reasons," which is also to say that my "reasons" are characterized by responsibility, reference to evidence, and a certain coherence. At the same time, I doubt, am anxious, am frustrated. So my "reasons" face my reasoning. I want to know the truth of my "reasons." It is not enough to *feel* secure, to *feel* sure. I have been disappointed often enough when my feeling secure turned dangerous. Intuitive certainty is typically the alternation of absolute confidence and utter despair. Reasoning, by contrast, makes me more secure by means of the very uses of uncertainty. I think, for example, of the reliability of scientific probabilities when contrasted with the terrors of faithfulness. At times, of course, reason is uninvited. I prefer to feel sure and resent my doubt. I enjoy my blindness—at least for a time and at least until, Oedipus-like time catches up with me. But even here—to reason, not to reason—I am embedded in passions.[22] At any rate, I am not a machinery and reason is not turned on or off at the touch of a switch.

Reason betrays its other nature—what it is besides definition, axiom, theorem, verification, and rules of procedure. It stirs up argument, advocacy, exploration, doubt, curiosity, commitment. There is a restlessness to reason so that even a successful "proof" leads me to ask: Is there a better way, a neater way, a prettier way to arrive at the "same" conclusion? Hence the distinction between the student who only satisfies the requirements of the classroom and the student who catches on to logic and mathematics. It is, no doubt, a sign of the impoverishment of reason that in a classroom the unexpected proof, the nontextbook proof, is greeted by doubt and disapproval. "Do it the right way" is reduced to pedestrianism.

For me, after first encountering him years ago, Spinoza remains the exemplar of reason just because he was also the "god-intoxicated man." And Euclid's geometry remains the ideal of rational achievement recalling the Pythagorean "music of the spheres" and the poet's line, "Euclid hath seen beauty bare." To be sure, with the notable exception of Plato, this passion is not often matched by style. Typically presented in antibiographical form, there is a deliberate suppression of passion in its communication. This "dispassionate" mood is said to be justified by the need for distancing myself from my prejudice. So it is almost as if there was something to be ashamed of in admitting that reason is a passion; reason thereby seems to become "irrational." Again, reasoning suggests shame's reason. Passion, as Spinoza noted, distorts our judgments and makes us slaves and even addicts. We are less free to dismiss, to ignore, to avoid. Reason's "objectivity" is meant to guard us against the disasters of infatuation. But we confuse things by thinking that all passion is blind, as if the lover cannot be critical of the beloved without ceasing to be the lover. Indeed, just because I care deeply, I must be truthful.

Each of us has known seduction by an idea, by a dream, by an ideal. Something attracts me, and I am drawn to it without knowing why. As I come closer, the attraction increases, and I come closer still. Yet some things attract me but do not seduce me. I find out that I am not interested or simply mistaken. To be sure, this does not happen all at once. The attraction may linger awhile, or I may think myself foolish to have been attracted and so, unwilling to admit the fool, blind myself to the fact that I am not really attracted any longer. Reason, however, also asks me not to dismiss foolishness too quickly, for sometimes the fool can do the work of reason too. The court jester, after all, could get away with being a social and political critic just because he was "unserious." Gilbert and Sullivan sing their criticism of imperial England. Thus too, Erasmus's "goddess of folly":

> But since my ancestry is not known to many, I shall try, with the help of the Muses, to reveal it to you. My father was neither Chaos, Orcus, Saturn, Jupiter, or any other representative of the ancient and moldy gods, but Plutus, God of Riches, the Father of Gods and men, despite the opinion of Homer, Hesiod, and Zeus himself. At his nod, now as before, all things sacred and profane are turned topsy-turvy. By his judgment, war, peace, empires, plans, judgments, assemblies, marriages, treaties, pacts, laws, arts, sports, important matters (my breath is almost gone)—in brief, all public and private affairs—are governed. Without his help that whole group of deities of the poets' making and even—I will speak more boldly—the most eminent gods themselves, either would not exist at all or certainly would live very meagerly at home. . . . I glory to have such a father. And he did not give birth to me from his brain as Jupiter begot severe and gloomy Pallas; but rather from "youth" the most beautiful nymph of all.[23]

As seduction matures, intelligence is joined with allure. I settle in to enjoy it.

Reason first attracted me by the power it gave me to dissect my opponents in an argument. It was then a young man's weapon, and, because it claimed the name of reason, it was a righteous weapon. After all, I did not, like some barbarian, want to destroy my opponent but only to force him or her to submit to my evident superiority. I wanted to expose error and truth in the belief that once exposed, rejection of the former and acceptance of the latter simply had to follow. But my opponent did not have the good sense to see it that way. The temptation to desert reason thus grew when I found I could not succeed in silencing my opponent. Fortunately, I did not have powers of destruction. I wonder, then, is reason "warfare by other means"? Perhaps that is the wisdom of Plato's notion that philosophy ought not to be undertaken before the age of forty, or is that only a type of special pleading as I grow older?

When my attack did not succeed, reason forced me to confront the stubbornness in the other and did not let me ignore the unreasonable in myself. Reason, in other words, behaved as its own cure. I began to encounter the fascinating game of "as if . . ." and so, Jesuitical, played out the reason of the other as if it were my own. By then, I had discovered that reason was an endless game too. Just as a demonstration seemed concluded, it was reopened again, and in a new and more interesting way. The seduction was transformed into love and even into affection.

Looking back, I am fascinated by the pathways along which I have been led by reason. It remains a game, and yet the ends of the game are serious. It lives for understanding, for explanation, opening the world to me. It is not accurate merely to call this opening up "science" or "scientific method" or even "organized intelligence," for these are too encapsulated to catch what I am doing and feeling and hoping as I live the life of reason. I am not only the romantic in a still and darkened night. I am on a journey in all the vast and wondrous array of space and time. I imagine moments of creation, massive release of energies, and massive occurrence of events: black holes and light years and expanding and contracting universes. Einstein spoke of this move of reason as driven by *heilige curiositat.* I learn to ask questions, to inquire. I am forced to master method and symbol and history. I take many false steps, pause and retrace, explain myself. The fascination will not let me go.

I look within to reasons of the heart, which are not only emotions and affections but distinctive structures of give and get, stimulus and response, desire and disappointment. I may be said to have and to feel. But it is not enough. I need to know why this having, this feeling. Needing to distinguish this from that and needing to know why is the continuing seduction of reason. I remember, years ago, conversations with a four year old as we sat together on a hillside. Every other word he uttered was *why*, almost to the point of distraction. From him—from children—I learned that it is in the impulse to ask questions that reason lives. I want to go on; I want to want to go on.

Reasoning is not very neat. Only later do I look back and describe it all "rationally," as in the textbook descriptions of *the* scientific method. It does not happen that way at all but is more like going back and forth and sideways, more like being attracted and repelled, going toward and deserting. I recall reading a brief essay on doing science. The author contrasted the article in a suitably refereed journal, with the process. In the former, hypothesis, data, controls, and conclusions are neatly arrayed. The process, however, might well begin, "I was noodling around and I stumbled onto . . ." Of course, the report has its uses. It allows me to enter the world of the reporter and to make it my own. And yet, standing by itself as reason's model, it misleads, for in the doing, reason is a "blooming buzzing confusion."

The seduction begins with a call to attention. It continues when I answer the call and ask, "What is it?" I find out, and yet I am not satisfied. I describe, catalog, name. I add and subtract, make or find categories. I enjoy a power over things, as all naming and organizing and describing are types of power. There is then something quite reminiscent of the most primitive and the most childlike in me when I catch reason at work. I am empowered to grasp the world, to paint the world picture over and over again, to unite and separate, to conjoin and distinguish, to connect and sever. When I realize that I am in power or perhaps in the power of another, I understand that "is" connects to why and wherefore and witherto. Yes, all of this "is," but it also "means." I am driven to penetrate that meaning and the meanings that follow. I come to know the elation and the fearfulness of reason.

I describe and name, reason about meaning, feel elation and passion and fear. As I do, I find out who and what I am. I thus search out my identity. At the same time, I detect you doing the same thing. Reason thus reveals me to you and you to me. This mutual revelation is the genius of the artifacts of reason, the classroom, the dialogue, the conversation. I struggle, then, finally with what it is to be myself and at the same time to be human, for which the simple phrase, a "rational animal," is only the first cue.

This putting together and taking apart is as much the work of reason as the theorem, the syllogism, and the propositional calculus. Reason is an art that leads me out of the routine. It leads me into other worlds and generates new images of this world. For all that reasoning seems to go on "in my own head," a little reflection shows how peopled my reasoning is with others and their reasonings. Of course, I reason in the present and apparently by myself, but the present is filled with stories of the past and imaginings of the future. I seize these through models—actual and remembered images—of the way I perceive that others thought and behaved. The models seem to be constructed by me and not dictated by others. Yet I do not experience a chaos of models; I find out that I cannot construct just anything I wish for. When I try to—try to escape reason—my imaginings melt into disconnected fragments, mere ephemera. Rescuing them from chaos, I find that my imaginings are ordered and orderly, although the organization may be unexpected.

In any event, my imaginings are not simply arbitrary. For all that I believe that I think "in my own head," I realize that my images are shared; the culture of reason appears again since not just any model will do. Language, for example, reveals both the individuality and the sociability of reason. If I am fortunate, I find myself in a life-world that is hospitable to my fancy. The culture of reason then initiates a criticism of society and in its own way asks for social reform. Thus, those remarkable moments appear as in fifth-century Athens or eighteenth-century America.

Even fiction has its rationality. I show you pictures of what might be or of what is hidden. I create a dialogue between us even in "my own head," think up your challenges and my responses. I am both caught by images of you and yet free to imagine you as you might be or might become. I am then a creature of history just when I think to reason, following Spinoza, *sub specie eternitatus*, and just when I try to escape to Plato's "heaven beyond the heavens." I am captivated by this miniaturized sociability inside me that is both under my control and yet controls me as well.

When all of this intersection of sociability and imagination accrues in a vision, an intuition, a grasp—the world is this way or that, people are this way or that, I am this way or that—reason whispers, "Enjoy it, but hold a moment. Is this really the way it is?" Reason leads me on to the testing of my imaginings. That is its virtue and its pain. That is, also, its distinctiveness from other ways of imagining that rely on dogmatic absolute. For reason, the next question always arises. Its seduction is another leading out and leading to.[24]

ENCHANTMENT

We are said to live in a demythologized and disenchanted world. Arnold Burms writes,

> Science is disenchanting because it shows that everything we experience as profound, evocative or deeply moving, can also be observed with a cold eye and treated as an aspect of an impersonal, meaningless universe. . . .
>
> However, . . . Douglas Hofstadter, author of the famous book, *Godel, Escher, Bach*, says that science is fascinating for him partly because of its disenchanting effects. What intrigues him is the possibility of seeing how scientific descriptions of a reality we experience as familiar and valuable turns that reality into something which does not any longer have its familiar and valuable features. . . .
>
> Something similar is to be said about Einstein's attitude toward disenchantment. . . . In his view, science allows us to catch a glimpse of a marvelous, cosmic

order which is awe-inspiring, but also beyond good and evil and indifferent to human concerns. The individual who is confronted with this reality, feels humility and gains a far-reaching emancipation from human worries and desires.[25]

However described—as fascination, as emancipation, as awe inspiring—enchantment cannot be evaded. I am led to ask: Is it that we are disenchanted, or is it only that today's enchantments are shallow and dull? Hence the dangerous appeal, in reaction, of the wildest flights of fancy, whether in religion or politics or philosophy or art. An air of unreality pervades our so-called realism. We live in a measured world, a timed world as if the intensity and variability of duration's rhythm had no place in our experience. We have forgotten the most elementary fact of realism, or any other "ism" for that matter: that I am shaped by spoken and unspoken life assumptions. To call for "just the facts" or the "bottom line" or the "operational directive"—the language of our peculiar "realism"—is already to report one kind of world vision and not another. To name it *the* scientific vision is to presume that there is some pure description of things as they "really are" and to think that science is an epistemological black box.[26]

Our world vision thus only poses as disenchantment, as demythology. It is, of course, more adequate than many of the alternative visions human beings have entertained. But offered as the final truth of the matter instead of as a useful art and pleasurable entertainment, it becomes arrogant. It thus replicates precisely the most problematic feature of enchantment itself: our vision is not known for the metaphor it is but instead tells us the way things really are. Reason's task—to ask next-questions—is truncated, limited to functional necessities and formalist structures. A range of ideas is ruled illegitimate by such separations as "fact and value" and left unexplored: What values justify this function rather than that? What necessities dictate this outcome rather than that? Moreover, the politics and preferences that work beneath the surface to shape the enchantment are hidden.

This betrayal of reason goes much deeper. We are scientifically illiterate not because we fail to know the bits and pieces of science but because we fail to grasp its narrative. It is through the lens of enchantment that science and technology can be understood. We are misled by the styled antisubjectivity of inquiry. We call it objectivity and regretfully confess that much as we might want things to be otherwise, the world does not respect our dreams and hopes.[27] A necessary caution against wishful thinking, our "realism" masks unacknowledged prejudices that the world neither dictates nor demands.

William James long ago identified temperament and mood as ontological and not just as psychological categories. Intellectualist presumptions have a way of shaping popular realism too. For example,

> Until the 1950s, social science research was generally done in the field, where people would directly observe other people. But today, much of it is done on computers which can tackle bigger problems faster—and can also be easily manipulated. . . . Computer models used for research are notoriously friendly to their sponsors' interests. A computer model found that if airlines could not hire replacement workers during a strike, fares would rise so high that only the rich could fly; the study was prepared for the Air Transport Association. A computer model showed that if advertising were taxed in Minnesota, the industry as well as the state's entire economy would be damaged; the study was sponsored by the Communications Industry Coalition. Computer models found that if the U.S. adopted a Canadian-style national medical plan, health-care costs would either increase by $38 billion (people who oppose such a plan) or decrease by $241 billion (people who favor it).
>
> Tactical research has dominated contemporary debates about abortion, gun control, family leave, recycling, school choice and the speed limit, just to name a few.[28]

Feminists and postmodernists have done us a service by calling attention to the arrogance of a reductive reading of reason, although at the needless cost of rejecting the sciences and technology in favor of one or another type of magic. The sciences do happen within histories and cultures and do not exist outside time and independent of human interests. The sciences share with other activities aesthetic, purposive, and agonistic characteristics. Continuing in the pragmatic spirit, a portrait of science as a human activity akin to art and sport emerges. Dewey wrote,

> Because the free working of mind is one of the greatest joys open to man, the scientific attitude . . . is something which adds enormously to one's enjoyment of existence. . . . Yet, they [the sciences] are now as restricted in quality as they are in the number of those who share them. That is to say, as long as "scientific" thinking confines itself to technical fields, it lacks full scope and varied material. . . . The mind that is hampered by fear lest something old and precious be destroyed is the mind that experiences fear of science. He who has this fear cannot find reward and peace in the discovery of new truths and the projection of new ideals. He does not walk the earth freely, because he is obsessed by the need of protecting some private possession of belief and taste.[29]

The old standbys—the story, the song, the artwork—enchant us still. But reason too has its own story and song.

Ancient images picture us as creatures with our eyes on the clouds and our feet in the dirt. Too often, however, enchantment disconnects us from the earth, and we are invited to build castles in air. Enchantment thus acquires a poor reputation among us. To be enchanted carries with it the worst accusation that can be made in our world: You are unrealistic! The advice quickly follows: Come back to earth. But often it is not easy to come back to earth. I realize that I do not always enchant myself. I can be the victim of a witchcraft that casts a spell over me that can only be broken by some equally magical act. The narrative is all too often a form of manipulation. I am thus presented to myself as easily put under the control of another. Enchantment, even the enchantment of reason, is appealing in its release of imagination, but it also can be, and historically has been, an invitation to unfreedom.

It is understandable that the children of the Enlightenment should suspect the narrative and that reason's acid should be used to dissolve its power over us. But reason is not privileged to escape the human situation. It has its forms of enchantment too. Modern cosmology, for example, working backward from what is, imagines what might have been. This suggests the romance of reason, the antiutility streak in the life of reason. I think of the controversies over big bang and steady-state universes, over whether the universe is shrinking or expanding. I compare these to the simple logic of Aristotle's "unmoved mover," and I understand what it means to talk of stretching the imagination. I know that Aristotle does not give an adequate account of the things we now know, but I envy the cosiness of his world and fear the galactic homelessness of the modern universe. Without detracting from their conceptual richness, our modern cosmological romances have yet encountered their implication.

I think, too, of how reason generates enigmas that are insoluble because of the presumptions and structures that reason itself creates. The puzzles of modern epistemology that plague the freshman student of philosophy come to mind: whether other minds, other selves, or the world itself exists. These are phantasms of a premise that, posing as common sense or self-evidence, is not recognized as a premise at all. We trap ourselves with the notion that experience comes to us in discrete bits from an "outside" through a sensuous doorway to an "inside." And yet the premise—which Alfred North Whitehead called the "fallacy of misplaced concreteness"—forces the conclusion that we cannot escape from the "inside" and so the "outside" is finally lost. We try to break out of the trap we have made for ourselves. For example, when John Adams wrote supporting Bishop Berkeley's skepticism, Thomas Jefferson, in Cartesian fashion, replied,

"I feel: therefore I exist." I feel bodies which are not myself: there are other existences then. I call them *matter.* I feel them changing place. This gives me *motion.* Where there is an absence of matter, I call it *void*, or *nothing*, or *immaterial space.* On the bases of sensation, of matter and motion, we may erect the fabric of all the certainties we can have or need. I can conceive *thought* to be an action of a particular organization of matter, formed for that purpose by its creator, as well as that *attraction* is an action of matter, or *magnetism* of lodestone. . . . When once we quit the basis of sensation, all is in the wind. To talk of *immaterial* existences is to talk of *nothings.* To say that the human soul, angels, god, are immaterial, is to say that they are *nothings*, or that there is no god, no angels, no soul. . . . [30]

Later, William James's "radical empiricism" attacked the premise of "inside" and "outside" with the counterpremise that our experience is already relational and continuous. Decision between the two starting points arises from yet another premise: that when dead-ended, I am authorized to begin anew unless it is my fate to go in circles. In this interplay of premises, enchantment reveals itself again. I am fascinated by puzzles, driven to solve them, unwilling to surrender.

Even as I write these words, I understand that the enchantment of reason is not found just in the premises I play with or the arguments I erect. Of course, I choose among premises led by an inveterate curiosity to see how things turn out. I do not give up even when, for a time, I am trapped by premises that seem unavoidable, or, to use the language of formalist reason, axiomatic. I continue to hunt for ways out despite frustration, and I do so despite the temptation to throw it all over as a bad job. I am, in other words, drawn back to my puzzle again and again. I am, in short, caught as a lover of reason, and like lovers everywhere this "splendid misery" has hold of me. And then, there is the saving grace of reason. Despite its enigmas, it satisfies me aesthetically and practically too. I can enjoy it as both a having and a doing. What is more, apparently, the world is more hospitable to reason than to its alternatives.

I love the other, who may or may not love me, as the world may not love me. I am elated and cast down. I am not clearheaded, although as a lover of reason, I am supposed to be. Santayana puts it well when he writes,

In the passion of love . . . a cause unknown to the sufferer, but which is doubtless the springflood of hereditary instincts accidentally let loose, suddenly checks the young man's gaiety, dispels his random curiosity, arrests perhaps his very breath; and when he looks for a cause to explain his suspended faculties, he can find it only in the presence or image of another being, of whose character possibly, he knows nothing and whose beauty may not be remarkable; yet that image pursues him everywhere, and he is dominated by an unaccustomed tragic earnestness and a new capacity for suffering and joy. If the passion be strong there is no previous interest or duty that will be remembered before it; if it be lasting, the whole life may be reorganized by it; it may impose new habits, other manners, another religion. Yet, what is the root of all this idealism? An irrational instinct, normally intermittent, such as dumb creatures share, which has here managed to dominate a human soul and to enlist all the mental powers in more or less permanent service, upsetting their usual equilibrium. This madness, however, inspires methods; and for the first time, perhaps in his life, the man has something to live for. The blind affinity that like a magnet draws all the faculties around it, in so uniting them, suffuses them with an unwonted spiritual light.[31]

Reason, however, is not a jealous lover. Indeed, it has attached itself almost promiscuously to a congregation of other loves. I can love God or love wisdom. I can fall in love with a piece of music or a painting or a sculpture. An idea, an ideal, a dream are likely objects as well. I know the pains of rejection too as when the beloved turns away for the last time or an idea is revealed as false or an ideal as empty.

When I consult my love of reason, I find that I see and hear and learn new things, unexpected things. I am held to account by reason and by the world it opens to me. I am jealous and yet generous, possessing my ideas and how I got them and yet anxious to talk of my love, to share my ideas and how I got them. A discovery, an insight is not merely informative but thrilling. I want to write reason's poetry or sing reason's song.

As a lover, of course, I cannot help but compare and contrast. I learn the distinction—reason again—between true and false loves. Reason announces its ability to distinguish, to separate the true and the false, the adequate and the inadequate. My love affair is thus corroborated; objectivity too acquires new meaning through the acts of loving, and this is quite different from distancing and impersonality. Even where disappointment and frustration appear, as they do in all love affairs, reason carries me forward, asking next questions, forcing reflection, correcting impressions, leading to further connection.

Finally, I would not ignore the fact that reason is of the body and not just of the mind, if that separation makes any sense at all. At night I lie half awake and rehearse my arguments. Even when exhausted, I cannot stop myself. And though I lie very still, the rhythm of my breathing changes, punctuates the argument. I think to have found my way to an answer, a solution, but sleep still does not arrive. Or, frustrated, I tell myself to forget it for now, but I cannot. I begin to doze off, and then I hear other voices and am driven to answer. So it is that when I reason, I am restless, and when I am restless I reason. Even when sleep comes and the body eases, I dream, and the interpretation of dreams, the "forgotten language" as Erich Fromm called it, is an ancient testimony to reason.

At the same time, reason is shaped by the body. Symmetries occur to me, not incidentally because I am bipedal and of a certain size and shape—"on the one hand" or "on the other," I argue. Loss of memory is notoriously a sign of aging, and with that reason's arsenal is difficult to sustain. The body's stillness invites one kind of reasoning; its activity, another. Sometimes I seem to do things "thoughtlessly," and yet reflection reveals the thought that was there but not known to be there. There is, in other words, a biology of reason that we miss when we model it after some mechanical image.

THE LIFE OF REASON

I do not think I am exaggerating the passionate quality of reason. Robert Davidoff makes the connection incarnate:

> Jefferson and Emerson had more to do with one another than most readings allow. The crucial connection of American democratic history is between those two because they represent the interesting, fertile, and manifestly creative adjustment of the smart to the most. Each figure had an acknowledged share of his century's intellectual achievement, was a noticed and admired participant in a worldwide development but central to the Enlightenment and Romanticism in America. . . . Jefferson was of the Enlightenment and did some of its significant work in a fully realized version of its human vessel, while Carlyle and Nietzsche read and admired Emerson, after all.[32]

The joining of reason and passion challenges our technicist images of reason. Modernist and postmodernist have become partners in a destructive reading of reason. Like the prisoners in Plato's cave, they see only the shadow of reason's reality. Against it, the children of the Enlightenment must struggle to make the life of reason actual, vital. What then finally is the life of reason?

It is useful to keep in mind that reason is a way of doing things one way rather than another and not just a way of thinking about things one way or another. Thus, when I am reasonable, I do not abbreviate experience. I reach out for the world and do not decide in advance that things must be only one way or only another. I let the world in and do not, in advance, set a doorkeeper to censor and eliminate. Of course, I include and exclude—but only after, and with hesitation and tentatively. The continuing act of the life of reason is the act of opening up to even the act of reopening up to. In that sense, despite the neatness of a geometric demonstration or a syllogism, reason is never perfected, and this is both its fascination and its frustration. Reason expects me, like Socrates at the end of the *Symposium* or the *Euthyphro*, to begin again.

This welcome to the world is denied by the enemies of reason who close in on a belief or an entity as if these were the only things that could claim loyalty and truth. Indeed, this closing down is not merely proclaimed as virtue but demanded as righteousness. Opening up to is, by contrast, the work of Satan. The accusations of "relativist" and "secularist" are not simply legitimate terms of criticism after the fact but of moralism in advance of any fact. At the same time, reason is not merely nihilism in disguise or relativism run wild. Much as it opens to the imagination without prescriptive limits, it always demands a return to the earth. Failing that, the earth makes its own demands, refutes reason in event.

But there is yet another paradox here, for if the life of reason commands a welcome to the world, then it must in some sense include a welcome to its enemies as well, for they too are of this world. Without that welcome, the lover of reason would merely belong to another sect. This is, in fact, just the way reason's postmodern enemies conceive the matter. So it is that to live the life of reason is to be ready to be in the place of another, to grasp the realities that move a fellow human being to close down and to close in. "Universality," writes Jean Grondin,

> as an aim of knowledge, is something one achieves by broadening one's horizons, by going beyond the particularity of our given nature, by learning from others who have bequeathed to us the wealth of their wisdom. This meaning of universality differs from the one we encountered in the scientistic picture. There, universality meant that a hypothesis is valid for all the occurrences of this or that general law. For humanism, universalism resides rather in the unending task of overcoming one's particularity or situatedness. And it is important that it be understood as a task because it is never achieved once and for all. For humanism, one never ceases to learn and to rise above one's own indigence through learning.[33]

And so toleration must be added to reason's lexicon, for the life of reason is an act of appreciation. Illustratively, my colleague Gerald Larue, for all his secularism, writes,

> Religious expression can move me and touch me deeply, because religious expression is part of the human tradition. In the ancient Egyptian temple of the god Amun, I feel chills run along my spine when I realize that, where I stand, the

> pharaohs of Egypt stood in worship millennia ago. . . . If I listen, perhaps I can hear the footsteps of the ancient priests of Amun echoing in the peristyle hall. I can feel with the pilgrims at the legendary birthplace of Jesus in Bethlehem, where for centuries millions have come to worship. In a Roman Catholic or Greek or Russian sanctuary, I can let the music move me as I watch the sunlight filter through the clerestory windows and seemingly hang suspended in the air. At the same time, I am sharply aware of human stupidities perpetrated in the name of the sacred and that these sanctuaries built to honor a god are really statements honoring the humans who designed, built and contributed to them.[34]

To live the life of reason then is to walk the path of argument and responsiveness, to sense when argument has turned into brutality, when responsiveness has turned into shapelessness.

There is a special texture to the life of reason. Perhaps I may call it ever-renewed expectation. Much as I go out to the world, I also receive it as it presents itself to me. I do not always—or even often—know what awaits me. Surprise is likely even though I seek to predict things in accordance with reason's structures. I build up habits of perception and of organization to protect me against the wildness of experience. But just when I settle in with the results of inquiry, something unforeseen comes along. This is just as likely to happen in the sciences as in less determinate experiences. Surprise is not turned away, however, as an "error" or an "evil." It is taken for what it is: a happening that is unforeseen. Of course, I resist letting go of my habits, but ultimately, the unforeseen is neither denied nor regretted.

The life of reason has its tragic and poignant sides as well. I follow an idea to its end and find that it has led me into a trap of my own making. I decide for this and against that, reasonably I presume, and discover in the outcome the opposite of my expectation. I defeat the argument of another only to discover the validities of his or her point and point of view. I exert my powers of reasoning to make this or that, only to find out later—sometimes much later, often too late—that I have created a monster in idealism's costume.

The life of reason is risky and adventurous. Yet I cannot opt for passivity either since reason forces me to understand that passivity is itself a choice. I discover that there is no escape, for I am what I am. There is a certain harshness in the life of reason. And yet, like the stoic, I do learn to accept as well as to act. This acceptance is itself a willing embrace of the world even as it eludes me.

There are moments in the life of reason when things become too much. I am tempted then to turn from it or turn it into what it is not. I recognize in such moments that the life of reason has its boundaries too. Perhaps I even take a holiday—a metaphysical holiday or an epistemological one. But soon or late, I am brought back to the world, for events do not go away, whether I will it or not. Of course I grow quiet, enjoy the solitude, reflect. At times, I retreat within myself or lose myself in music or poetry or revery. But something of me knows what I am doing and knows that it is of the moment.

Fortunately the life of reason is not lonely. Reason, I recall, is a generous love. When things grow too much for me, there are others I may call upon. Opening up to the world reveals its diverse peoples, and I have not put walls around them. I open up to other worlds too—to the pasts that I have learned and enjoyed, to the futures that I can only imagine. Both tradition and art thus acquire therapeutic meaning—not as in the physician's treatment room but as in Aristotle's notion in *The Poetics* that tragedy, by evoking "pity and terror," is cathartic, cleansing.

I am found always in the company of other persons, real and present or remembered and imagined. This sociability is an existential fact. I exhibit it in my biology and in my languages, my costumes, my arts, my responses. I exhibit it, above all, in my ability to enter into the life of another as one who cares and one who needs to be cared for.[35] I am always connected—that was what appealed in the socialist ideal of human solidarity. However, solidarity so conceived was too harshly utilitarian, even legalistic and merely public. By contrast, Carol Gilligan remarks—and this is closer to the sensibility of the life of reason, I think—that life is a network, a web, and not an isolated path.[36]

Nature, for all that it threatens me with its uncertainties, is a companion too, for the life of reason teaches that I am in the world and of it. So it is that when things grow too much for me, I can turn to it as well. When things grow too much for me, I am recalled to the fact that there are always other things too—to question, explore, do with, enjoy, respond to. The world will be there for me as an "environing reality," which is secured to me by my presence in it and its presence in me. The naturalism with which I began this book now returns as I move toward my conclusion.

Finally, reason is recognition. I am witness to my reasoning; I am witness to yours as well. We encounter each other in many ways as friends, allies, and lovers but also as enemies and strangers. I find you also in your reasoning. You become clear to me, and I become clear to you. The life of reason will not let us stay out of view. In that recognition is a form of transcendence of culture, of race, of gender, even of time. Reason thus recalls a rightful cosmopolitanism.

In short, the Humanist knows—but too often forgets—that reason is the living out of reason.[37] Sadly, it is this forgetting that has invited reason's enemies to the table. Yet, before philosophy, before science, there was the human being at work in his or her reason. But "before" is misleading—as if the life of reason followed some more primitive origination. Better then to say that around and beyond and even within. Reason is environmental before it is instrumental, biographical before it is technical. Embedded in the lived experience, reason identifies and contrasts that experience with those that suppress, deny, ignore it. It is, of course, possible for the lived experience to be a destruction, a disaster. Yet it is what we are and what we have. To turn from it is to abdicate the being of the human being. To embrace it, terrors and all, is to refind the Humanist voice, to know that the life of reason may be out there between us and the world, but it is ultimately intimate between myself, my self and you.

NOTES

1. It may seem strange for a secular Humanist to conclude by reference to George Santayana, a philosopher apparently unsympathetic to the ideas of the children of the Enlightenment. Yet is is in his work that I find a clue to the recovery of the genius of rationality. I am particularly helped by his ideas on natural piety, his corrective to an uncritical optimism, his attentiveness to the personal, his striking combination of stoicism, naturalism, and faith. Summing up his position, Elizabeth Flower and Michael Murphy write,

> Santayana's great virtue to the student of the history of philosophy in America lies in the radical contrast between his work and that of every other American thinker. A Catholic in a Protestant country, a humanist in an age of science, a pessimist in a nation in which optimism was a national religion, a fatalist in a culture which preached the ability of creative intelligence to master the world, a man who advocated resignation as a cardinal virtue in a land wedded to activism, Santayana provides a reference point by comparison with which the differences between other American thinkers dwindle into insignificance and their common orientations stand out starkly. . . . but however alien Santayana's voice may seem in comparison to the prevailing American tradition, it is a voice which must be heard, for the world view Santayana articulated is an authentic alternative to the optimistic, activistic, practicalist view which has dominated American thought.

Elizabeth G. Flower and Michael Murphy, *A History of Philosophy in America* (New York: Capricorn Books, 1977), 2: 774.

2. For a discussion of this theme, see James Turner, *Without God, without Creed* (Baltimore: Johns Hopkins Press, 1985).

3. Steven Rockefeller, *John Dewey—Religion, Faith and Democratic Humanism* (New York: Columbia University Press, 1991), p. 477.

4. A good example of this dismissal of the Enlightenment from a Christian but nonfundamentalist point of view is George H. Hunter II, *How to Reach Secular People* (Nashville, Tenn.: Abingdon Press, 1992), pp. 37–38.

5. Felix Adler's last major work was *The Reconstruction of the Spiritual Ideal* (New York: D. Appleton, 1924; reprinted, New York, AMS Press, 1979) and typically, John Dewey published his critique of contemporary thought under the title *Reconstruction in Philosophy* (New York: Henry Holt, 1920).

6. Thomas McCarthy describes Max Weber's criticism of this departure in the following way,

> The first classical social theorist Habermas discusses in this book, Max Weber, directly challenged all these tenets of the Enlightenment faith in reason and progress in ways that remain relevant for us today. In his view, the rationality that defines modernity is at bottom a Zweckrationalitat, a purposive or means/ends rationality. . . . As a consequence, the growth and spread of reason does not, as Enlightenment thinkers supposed it would, furnish a new, nonillusory center of meaning in modern culture. It does, to be sure, gradually dissolve traditional superstition, prejudices and errors; but this "disenchantment of the world," as Weber calls it, does not replace traditional religious world views with anything that could fulfill the functions of, for instance, giving meaning and unity to life. Rather, the disenchanted world is stripped of all ethical meaning.

Jurgen Habermas, *The Theory of Communicative Action*, vol. 1: *Reason and the Rationalization of Society*, trans. Thomas McCarthy (Boston: Beacon Press, 1984), p. xvii.

7. It is true that Adam Smith's *The Wealth of Nations* was published in 1776. Forgotten, however, in the effort to interpret Smith as an advocate of the "free market" as an adventurer's paradise, is his *Theory of Moral Sentiments* (1759). In his view, "self-interest" is disciplined by the operations of human empathy and sympathy as well as by the guidance of an invisible hand that ensured a just and reasonable market outcome for the public good.

8. Richard Tarnas, *The Passion of the Western Mind* (New York: Ballatine Books, 1991), p. 401.

9. For a discussion of differing models of democracy, see Howard B. Radest, *Community Service: Encounter of Strangers* (Westport, Conn.: Praeger, 1993), chap. 9.

10. Steven Rockefeller identifies this enlarged sense of democracy:

> Whitman's naturalism, humanism, and individualism are coupled with a very real moral and religious concern. In *Democratic Vistas*, he calls for "a sublime and serious Religious Democracy." It is rooted in an individual awareness that "there is a moral purpose, a visible or invisible intention certainly underlying all" and a "belief in the wisdom, health, mystery, beauty of every process, every concrete object, every human or other existence, not only considered from the point of view of all, but of each." . . . It is in this connection that he argued that if the United States is to fulfill its "spiritual and heroic" destiny, it needs most of all "more moral identity," a greater sense of common purpose.

John Dewey—Religion, Faith and Democratic Humanism (New York: Columbia University Press, 1991), p. 153.

11. For an incisive and definitive discussion of this theme, see Robert B. Westbrook, *John Dewey and American Democracy* (Ithaca, N.Y.: Cornell University Press, 1991). Chapter 13, "Their Morals and Ours," is particularly relevant to my theme.

12. See Radest, *Community Service.*

13. Robin Horton, "African Traditional Thought and Western Science," in Bryan Wilson, ed., *Rationality* (London: Oxford, 1970), p. 170.

14. Nel Noddings, "Conversation as Moral Education," *Journal of Moral Education* 23, no. 2 (1994): 109.

15. Summing up the postmodern indictment of reason, Pauline Marie Rosenau writes,

> Reason is the product of the Enlightenment, modern science, and Western society, and as such for the post-modernists, it is guilty by association of all the errors attributed to them. Reason, like modern science, is understood to be dominating, oppressive, totalitarian. Assuming a "best answer" or a "unique solution," it thus precludes diversity and tolerance. . . . The post-modernists focus on how reason and rationality are employed as legitimating devices to defend modern bureaucracy, law, economics, and politics. . . . Abandoning reason means, for post-modernists, liberation from modernity's preoccupation with authority, efficiency, hierarchy, power, technology, commerce . . . administration, social engineering.

Pauline Marie Rosenau, *Post-Modernism and the Social Sciences* (Princeton, N.J.: Princeton University Press, 1992), pp. 128–129.

16.

> Let us admit the case of the conservative: if we once start thinking, no one can guarantee where we shall come out, except that many objects, ends, and institutions are doomed. Every thinker puts some portion of an apparently stable world in peril and no one can wholly predict what will emerge in its place.

John Dewey, *Intelligence in the Modern World*, ed. Joseph Ratner (New York: Modern Library, 1939), p. v.

17. Richard Bernstein, *Beyond Objectivism and Relativism, Science: Hermeneutics and Practice* (Philadelphia: University of Pennsylvania Press, 1988), p. 19.

18. There is even an available theoretical denial of this notion in Gödel's theorem, which holds:

> In any formal system adequate for number theory there exists an undecidable formula—that is, a formula that is not provable and whose negation is not provable. . . .
>
> A corollary to the theorem is that the consistency of a formal system adequate for number theory cannot be proved within the system.

J. Van Heijenoort, "Gödel's Theorem," in *The Encyclopedia of Philosophy*, ed. Paul Edwards (New York: Macmillan, 1972), p. 348.

19. Howard B. Radest, "The Humanist Imagination," *Journal of Humanism and Ethical Religion* 2, no. 1 (Fall 1989): 51.

20. Cited in Daniel J. Boorstin, *The Lost World of Thomas Jefferson* (Boston: Beacon Press, 1948), p. 125.

21. While I grow impatient with Emerson's effort to elevate Reason at the expense of reason, I think there is legitimate insight hidden away in the distinction. It will not do to reduce reason to a technical discipline. Like other human capacities, reason disembodied ceases to perform its life-task. Mere "method" is an illusion. Feminists, for example, may be faulted for political exaggeration in accusing rationality of gender bias, but they are not incorrect in identifying reason—I would say our picture of reason—with particular political and cultural roots and purposes. In a similar way, Calvin Schrag writes,

> Reason becomes within this broader scheme of things a posture of vision and insight, commemoration and foresight, that envelops not only the intentionality of categorical thinking but also the interpretive understanding with the texture of lived experience. . . . This expanded and vitalized notion of reason finds articulation in the intentionality of gestures, the lived-body as a comprehension of the world, the dialogic encounter of selves in conflict and community, the planning that goes on in the sector of public affairs, the ritual and rhetoric of religion and the work of art.

Radical Reflection and the Origin of the Human Sciences (West Lafayette, Ind.: Purdue University Press, 1980), p. 104.

22. Spinoza, certainly no stranger to reason—his *Ethic*, after all, is developed according to the "way of geometry"—suggests a moral psychology that is appropriate here. Unlike the "rationalist" of the shadow enlightenment, he knew that human beings cannot be argued into shifting belief or attitude or life stance, that a "passion" must be confronted by a stronger "passion." So, for example,

> Prop. VII. *An affect cannot be restrained or removed unless by an opposed and stronger affect.*
>
> Demonst. An affect, in so far as it is related to the mind, is an idea by which the mind affirms a greater or lesser power of existence for its body than the body possessed before. . . . Whenever, therefore, the mind is agitated by any affect, the body is at the same time affected with an affection by which its power of action is increased or diminished. Again, this affection of the body . . . receives from its own cause a power to persevere in its own being, a power, therefore, which cannot be restrained nor removed unless by a bodily cause . . . affecting the body with an affection contrary to the first, . . . and stronger than it.

Ethic, ed. John Wild (New York: Charles Scribner's Sons, 1930), Proposition VII, Fourth Part, Of Human Bondage or of the Strength of the Affects, pp. 292–293.

23. Erasmus, "In Praise of Folly," in *The Essential Erasmus*, ed. John P. Dolan (New York: New American Library, 1964), pp. 103–104.

24. In other words, the "Socratic impulse" is not merely a philosopher's disease. For an extended discussion, see Howard B. Radest, *Can We Teach Ethics* (New York: Praeger, 1989), chap. 7.

25. Arnold Burms, "Disenchantment," *Ethical Perspectives* 1, no. 3 (September 1994): 146.

26. For an interesting and revealing discussion of this theme, see Richard Rorty, "Does Academic Freedom Have Philosophical Presuppositions?" *Academe* 80, no. 6 (November–December 1994): 52–63.

27. A recent instance of this "hard-nosed" realism is to be found in Richard J. Herrnstein and Charles Murray, *The Bell Curve* (New York: Free Press, 1994), the latest instance of mixing a responsible collection and reporting of data with derived conclusions and recommendations that are only options among many interpretive alternatives. That these conclusions just happen to accord with both the biases of the authors and the temper of the American majority is, no doubt, fortuitous. At any rate, an epistemology that presumes one best answer to the findings of empirical research is questionable at best.

28. Cynthia Crossen, "How 'Tactical Research' Muddied Diaper Debate," *Wall Street Journal*, May 17, 1994, p. B1, adapted from Crossen, *Tainted Truth: The Manipulation of Fact in America* (New York: Simon & Schuster, 1994).

29. John Dewey, *Individualism Old and New* (1929, 1930) (New York: Capricorn Books, 1962), pp. 161–162.

30. Thomas Jefferson to John Adams, 1820, cited by Flowers and Murphy, *A History of Philosophy*, 1: 301–302.

31. George Santayana, *The Life of Reason* (New York: Charles Scribner's Sons, 1954), p. 7.

32. Robert Davidoff, "The Jeffersonian Option," *Political Theory* 21, no. 3 (August 1993): 439.

33. Jean Grondin, "Humanism and the Limits of Rationality," *Graduate Faculty Philosophy Journal* (New School for Social Research) 16, no. 2 (1994): 422.

34. Gerald Larue, "Positive Humanism," American Humanist Association, pamphlet reprinting the lead essay from *The Way of Positive Humanism* (Los Angeles: Centerline Press, 1989).

35. As Nel Noddings describes it,

> Caring involves, for the one-caring, a "feeling with" the other. We might want to call this relationship "empathy" but we should think about what we mean by this term. *The Oxford Universal Dictionary* defines *empathy* as "The power of projecting one's personality into, and so fully understanding, the objects of contemplation." This is, perhaps, a peculiarly rational, western, masculine way of looking at "feeling with." The notion of "feeling with" that I have outlined does not involve projection but reception. I have called it "engrossment." I do not "put myself into the other's shoes" so to speak, by analyzing his reality as objective data and then asking, "How would I feel in such a situation?" On the contrary, I set aside my temptation to analyze and plan. I do not project; I receive the other into myself

> and I see and feel with the other. I become a duality. . . . The seeing and feeling are mine, but only partly and temporarily mine, as a loan to me.

Caring (Berkeley: University of California Press, 1984), p. 30.

36. See Carol Gilligan, *In a Different Voice* (Cambridge, Mass.: Harvard University Press, 1982).

37. Following Santayana, the life of reason is methodological and biographical, to be sure. But it is above all ontological—a natural way of being in a natural world that is "precarious and stable" (Dewey). As Santayana writes,

> The universe, so far as we can observe it, is a wonderful and immense engine; its extent, its order, its beauty, its cruelty, makes it alike impressive. If we dramatise its life and conceive its spirit, we are filled with wonder, terror, and amusement, so magnificent is that spirit, so . . . inexorable, grammatical, and dull. Like all animals and plants, the cosmos has its own way of doing things, not wholly rational nor ideally best, but patient, fatal, and fruitful. Great is this organism of mud and fire, terrible this vast, painful, glorious experiment. Why should we not look on the universe with piety? Is it not our substance? Are we made of other clay? All our possibilities lie from eternity hidden in its bosom. It is the dispenser of all our joys. We may address it without superstitious terrors; it is not wicked. It follows its own habits abstractedly; it can be trusted to be true to its word. Society is not impossible between it and us, and since it is the source of all our energies, the home of all our happiness, shall we not cling to it and praise it, seeing that it vegetates so grandly and so sadly, and that it is not for us to blame it for what, doubtless, it never knew it did? Where there is such infinite and laborious potency, there is room for every hope.

George Santayana, *Reason in Religion, The Life of Reason* (New York: Scribner's 1905), 3: 191–192.

BIBLIOGRAPHY

Adler, Felix. *An Ethical Philosophy of Life.* New York: Ethica Press, 1986.

———. *The Reconstruction of the Spiritual Ideal.* New York: AMS Press, 1979.

Amery, Jean. *Radical Humanism: Selected Essays.* Edited and translated by Sidney Rosenfeld and Stella P. Rosenfeld. Bloomington, Ind.: Indiana University Press, 1984.

Arendt, Hannah. *Eichmann in Jerusalem.* New York: Viking, 1963.

Austin, John L. *How to do Things with Words.* Oxford: Oxford University Press, 1962.

Bellah, Robert N., et al. *Habits of the Heart.* New York: Harper & Row, 1985.

Bernstein, Richard J. *Beyond Objectivism and Relativism, Science: Hermeneutics and Practice* (1983). Philadelphia: University of Pennsylvania Press, 1988.

Black, Algernon D. *Without Burnt Offerings.* New York: Viking, 1974.

Blau, Joseph L. *Men and Movements in American Philosophy.* New York: Prentice-Hall, 1952.

Boorstin, Daniel J. *The Lost World of Thomas Jefferson.* Boston: Beacon Press, 1948.

Buber, Martin. *I and Thou.* Translated by Ronald Gregor Smith. New York: Scribner and Sons, 1958.

Burtt, E. A. *The Metaphysical Foundations of Modern Physical Science.* London: Routledge, Kegan Paul, 1924.

Campbell, Joseph. *The Hero with a Thousand Faces.* New York: Meridian Books, 1956.

Camus, Albert. *The Fall.* Translated by Justin O'Brien. New York: Alfred A. Knopf, 1956.

———. *The Myth of Sisyphus and Other Essays.* Translated by Justin O'Brien. New York: Vintage Books, 1955.

Coles, Robert. *The Call of Stories.* Boston: Houghton Mifflin, 1989.

Dean, William. *The Religious Critic in American Culture.* Albany, N.Y.: State University of New York Press, 1994.

Derrida, Jacques. *Of Grammatology.* Translated by Gayatri Chakravorty Spivak. Baltimore: Johns Hopkins Press, 1976.

Dewey, John. *Art as Experience*. New York: Milton Balch and Company, 1934.
———. *A Common Faith*. New Haven: Yale University Press, 1934.
———. *Human Nature and Conduct*. New York: Henry Holt and Company, 1992.
———. *Individualism Old and New* (1929–1930). New York: Capricorn, 1962.
———. *Intelligence in the Modern World.* Edited by Joseph Ratner. New York: Modern Library, 1939.
———. *Logic: The Theory of Inquiry*. New York: Henry Holt and Company, 1938.
———. *Reconstruction in Philosophy*. New York: Henry Holt, 1920.
———. *The Influence of Darwin on Philosophy and Other Essays in Contemporary Thought.* New York: Holt, Rinehart and Winston, 1910.
———. *The Philosophy of John Dewey.* Edited by John D. McDermott. Chicago: University of Chicago Press, 1981.
Dostoyevsky, Fyodor. *Notes from Underground.* Translated by Andrew R. MacAndrew. New York: New American Library, 1961.
Emerson, Ralph Waldo. *Selected Essays*. Edited by Larzer Ziff. New York: Penguin, 1982.
Engels, Frederick. *The Condition of the Working Class in England* (1892). London: Panther Books, 1969.
Erasmus. *The Essential Erasmus.* Edited by John P. Dolan. New York: New American Library, 1964.
Fairfield, Roy, ed. *Humanizing the Workplace*. Buffalo, N.Y.: Prometheus Press, 1974.
Flanagan, Owen. *Varieties of Moral Personality: Ethics and Psychological Realism.* Cambridge: Harvard University Press, 1991.
Flower, Elizabeth G., and Murphy, Michael. *A History of Philosophy in America.* 2 vols. New York: Capricorn Books, 1977.
Foucault, Michel. *Madness and Civilization: A History of Insanity in the Age of Reason* (1961). Translated by Richard Howard. New York: Vintage Books, 1973.
———. *The Archeology of Knowledge* (1969). Translated by A. M. Sheridan Smith. London: Tavistock Publications, 1972.
Frolov, Ivan. *Man-Science-Humanism: A New Synthesis.* Moscow: Progress Publishers, 1986.
Fromm, Erich. *Escape from Freedom.* New York: Rinehart and Company, 1941.
———. *Man for Himself.* New York: Rinehart, 1947.
———. *Marx's Concept of Man*. New York: Ungar, 1966.
Gadamer, Hans-Georg. *Reason in the Age of Science* (1981). Translated by Frederick G. Lawrence. Cambridge, Mass.: MIT Press, 1990.
Galbraith, John Kenneth. *The Culture of Contentment*. Boston: Houghton Mifflin, 1992.
Gilligan, Carol. *In a Different Voice*. Cambridge, Mass.: Harvard University Press, 1982.
Gleick, James. *Chaos: Making a New Science*. New York: Viking, 1987.
Goicoechea, David; Luik, John; and Madigan, Tim. *The Question of Humanism Challenges and Possibilities*. Buffalo, N.Y.: Prometheus Books, 1991. (See pp. 20–22 for a quick summary of Humanisms and anti-Humanisms.)
Habermas, Jurgen. *The Theory of Communicative Action* (1981). Vol. 1: *Reason and the Rationalization of Society*. Translated by Thomas McCarthy. Boston: Beacon Press, 1984.

———. *The Theory of Communicative Action* (1985). Vol. 2: *Lifeworld and System: A Critique of Functionalist Reason.* Translated by Thomas McCarthy. Boston: Beacon Press, 1987.

Heidegger, Martin. *Basic Writings, from Being and Time (1927) to The Task of Thinking (1964).* Edited by David Farrell Krell. New York: Harper & Row, 1977.

———. *Existence and Being.* Chicago: Henry Regnery Company, 1949.

Hinnels, John R., ed. *A Handbook of Living Religions.* London: Penguin Books, 1984.

Horvat, Branko; Markovic, Mihailo; and Supek, Rudi, eds. *Self-Governing Socialism: A Reader.* 2 vols. White Plains, N.Y.: International Arts and Sciences Press, 1975.

———. *Humanist Manifestos* I and II, Buffalo, N.Y.: Prometheus, 1973.

Hunter, George H., II. *How to Reach Secular People.* Nashville, Tenn.: Abingdon Press, 1992.

James, William. *Essays on Faith and Morals.* New York: Meridian Books, 1962 .

———. *Some Problems of Philosophy.* London: Longmans Green and Co., 1948.

———. *The Principles of Psychology* (1890). New York: Dover, 1950.

———. *Varieties of Religious Experience.* New York: Macmillan, 1961.

Jaspers, Karl. *Way to Wisdom.* Translated by Ralph Mannheim. New Haven: Yale University Press, 1954.

Jefferson, Thomas. *The Portable Thomas Jefferson.* Edited by Merrill D. Perterson. New York: Viking Penguin, 1975.

Jung, Carl G. *Man and His Symbols.* Garden City, N.Y.: Doubleday, 1964.

———. *Synchronicity.* Princeton: Princeton University Press, 1960.

Kant, Immanuel. *Critique of Judgement.* Translated by J. H. Bernard. New York: Hafner, 1951.

———. *Critique of Practical Reason.* Translated and edited by Lewis White Beck. Chicago: University of Chicago Press, 1949.

Kaufmann, Walter. *Existentialism from Dostoevsky to Sartre.* New York: Meridian Books, 1956.

———. *Nietzsche: Philosopher, Psychologist, Antichrist.* Princeton, N.J.: Princeton University Press, 1950.

Kierkegaard, Soren. *A Kierkegaard Anthology.* Edited by Robert Bretall. Princeton, N.J.: Princeton University Press, 1947.

Kuhn, Thomas. *The Structure of Scientific Revolutions.* Chicago: University of Chicago Press, 1970.

Kurtz, Paul. *The Transcendental Temptation.* Buffalo, N.Y.: Prometheus, 1986.

Lamont, Corlis. *The Philosophy of Humanism.* New York: Ungar, 1982.

Larue, Gerald. *The Way of Positive Humanism.* Los Angeles: Centerline Press, 1989.

Lifton, Robert Jay. *Human Resilience in an Age of Fragmentation.* New York: Basic Books, 1994.

MacIntyre, Allisadair. *After Virtue.* Notre Dame, Ind.: University of Notre Dame Press, 1981.

Mannheim, Karl. *Ideology and Utopia.* Translated by Edward Shils and Louis Wirth. London: Routledge & Kegan Paul, 1936.

Marty, Martin E., and Appleby, R. Scott, eds. *Fundamentalism Observed.* Chicago: University of Chicago Press, 1991.

Maslow, Abraham. *Religion, Values, and Peak Experiences.* New York: Viking, 1970.

———. *The Psychology of Science.* New York: Harper & Row, 1966.

———. *Toward a Psychology of Being.* New York: Van Nostrand, 1968.
Miller, Charles A. *Jefferson and Nature.* Baltimore: Johns Hopkins University Press, 1993.
Miller, Perry. *The American Transcendentalists.* New York: Doubleday, 1957.
Nietzsche, Friedrich. *The Birth of Tragedy* (1872). pp. 1–146, *The Genealogy of Morals* (1887). pp. 149–299. Translated by Francis Golffing. Garden City, N.Y.: Doubleday Anchor Books, 1956.
Noddings, Nel. *Caring. A Feminine Approach to Ethics and Moral Education.* Berkeley: University of California Press, 1984.
Novak, Barbara. *Nature and Culture.* New York: Oxford University Press, 1980.
Olds, Mason. *Religious Humanism in America.* Washington, D.C.: University Press of America, 1978.
Pagel, Henry. *The Dreams of Reason: The Computer and the Rise of the Sciences of Complexity.* New York: Simon & Schuster, 1988.
Paine, Thomas. *The Age of Reason.* New York: Truth Seeker Company, n.d.
Perry, Lewis. *Intellectual Life in America.* New York: Franklin Watts, 1984.
Persons, Stow. *Free Religion.* New Haven, Conn.: Yale University Press, 1947.
Petrovic, Gajo. *Marx in the Mid-Twentieth Century.* Garden City, N.Y.: Doubleday Anchor Books, 1967.
Radest, Howard B. *Can We Teach Ethics.* New York: Praeger, 1989.
———. *Community Service: Encounter of Strangers.* Westport, Conn.: Praeger, 1993.
———. *The Devil and Secular Humanism.* New York: Praeger, 1990.
———. *Toward Common Ground.* New York: Ungar, 1969.
Rawls, John. *A Theory of Justice.* Cambridge, Mass.: Harvard University Press, 1971.
Richard, Carl J. *The Founders and the Classics.* Cambridge, Mass.: Harvard University Press, 1994.
Rockefeller, Steven C. *John Dewey—Religion, Faith and Democratic Humanism.* New York: Columbia University Press, 1991.
Rogers, Carl. *On Becoming a Person.* Boston: Houghton Mifflin, 1961.
Rorty, Richard. *Contingency, Irony, and Solidarity.* Cambridge: Cambridge University Press, 1989.
———. *Philosophy and the Mirror of Nature.* Princeton, N.J.: Princeton University Press, 1979.
Rosenau, Pauline Marie. *Post-Modernism and the Social Sciences.* Princeton, N.J.: Princeton University Press, 1992.
Santayana, George. *The Life of Reason.* 5 vols. New York: Scribner's, 1905.
———. *The Life of Reason.* 1 vol. Rev. with Daniel Cory. New York: Charles Scribner's Sons, 1954.
Sartre, Jean-Paul. *Existentialism and Human Emotions.* Translated by Bernard Frechtman. New York: Philosophical Library, 1957.
———. *Nausea.* Translated by Lloyd Alexander. London: Purnell and Sons, 1949.
———. *No Exit and Three Other Plays.* Translated by S. Gilbert. New York: Vintage Books, 1955.
———. *Truth and Existence* (1948). Translated by Adrian Van Den Hoven, edited by Ronald Aronson, annotated by Arlette Elkaim-Sartre. Chicago: University of Chicago Press, 1992.

Schrag, Calvin O. *Radical Reflection and the Origin of the Human Sciences.* West Lafayette, Ind.: Purdue University Press, 1980.
Silverman, Hugh J., ed. *Derrida and Deconstruction.* New York: Routledge, 1989.
Simmons, J. L. *The Emerging New Age.* Santa Fe, N.M.: Bear and Co., 1990.
Skolnick, Arlene S. and Jerome H., eds. *Family in Transition.* 5th ed. Boston: Little, Brown, 1986.
Spinoza, Benedict. *Ethic.* Edited by John Wild. New York: Charles Scribner's Sons, 1930.
Stack, George J. *Nietzsche and Emerson: An Elective Affinity.* Athens, Ohio: Ohio University Press, 1992.
Storer, Morris B., ed. *Humanist Ethics.* Buffalo, N.Y.: Prometheus Press, 1980.
Tarnas, Richard. *The Passion of the Western Mind.* New York: Ballantine Books, 1991.
Thoreau, Henry David. *Walden.* New York: Oxford University Press, 1906.
Tillich, Paul. *The Future of Religions.* Edited by Jerald C. Brauer. New York: Harper & Row, 1966.
———. *The Shaking of the Foundations.* New York: Charles Scribner's Sons, 1948.
Turner, James. *Without God, without Creed.* Baltimore: Johns Hopkins University Press, 1985.
Vahanian, Gabriel. *The Death of God.* New York: George Braziller, 1957.
Weinstein, Gregory. *The Wilderness and the City.* Boston: University of Massachusetts Press, 1982.
West, Cornel. *The American Evasion of Philosophy.* Madison: University of Wisconsin Press, 1989.
———. *The Ethical Dimensions of Marxist Thought.* New York: Monthly Review Press, 1991.
Westbrook, Robert B. *John Dewey and American Democracy.* Ithaca, N.Y.: Cornell University Press, 1991.
Whitman, Walt. *Leaves of Grass.* Philadelphia: David McKay, 1900.
Wilson, Brian, ed. *Rationality.* London: Oxford University Press, 1970.
Wood, Gordon S. *The Radicalism of the American Revolution.* New York: Alfred A. Knopf, 1992.
Wright, Conrad. *A Stream of Light.* Boston: Unitarian Universalist Association, 1975.

INDEX

About the Author

HOWARD B. RADEST is Adjunct Professor of Philosophy at the University of South Carolina-Beaufort. He is the founding Dean and now Dean Emeritus of The Humanist Institute. His books include *Community Service: Encounter with Strangers* (Praeger, 1993), *The Devil and Secular Humanism* (Praeger, 1990), and *Can We Teach Ethics?* (Praeger, 1989).

ISBN 0-275-94969-9
90000>
EAN
9 780275 949693
HARDCOVER BAR CODE